TOM BENNETT

RUNNING THE ROOM

THE TEACHER'S GUIDE TO BEHAVIOUR

First Published 2020

by John Catt Educational Ltd,
15 Riduna Park, Station Road,
Melton, Woodbridge IP12 1QT

Tel: +44 (0) 1394 389850
Email: enquiries@johncatt.com
Website: www.johncatt.com

Cover concept by Florence Bennett

Opinions expressed in this publication are those of the
contributors and are not necessarily those of the publishers
or the editors. We cannot accept responsibility for any
errors or omissions.

ISBN: 978 1 913622 14 5

Set and designed by John Catt Educational Limited

PRAISE FOR *RUNNING THE ROOM*

When Tom Bennett writes, common sense leaps off the page and slaps you in the face. You will find yourself engrossed, helplessly nodding in total agreement as he shares his years of research, experience and first-hand accounts from schools.

It is hard to imagine anyone reading this book and not improving their thinking and day-to-day classroom practice.

Tom's tales will engage and amuse you, the practical advice will inspire you, but most importantly this book will change the way you think about school culture and its impact on pupil behaviour.

Damian McBeath,
Regional Director for Ark Schools, London and Portsmouth

In this masterful volume, Bennett outlines the highest-impact theories and strategies to be able to – as it says on the tin – run the room. Bad advice is everywhere when it comes to behaviour, and no other book explains easily actionable and effective techniques so clearly. This is the book I needed years ago; how much time have I wasted discovering for myself a fraction of the techniques and routines clearly outlined in this book? Readers are indeed lucky to have access to it as I have no doubt it will improve the practice of teachers with all levels of experience.'

Adam Boxer, Chemistry teacher,
Editor of *The researchED guide to explicit and direct instruction*

As always, Tom gives pragmatic and sensible advice for managing behaviour. The anecdotes he shares from early teaching are both devastating and hilarious, but ultimately serve as a reminder that great teachers are made, not born. A really helpful book for any teacher who wants to improve their craft.

Natasha Porter,
Founder and CEO of Unlocked Graduates

Wise, clear, and eminently practical, this book will help teachers create a classroom atmosphere where students feel valued and ready to work.

Professor Daniel Willingham,
Professor of Psychology at the University of Virginia

A nuanced and comprehensive approach to behaviour that provides practical guidance while exploring the complex fields of psychology and motivation. The book is vital reading for everyone facing the challenge of controlling a classroom. Even more importantly the methods in this book will help children develop and find purpose as individuals.

Rachel de Souza,
CEO at Inspiration Trust

Practical, sensible, step by step, very thorough. There's a lot more to this book than first meets the eye. Read it carefully. Read it again. Keep coming back to it. Apply it. You won't regret it.

Barry Smith,
Headteacher

Running the Room offers the training we deserved but did not receive. This book champions behaviour as the number one school improvement driver. If you want happy staff, if you want pupils to learn, if you want parents to pick your school, if you want teachers to be able to teach, then treat behaviour as an integral part of the curriculum. Above all else, teach behaviour and teach it some more. Packed with research, hints, tips and strategies to support anyone of any level with behaviour, this is a must read. Tom nails it!

Sam Strickland,
Headteacher

Tom Bennett honestly and humbly recounts how he learned to manage a classroom: a slow process of trial and error, which served him and his students poorly. In this book, he combines his experience, wisdom and the evidence to help us avoid his mistakes. With a light touch, he shows how running the room can ensure all students thrive in school.

Harry Fletcher-Wood,
Associate Dean at Ambition Institute

The what, why and how of behaviour – this book helps teachers explore behind the behaviour, understand the challenges students face in the classroom and how we can build a culture that helps students to engage in a productive way.

A great book to help teachers get ahead of the behaviour and create a calm and cohesive classroom where everyone feels safe, allowing teachers to get on with the job of helping students to flourish and learn.

Craig Benham,
SCITT Development Manager, Leicestershire Secondary SCITT

Running the Room is a unique book. It's a rare combination of erudition and anecdote, gravity and wit, failures and triumphs, self-deprecation and swank, trials and tribulations and optimism. In a style that often made me think of Samuel Clemens (Mark Twain), Tom shows us how running the room is the teacher's ultimate act of love and dedication to education and their students.

Professor Paul Kirschner,
Emeritus Professor of Educational Psychology and Guest Professor,
Thomas More University of Applied Science

This is classic Tom Bennett – funny, practical and wise insights into classroom management.

Daisy Christodoulou,
Director of Education at No More Marking

This is a must-read, not only for new teachers, but for anyone who spends time in classrooms of any kind.

Tom Bennett understands that behaviour in school is nuanced; there are no clear black-and-white rules that work for all teachers in all schools. There is no magic wand.

Establishing excellent behaviour in schools is as much about subtleties, persistence and culture as it is about clarity, transparency and consistency. It can be taught – and this is how.

Clare Wagner,
West London Free School

Tom's extremely readable style (often entertaining; always enjoyable) makes a complex and fraught area of classroom practice accessible and actionable to a new teacher. We know behaviour is one of the greatest sources of anxiety for teachers and potential barriers to learning for pupils. This book does much to alleviate both problems and will be a useful addition.

Professor Sam Twiselton,
Sheffield Hallam University

In some areas of education, there is lots of high-quality research evidence about the 'best bets' for improving one's practice. For these areas, my advice is simple: read the research and figure out what this might mean for your own practice. In other areas, like behaviour management, where the research evidence is thin, weak, or contradictory, my advice is different, but equally simple. Find people who know what they are talking about, and listen to what they have to say. Like Tom Bennett.

In *Running the Room*, Tom condenses all he has learned about managing student behaviour – from his experiences as an inner-city school teacher, by observing hundreds (thousands?) of classrooms, and by carefully researching what good research there is – into a wonderfully accessible, practical – and, yes, funny – guide to classroom management. This book is the best guide I have ever read on getting good behaviour in classrooms. It should be required reading for those training to teach, but experienced teachers will also find a lot here to reflect on, and to use. Highly recommended.

Dylan Wiliam,
Emeritus Professor, University College London

Tom Bennett has written the book we all needed at the start of our teaching careers. With characteristic wit and wisdom, Tom describes what some of the most effective teachers have done to create the best learning environments. It's kind, searingly honest, and stuffed full of concrete examples that'll help trainees through to headteachers. If you're at the start of your teaching career: read it. If you're 20 years in like me: read it.

Claire Stoneman,
Teacher and School Leader

Running the Room is a funny, perceptive exploration of the philosophy underpinning behaviour in schools. It will help even the veteran teacher understand why certain strategies work. Bennett argues with a charm that convinces and I can't wait to get several copies for our staff library.

Katharine Birbalsingh,
Headteacher, Michaela Community School

This book is brilliant. It will make you a much better teacher.

You probably already know all of this. Tom is the founder of researchED, the game-changing teacher-led international education movement. He is a published author, speaker, trainer, teacher. He is the DfE's national behaviour adviser and is frequently in the national media defending teachers from nonsense ideas that do damage. The *TES* famously referred to him as 'the voice of the modern teacher'. There isn't a more helpful, credible, kinder voice in education who will give you the tools to be effective in the classroom when you are young people's best hope of making their own destiny.

Running the Room is practical, funny and wise and it does not patronise you. Reading it is like your glamorous older brother has returned from university for a spell and unexpectedly taken you to the cinema. You will read it goggle-eyed and gripped, running through an action-adventure story feeding your emotions and educating your wits. Except it is all rooted in evidence, practice and hard-won fact. Do you want to know how to run a classroom with compassion, high standards and with learning at its heart? Of course you do, that's why you're a teacher! Tom will tell you how.

Jude Hunton,
Principal, Skegness Grammar School

'Practical' is the standard praise for a book on behaviour, but Bennett's book is something different: a thing of beauty. And not just because of his humility, humor and occasionally elegiac prose. Because the truth is beautiful. To love children is to ensure that our classrooms protect them and honor their chance at learning – bring out the best in each of them and teach them to be giving and positive members of the society we share. Sadly the first response when adults find themselves unable to ensure such an outcome is often to argue that it is unnecessary. Rarely has anyone explained so clearly an alternative and provided as practical (and beautiful) a guide to accomplishing it.

Doug Lemov,
Author of *Teach Like a Champion*

For Gabriella and Benjamin, who astonish, delight and perplex me on a daily basis, and who constantly remind me that the Good Life is built on loving one another.

For Anna, who changed my life so profoundly for the better that I now divide it into two eras: BA and AA. I carry your heart.

And for Annie McGhee, the best of us, now at rest with the Saints. Thank you for the words, and the toffee and your unconditional love. A small boy is forever grateful to you.

'It is only that I dislike the whole notion of subordination. The corporal lurks in almost every bosom, and each man tends to use authority when he has it, thus destroying his natural relationship with his fellows, a disastrous state of affairs for both sides. Do away with subordination and you do away with tyranny: without subordination we should have no Neros, no Tamerlanes, no Buonapartes.'

'Stuff,' said Jack. 'Subordination is the natural order: there is subordination in Heaven – Thrones and Dominions take precedence over Powers and Principalities, Archangels and ordinary foremast angels; and so it is in the Navy.

'You have come to the wrong shop for anarchy, brother.'

Stephen Maturin and Captain Jack Aubrey
The Ionian Mission, **by Patrick O'Brian**

CONTENTS

THE PRINCIPLES OF THE CLASSROOM

These principles underpin everything I have learned about excellent classroom management. Some of them may seem obvious, some of them may seem ambiguous. Throughout this book, I will refer or allude to these principles, and my hope is that by the end, they will make sense, seem sensible, and make a difference in your own understanding. Which, with luck, will direct your behaviour, and that of your students.

1. Behaviour is a curriculum
2. Children must be taught how to behave
3. Teach, don't tell, behaviour
4. Make it easy to behave and hard not to
5. No one behaviour strategy will work with all students
6. Good relationships are built out of structures and high expectations
7. Students are social beings
8. Consistency is the foundation of all good habits
9. Everyone wants to matter
10. My room, my rules

INTRODUCTION
SECRET ORIGINS

Until I became a teacher, I ran nightclubs in central London. I was confident, relaxed and comfortable managing drunks, bouncers, bartenders, and every shadowy citizen of Soho. None of this made any difference when I became a teacher. This was because:

- The skills I had learned were not useful in any obvious way.
- Anything clubs and classrooms had in common would take me years to discern.

What I thought would be a useful preparation provided me with no skills or aptitudes in a portable form. I was so used to telling people what to do, I imagined it was a magical gift I possessed, given to me by three fairies in the crib. I had 'authority', but only in the boundaries of my club; I did not possess a nebulous, intangible miasma called 'authority'. I could not command the driver of a bus to take me to Vauxhall if the destination read 'Tottenham'. I could read a crowd well enough to know when horseplay was about to turn into a saloon brawl. But I could not discern the mood of a class clearly enough to see the difference between the compliance of boredom and quiet focus.

As to that, on paper I looked a very good bet. A 30-year-old man with management and leadership experience, years of social interaction with the public, and a career that required discipline, self-regulation and resilience.

Were those features easily transferred into other domains, I would have flourished. Instead, I floundered. The confidence I felt in the clubs, where I could snap my fingers and have 300 people removed, melted like frost on a car bonnet at sunrise. The certainty with which I issued instructions became speculation; the persuasiveness I routinely displayed in dissolving ardour, anger or anguish in the fraught centrifuge of a nightclub became hollow and inept. All of it dashed against the cliffs of the children's indifference.

My crowd control – my behaviour management, if you will – was not a magic quality I possessed. I did not have *the Force*. You do not have the Force either. Untrained and hapless, for at least three years I ran classes badly. Rather, they ran me.

Many of the skills we believe we have are domain specific. We have always known this, until we forgot. As Thorndike said in the early 20th century:

> Common observation should teach that mental capacities are highly specialised. A man may be a tip-top musician but in other respects an imbecile: he may be a gifted poet, but an ignoramus in music: he may have a wonderful memory for figures and only a mediocre memory for localities, poetry and human faces: school children may reason admirably in science and be below average in grammar: those very good in drawing may be very poor in dancing.[1]

I entered teaching with nervousness, but high hopes. I knew it would be hard, but I knew I could do it. On the last count, I was spectacularly wrong.

My first few years in teaching were a Dickensian misery memoir. Every day was a gauntlet. In part it was because I had no idea what I was teaching. In what will eventually – I hope – be seen as a scandal, it had been possible for me to become an actual teacher with the most flimsy grasp of my subject or pedagogy. Teacher training was a well-meant but woefully undercooked half-preparation for the classroom. It was simultaneously too theoretical and maddeningly over focused on microscopic details of practice. We spent a whole day comparing how we had made a poster for our subject, a day on how to use a PowerPoint, but almost nothing on pedagogy, the principles of instruction, or behaviour management. It was like preparing someone to defuse bombs by sending them to a seminary.[2]

Like many teachers, I worried constantly that I was a fraud. In my case, my fears were legitimate. And like most early-career teachers, one of my primary concerns was 'Would I have enough material to last a whole lesson?'

My next concern – equally valid – was 'What if they don't do as I ask?' And I soon found out that this was central to everything else. If they wouldn't follow simple instructions, then no learning would take place. I was often left alone in the classroom after my first few days, and my classes worked exactly as they pleased, no more, no less. If they felt like it, they would; if not, then not. My anxious directions to them were as trivial as a breeze to a mountain.

---

1. Thorndike, E. L. (Edward Lee) (1906) *The principles of teaching, based on psychology.* New York, NY: A. G. Seiler.
2. The Holy Hand Grenade of Antioch notwithstanding.

This was mentally and emotionally harrowing. I simply assumed I was a terrible teacher. I was right. I planned lessons alone all evening until I fell asleep at the desk, and dreaded the morning. On Sunday, I worked; and Saturdays, I hid in bed, a brief respite from the grinding and flavourless week. I would have quit, but I had no off-ramp.

I confess this is not an inspirational vignette, but an unattractive and boring time filled with quiet despair. I was bottoming out, but I was too tired to quit. I only persisted because I lacked the willpower or wit to give up.

Poor classroom behaviour was central to my problems, and to my mindset. I barely knew what I was teaching, I had no idea how to teach it, and I had no idea how to get students listening and learning. If they had done so, I could have devoured the day. Instead, it devoured me.

The students...ah, Lord. They were a perfect microcosm of humanity. Some of them would do anything you asked and were power-ups in a game designed to drain you. These cheering few were a minority. Then there was a substantial middle who were partially receptive to listening if you could only find something they wanted to listen to. They were hard work, but the real difficulty lay with the bottom third who seemed determined to do the opposite of anything asked. They openly mocked all adults, and me, my clothes, my accent, told me to go back to Scotland, that I wasn't a real teacher, I was boring, I wasn't funny.

They sneered at any warmth and ignored me to my face when I addressed them. As I was advised by my trainers, all my energy was invested in building relationships with them, but with no impact. The well-behaved barely saw me. I would spend entire lessons bogged down in chaos. One day was lost arguing with someone who had dribbled a ball into the classroom and who then refused to stop playing keepy-up in front of my desk. I snatched the ball away, and he screamed assault, laughing as he did so. Students ran out of other classrooms to watch and laugh.

At the end of every day, I would wait glumly for students to return for a healing conversation, but the only ones who ever did were students the least in need of it. I reported absences; perhaps something happened as a result, but I never knew. My colleagues were all incredibly kind, but many of them also struggled with behaviour. It seemed that they had achieved a strained and fragile détente with their classes, permitting them to teach. But this was achieved by having been there for many years. Their advice was often, 'Wait until they get to know you.' I shuddered to think the only remedy to my predicament was to endure until everyone got tired and just behaved out of pity or boredom. It felt like a siege.

Other advice at this time seemed to revolve around 'engaging with the children' or giving them tasks to perform that they enjoyed. But when I tried – through humour, or through devising ways to disguise learning as a game, they seemed equally scornful, like a dog who has correctly discerned a worming tablet crushed into its feed.

I had intermittent successes, lessons where they would sit and listen to the content, or try a worksheet, or discuss a topic for a short time. But I had no idea why and how this happened. It was lightning in a bottle, it came and went when the gods willed, and what flew one day stalled the next. Added to this was the sheer exhaustion of the job – even as a training teacher, it felt like every minute you were in front of a carousel of classes that strobed past you like a zoetrope. The job was a lumpy gravy of unfamiliar faces, drowning in open hostility, and feeling a failure with every step.

Over the next three or four years, and as I moved schools, it got better, but slowly. As my subject knowledge improved and I stayed in one place, I got to know the students better. Crucially, I found my 'in' with them. For me it was telling stories about my previous career in nightclubs and threading stories about that into lessons that grazed thematically close to the narratives.

I started to relax a little, but I also picked up bad habits with the good. I learned that with some kids, the easiest way to avoid their endless meltdowns was to placate and contain them, ignore their low output, expect little and get it. I learned that some children will behave perfectly well *as long as you don't ask them to do anything they don't want to do*. Which at least allows you to focus on the ones who are amenable to a little learning. It's suboptimal, but you learn that teaching is the art of the possible, not the perfect. I learned that what you had to do to cope in an insane job was the same thing you do to survive on the ledge of a skyscraper: hang on by your fingernails and never look down.[3]

It only struck me years later that this was a mess. Like a fish immersed in teaching culture, I had been unable to conceive of anything but the turbulent

---

3. Paraphrased slightly from Rorschach in Alan Moore's 1986 comic book series *Watchmen*.

water in which I swam. I assumed that was all you could expect – not only from the students, but from the system we inhabited.

Eventually I recognised that there were some techniques you could use that seemed to work better than others. I couldn't quite verbalise it, but it seemed to be a combination of maintaining an even temper, balancing a sense of humour with performative gravity, and also something to do with pace, voice, and gesture. How I explained the topics I taught also seemed to matter. I discovered a hidden knack for explaining things well. People would listen and regurgitate it on command to some extent, but I had no idea what principles underpinned rhetorical success, let alone pedagogical success. Setting detentions helped a little to deter the worst offenders, as did parking students (sending them into another classroom) when necessary. Things got better.

But they got better by trial and error, and much of my time was spent on the error. The gains were bought at a high price, and too slowly for words. Worse, discerning error from the correct principles seemed impossibly cryptic. How did you know something was working with them unless you had some immediate feedback?

But still, things improved. As years passed, my cohorts grew older with me, and by the time they went through their examination years they usually had excellent behaviour. We all knew what to expect from one another, and that seemed to matter. That fed back into my efforts with new classes, or younger classes, and I applied my burgeoning skills in cycles. But it was still largely sub-verbal, and intuitive. I could probably tell you when another teacher was doing something wrong behaviourally, but I couldn't express what they were doing right, or suggest ways they could improve.

It continued to get better as I reflected on my own practice and read as much as I could. I attended every course my school would pay for on behaviour, and I read everything I could find about it like a man facing the gallows. Much of what I read seemed either obvious or absurd, focusing on ways to deal with children that were already impeccably behaved. Little of it seemed very practical, and much of it seemed to have little relevance to the difficulties I faced in a challenging school. Still, I got better by centimetres.

I started to find interesting material in fields tangential to education, such as cognitive and developmental psychology, behavioural economics, sociology and anthropology.

21

Ironically, I found political philosophy far more important than I had ever imagined. This was an area that had been considered exhaustively for centuries. How should we be governed? By what right? How do people coexist in ways that maximise their aims – justice, liberty, equality, income, resources, or some combination of all of these? But these became relevant only once I had absorbed enough experience to understand it. Classrooms are stubbornly physical places. Theory can only take you so far by itself. You can follow a recipe and still cook abysmally.

Years passed, and I took a sabbatical at the University of Cambridge as a teacher-fellow of Corpus Christi. Time away from the classroom was like breaching the surface of the ocean after a long dive, and I gulped at the air before falling back into teaching, invigorated. I started to write: blogs, articles, then books that specialised in behaviour. I ran the online behaviour advice forum for the *TES*, and for years contributed hundreds of pieces on behaviour. That took me into school after school after school, until what I learned there could be shared tentatively with others.

By now I estimate I've probably been to around 400 schools in the UK and abroad, principally to look at their behaviour systems. I am currently the UK Department for Education's Behaviour Advisor. *None of this makes me any better than a good teacher in any school.* The only advantage I do have is the privilege of having seen what extraordinary teachers do all over the UK and around the world.

And it convinced me – and continues to do so – that good behaviour should be the central concern of any teacher. If your classes behave well already, you may not think so. But the minute you try to teach in an even partially challenging environment, you realise that if they aren't behaving, they aren't learning.

Teaching saved me. Aimless, it gave me direction. Selfish, it forced me to focus on others. Unhappy, it brought me purpose – and with it, joy. None of that became possible until I started to understand the need to direct student behaviour, and until I began to understand how to do it.

The same small, good thing

Teaching changed my life immeasurably for the better. It has the power to do the same for so many. It reminds me of the story of Tom Junod's article on Fred Rogers. In 1988 Junod, feature writer for the American magazine *Esquire*, wrote an article[4] about Rogers, the avuncular and beloved host of *Mister Rogers' Neighbourhood*, which was a cornerstone in American children's broadcasting for decades. The cynical Junod was initially sceptical of Rogers's saintly reputation, but he eventually said that meeting him had changed his entire perspective on life. And with impeccable economy, he described Rogers's life's work as 'doing the same small good thing for a very long time'.

And that's exactly what teachers do: the same small good thing for a very long time.

In a world drunk on spectacle, impatient for instant results, and addicted to even the most diaphanous of glories, that's a rebellious act. It's the most wonderful thing you can do – and wonderfully, also the most effective. I recommend it. Go you and do likewise.

---

4. Junod, T. (1998) 'Can you say hero?' *Esquire Magazine*, November 1998.

SECTION 1:
HUMAN NATURE

BEHAVIOUR IS A CURRICULUM

Being well-behaved is a combination of skills, aptitudes, habits, inclinations, values, and knowledge. These can be taught.

CHAPTER 1

THE BASICS

Can anyone teach?

'Some are born great, some achieve greatness, and some have greatness thrust upon them,' as Malvolio says in *Twelfth Night*. Often, I am asked if some people naturally make better teachers. This is because of some fear that despite their best efforts, new teachers will always be fighting a battle against their inbuilt limitations. This fear is understandable, but I believe that *almost* everyone can become a competent teacher, with sufficient high-quality training.

There are undoubtedly people who enter the profession with character traits that make professional development easier, e.g. tenacity; a reasonably thick skin; the ability to stay calm under pressure. We might call these habits or tendencies to react in a certain way. Certainly, the nervous practitioner, the easily angered, the over-sensitive personality will find themselves at a disadvantage in the tumultuous and emotionally demanding classroom. But character traits can be improved. Timidity can be managed by experience; so can a short fuse, or the tunnel vision that stress can generate.

Crucially, most parts of the professional's toolkit are learnable, and therefore teachable. There are a thousand microscopic skills that individually seem unimportant but constitute a greater whole. Seen up close, they seem trivial: how to stand at a door waiting for students, how to eyeball an off-task student, how to reprimand an anxious student while also encouraging them during a test, etc. These can all be improved. But – and this is the biggest but – this is best done through a structured training process that many teachers simply do not receive.

This has always struck me as one of the most glaring deficiencies in the education universe: that teachers, one of the largest professional sectors (and one of the most vital), are often insufficiently prepared by their induction. It is often assumed that many aspects of the job will be acquired, presumably osmotically, once in the role. This paradigm is about as practical as hoping that a pilot will decipher the mysteries of the flight deck by sitting in the cockpit and seeing what the buttons do. As they say, 'In theory there is no difference between theory and practice. In practice there is.'[1]

Doing, blindly, is not learning. Discovery learning, that pedagogy so beloved of education antiquarians and people who have never taught, only starts to become effective when one already possesses some expertise. Novices don't know where to begin.[2] They don't even know when they're wrong. And they don't know what they don't know. We condemn generation after generation of teachers to the Hell of Guesswork in the vital field of behaviour management, then wonder why they leave.

Summary: *everyone can improve. Almost everyone can be a good teacher if they are trained well. But they must be trained.*

Finally, I am often asked if gender, size, etc. makes a difference. I am frequently told that 'men have it easier' at behaviour management, or tall people or those with deep voices dominate without trouble. I haven't seen any evidence of this, and think such statements often reflect the anxieties of the person making them. Children don't behave for you because you look scary or massive (and if they do, I would question the integrity of your classroom). I have seen students behave impeccably for the tiniest of women and circle a tall man like Morris dancers around a maypole. It is what we do with the students, what we say to them, the relationships we build with them, that drives the behaviour. Napoleons and Yodas teach us that status doesn't come from broad shoulders but broad spirit. It is not the size of the dog in the fight, but the size of the fight in the dog.[3]

Why is behaviour so important?

We can answer that question with another. What do you think the aim of education is? Asking this of any room will produce dozens of different answers. Common answers include:

---

1. Attributed to Benjamin Brewster

2. Kirschner, P. A., Sweller, J. & Clark, R. E. (2006) 'Why minimal guidance during instruction does not work: an analysis of the failure of constructivist, discovery, problem-based, experiential, and inquiry-based teaching', *Educational Psychologist*, 41:2, 75-86.

3. Attributed to Mark Twain. It's usually a safe bet.

- Good grades
- Creating informed citizens
- Creativity
- Democratic participation
- Building character

And so on. I don't believe education has one intrinsic aim; I believe people have aims for education. Whatever you believe the aim ought to be, every single one of them is achieved more successfully when students are taught to behave. This may seem obvious, but it is not obvious to everyone. I frequently hear arguments like 'They're all a bit rowdy, but they're learning because they're excited' or 'Making them all listen at once is just cattle herding, not teaching – they need to come to the learning themselves' or similar. These are absurd things to say. Noisy classes mean that some or many of the children can't focus or listen *when they need to*.

Sometimes these arguments are backed up by references to anecdotes. But every conceivable aim of education is supported by better behaviour.

You value creativity? Shakespeare was no peasant who sprang from the mud- he went to a grammar school, where he was taught to memorise the Bible. That's probably not a great template for all education, but you can see the dense familiarity with canon texts dripping off every page.

Gandhi, one of history's greatest revolutionaries, studied law at University College London before he became the great catalyst for Indian political reform. It is reasonably certain that Gandhi did not spend his days in the student bar, learning to fold crisp packets into triangles while drinking snakebite, or snoring through lectures. Self-discipline, self-regulation, hard work, patience and effort are all enormously important characteristics of successful people in a variety of contexts.

Or perhaps you want children to pass examinations; they also need to learn to focus, listen, speak well, ask intelligent questions, read, and do all of this independently when required. You want children to leave school as model citizens and informed democratic participants? They need to know what democracy entails, the values it embodies, and how to be informed enough about the world to make judgements in a ballot about who best represents us. You want schools to provide vocational opportunities? No craft was ever gained by sleeping in the machine shop. Everything of value you can conceive of was acquired through sustained effort, practice, and delayed self-gratification.

And none of that happens by itself. It must be taught. Some children are taught these qualities from the minute they are born, raised in fortunate familial circumstances that provide patience, love and structure like an invisible womb. Many are not so fortunate. Many more are somewhere in between. You teach many of all these children. They possess a broad mixture of abilities, vocabulary, character, habits and expectations. You cannot do anything about what walks into your classroom. But you can do two things: you can anticipate what your students' baseline abilities are and what they will need to learn in order to flourish; and you can make sure that as many of them as possible are well instructed in the behavioural skills that they will need to be learners.

Safety

There is another, sombre side to all of this. Well-managed, well-behaved school spaces are essential for children to be safe.

> **Almost** 30,000 reports of children sexually assaulting other youngsters, including 2625 alleged attacks on school premises, have been made to police in the last four years, figures reveal … reports of so-called 'peer on peer' abuse rose from 4603 in 2013 to 7866 last year – an increase of 71% … The investigation found that 2625 reported sexual offences, including 225 alleged rapes, carried out by under-18s on other children happened on school premises, including primary school playgrounds, across 31 force areas.[4]

> **Assaults** on school premises have soared 72 per cent in the past four years, with 27,805 reports received by the police since 2015.[5]

> **In 2018**, the Union's Big Question survey of over 7000 teachers throughout the UK found that in the past 12 months:

> - more than one in ten teachers (11%) had been physically assaulted by a pupil;
> - one in seven (14%) had been threatened with physical assault by a pupil; and
> - more than half (51%) had been verbally abused by a pupil.[6]

---

4. www.bit.ly/31U7yvY

5. www.bit.ly/3e7z9Mk

6. www.bit.ly/2Z5bFTP

The NASUWT also reported in 2016 that 72% of teachers surveyed believed 'there is a widespread problem with pupil behaviour in schools today.'[7]

Students deserve to be safe. So do teachers and other staff. Worrying about the threat of violence or humiliation should be the least part of classroom life. Teachers and students should never be expected to tolerate these things. We should never accept it as normal or think 'that's just the job'. We would never accept this for our own children, and yet I frequently meet people who appear comfortable to accept this for other people's children. Schools are not usually systemically violent, but there are too many schools where violence is not uncommon, where bullying is normal, where teachers feel scared to walk down a busy corridor at break time. Too many children live in fear of persecution or spend their lunches weeping in secret places only they know about; too many teachers brace themselves for a gauntlet when they go into lessons; too many teachers take a bruise and get asked to chalk it up to the job.

Enough. Enough. We cannot make the world or classrooms risk free. But we can do everything we can to make classrooms calm, safe spaces where everyone flourishes as best they can. That is the lowest possible bar that should be acceptable.

Potential

And finally, better behaviour is essential if you have any concern at all for children – all children – being happy and well. Not just in regard to their safety, but in regard to the possibilities they possess. People often talk about potential. 'You need to unlock their potential,' they say, as if potential were a ruby locked in the treasure chests of their hearts, and we need only use love to turn the key. This is a popular trope in fiction and fantasy; the mundane boy in mundane circumstances discovers he is the chosen one and he's really magic. The Dead Poets, the Dangerous Minds, just waiting for someone to awaken the giant within. This is a concept beloved of those who believe that potential is, like the statue of David, buried beneath the block of marble, waiting to be let loose.

Potential isn't like that. The problem with the metaphor of *David* and the marble block is that he is not discovered, he is *carved*. You could just as easily find a hundred garden gnomes or a thousand bathroom tiles – or two tonnes of rubble – in the same block. Potential is overrated. That kind of potential is the

---

7. www.bit.ly/2O4nIKQ

plot line to a Disney film: *believe in yourself and follow your dreams.* Try telling that to a pyromaniac, or Charles Manson.

It's enormously patronising. It tells students they don't have to work hard or dedicate themselves to their improvements. The mansion is already built, and someone needs to simply pull away the curtain. It's dangerously close to moral subjectivism, that everyone is just fine the way they are because no one is better than anyone else.

I think potential isn't discovered; it's carved or built. It takes effort and skill and patience and probably a lot of luck. It usually takes skilled sculptors working sensitively with the material that they have, albeit with more agency on the statue's part. But it isn't released just because someone looks into your heart and says, 'You're magic; fly free, you beautiful dreamer.'

And that is why behaviour matters. Because too many kids who behave badly could be persuaded or taught or helped not to. Who, instead of enduring school, ricocheting through it like a dirty comet, could do better. Who, if they were patiently shown how to behave, could be more than just the kid who was, in the words of A.A. Gill, 'bottom of the class at pretty much everything except the nature table'.[8]

They need us. They need our help to behave, and to flourish.

Summary:

- *Better behaviour improves every aim of school we can imagine.*
- *Improving behaviour should be the common goal of everyone in education.*
- *Better behaviour is essential to good learning.*

Good behaviour takes constant effort

In restaurants, you often see this ticket system: the waiter types your order, and a ticket comes up on the kitchen printer. The window man reads this and calls out to the line chefs: a medium-rare fillet, an enchilada, a plate of wings, and so on. When the chefs have cooked them off, they pass it to the window man who gathers the dishes in the hot window, until the ticket is complete. Then he calls the expeditor on the other side of the window to collect and dress the food, and

---

8. Gill, A. A. (2018) *The Best of A. A. Gill.* London: W&N.

have it sent front of house. This bit is called 'selling your ticket'. Once the ticket is sold, it's gone. He can forget about it forever.[9] Life is good.

In teaching, you never sell your ticket. Tasks roll over into the next day and the next. Educating a class is a commitment spanning years, thousands of days, moments and conversations. You never get to 'perfect' behaviour. There is no point at which you can say, 'My job here is done; I need do no more.' Ensuring good behaviour in a classroom is an act of maintenance; it is an act of constant creation. It is like a song, or juggling: it only exists as long as you put effort into it. Entropy constantly nips at your heels.

You will – hopefully – see your classes behave wonderfully, but even then you can never relax. Good habits slip; people forget themselves; dynamics change; moths and rust take all the treasures of the earth. Everything is impermanent.[10] Your job is keeping the train on the tracks; keeping the plates spinning. Teachers need to understand their constant effort is crucial to sustaining the permanent forward motion. Behaviour management is like juggling three balls. You stop juggling, your balls drop.

But then, nothing valuable can endure without maintenance. A house must have its roof mended; teeth need cleaning; relationships take work; a six-pack demands abstinence and horrific levels of calorific austerity. Maintaining it can be immensely rewarding, so long as you keep reminding yourself how much you have achieved, how far you have come, and what your goal is.

When you forget this, behaviour can go off the rails quickly. I once saw behaviour deteriorate from excellent to terrible in a matter of a few weeks. The school had a challenging demographic, but the behaviour was good because the senior staff led a team of motivated teachers in a rigorous way. Then along came a new head, whose first words to the students were, 'I want you to see me as a friend,' and 'I will always give you another chance.' Within a week, the most ambitious of students had tested his word and found that he would indeed permit anything as long as they thought he was a nice guy. Within a second

---

9. Until someone complains that the walnut cake contains nuts, or their chips aren't pointing the right way, or it's Tuesday or something.

10. In Buddhism this is called *annica*, and forms one of the religion's three essential doctrines. In some forms of Hinduism, the god Vishnu reclines in the coils of the serpent Shesha, as he dreams the world into existence. When he wakes up, the dream ends. In your classroom, when you wake up, the nightmare starts.

week, the change in behaviour was palpable. A month later, with little support, teachers started to give up. The school went into a terminal nose spin. But it was OK: the school head moved on after a few years to another school, and no one was hurt apart from thousands of children who had their futures shredded by naivety, incompetence and the fairy tales we tell ourselves to feel good.

Summary: *getting behaviour right can take some time. For example: forever.*

Some schools are harder than others

I want to paint an optimistic picture: everyone can improve, and miracles are indeed possible. It also takes time to get this right. Good classroom behaviour takes high levels of commitment, because they require high levels of consistency, and there is simply no way around this. Like losing weight has no short cuts, unless you count liposuction or gastric bands, the medical equivalent of excluding all your naughtiest children: possible, but you haven't solved the reasons things got so bad.

Also, some classes and school demographics are much harder than others. If you teach the children of Swiss diplomats, then you may enjoy a classroom of some calm and fragrancy. If you teach comprehensive cohorts from complicated backgrounds of disadvantage, dislocation or lack, then you will be struggling uphill with behaviour. It's still possible, but it is the difference between sprinting 100 metres in lycra versus doing it in a frogman's suit. You *can* still do it, but get ready to work ten times as hard.

This isn't going to be easy

But to go back to the cheerier end of this vision: none of what needs to be done to get good behaviour is rocket science. It's hard to do but reasonably easy to grasp. For the most part, the techniques that create calm, safe classrooms are relatively straightforward and basic. The principles of good behaviour management are as simple as the principles of good diet. Which is lucky, because at a societal level we need so many teachers, it would be a disaster if they all had to have PhDs in psychology to make the difference they needed.

What it does take, however, is dedication, persistence, and consistency. That is unavoidable. Work hard at this, forever. That's all I have to offer you: blood, toil, tears and sweat, because that's all there is. The fruits, however, are extraordinary. As Marzano says, 'Research[11] tells us that the teacher is the single most important factor affecting student achievement – at least the single most important factor that we can do much about.'[12]

How responsible are students for their own behaviour?

This is a good question. We need to confront some basic philosophical questions about human behaviour: do we choose to act freely, or is all of our behaviour caused by external and internal forces beyond our control? This is important, because if students' actions are all caused by, for example, their upbringing or their genes, then it is hard to hold them responsible for their behaviour. We would not be able to blame or praise them for their actions, any more than we would blame or praise the sun for shining. That would then have an impact on our attitudes to, for example, using sanctions or rewards. If students aren't responsible for their actions, then why should we condemn or applaud anything they do?

Practically, it is useful to draw distinctions between three categories of student behaviour:

1. Behaviour they cannot choose *not* to perform. A good example of this would be a student with Tourette syndrome who often finds it impossible to restrain their verbal tics spilling over into e.g. profanity or inappropriate comments.
2. Behaviour they find *hard* to perform. This could mean that students who have been raised to behave a certain way – e.g. to shout or be demanding when they want attention – will do so if not challenged to do otherwise
3. Behaviour they freely choose to perform and could do otherwise if they wished. This could include showing off to one's friends, being lazy because they find a task challenging, and so on.

Many would say these categories are not distinct, and blend easily into one another; others would say that they all collapse into one category – because 'all

---

11. Sanders, W. L., Wright, S. P. & Horn, S. P. (1997) 'Teacher and classroom context effects on student achievement: implications for teacher evaluation', *Journal of Personnel Evaluation in Education,* 11, 57–67.

12. Marzano, R. J., Marzano, J. S. and Pickering, D. (2003) *Classroom management that works: research-based strategies for every teacher.* Alexandria, VA: Association for Supervision and Curriculum Development.

actions are caused by prior events, and we have no free will.' This is a debate that has raged, unsettled, for millennia.

Happily, you do not have to solve it. This trinity of distinction is still useful. Some things can be affected by the student's willpower, and some cannot. We should no more reprimand an autistic student who screams because they are touched when they do not wish to be than we would a student in a wheelchair for failing to run a 400-metre relay. Many things are beyond our ability to control.

It is essential that teachers are alert to when behaviour is voluntary and when it is involuntary. If a student misbehaves, the wise teacher should investigate if there is some exceptional cause. It might, for example indicate something important or more serious. I once taught a student who behaved terribly on Friday afternoons only, resulting (without exception) in a detention on that day. And then we discovered his father, with whom he spent the weekends, battered him. His misbehaviour was a way to delay that, even for an hour. Or the girl who was late every Monday and Tuesday (and sanctioned accordingly) until we discovered she was the primary carer for her disabled parents on both of those days' mornings, dressing and washing them, and making her late. We changed our response.

But most misbehaviour is not like this. In most *mainstream* classrooms, *most* misbehaviour is avoidable. Most students could, if they decided, do otherwise. In other words, most misbehaviour can be modified. It's often done for the most human of reasons: to amuse, to distract, to win esteem or status from their peers. It is usually not some symptom of a shadowy cause. Realising this is useful to the classroom teacher because it means that we can proceed in most instances as if behaviour were the responsibility of the student and react (or anticipate) accordingly. In fact, as we shall see, treating students as having responsibility over their actions is vital if we are to teach them how to accept responsibility for themselves, to manage their own lives, and grow in maturity.

CAUTION 1: the flip side is that teachers must be on the lookout for signs that a student's behaviour does require more support, especially where we know the student faces burdens and challenges in their home or mental circumstances.

CAUTION 2: in more specialised learning environments (e.g. special schools), the frequency with which trauma, mental health issues, and far more serious behavioural causes occur is obviously much, much higher.

This is important (and useful) because if we insist on treating every act of misbehaviour as an inscrutable riddle to be unwrapped, as if we were some kind of classroom Poirot, it becomes impossible to actually teach. We permit too much misbehaviour while we explore its reasons and lose more time than we possess. More importantly, whatever the reason for the behaviour, usually the initial response is the same. For example, if a student swears in class, or uses racist language, then they need to be dealt with immediately, whether or not their behaviour springs from some terrible internal conflict, or merely malice. The safety and dignity of the class are paramount, and students (and staff) must be protected from abuse – this is the primary duty of the teacher. This is part of the moral compass core of running the room.

The prime directives of teaching

The classroom teacher has two prime directives:[13]

1. To protect
2. To educate

To protect

The most basic role of the teacher is to make sure students are safe from harm. This seems so obvious, it hardly needs stating; but if we do not state it, we find ourselves permitting some peculiar dangers. I became acutely aware of this when my own children started to go to elementary school, and they would come home with the inevitable scratches and bumps the rough edges of the world send us. The reaction you feel as a parent in such circumstances is visceral: *Who did this to my perfect child? Why were they not protected and shielded from this inequity?* Of course, no such invulnerability is possible. Small people running in playgrounds will race, giggle, trip and weep for their troubles. When we place the care of our fragile children with others – an institution, the state – the very least we can expect as adults is that the room they are in, if nothing else, is as safe as possible. They must be returned to the parents in the same physical state they arrived in.

This also necessarily implies that we cannot permit anything to happen to them that we would not wish on our own children. We must work tirelessly to root out and eliminate bullying; prevent them from being harassed or mocked or any other attempt to threaten their safety by fellow classmates. Also, if children are not safe, they cannot learn – at least, not what we want them to learn. If we cannot guarantee their safety, then we have not performed our duty.

---

13. Sadly not 'Serve the public trust; protect the innocent; uphold the law.' But not far off it.

When I was a new teacher, I taught a very hard class of 24 capering, rough boys, and one quiet girl. It was a 'bottom set' class for low ability. Most of the boys were there because they didn't behave and didn't achieve much. The girl, a recent immigrant from Slovakia, was there purely because English was her second language. The boys were as predictably awful as you would fear, ogling and mocking her. I was fresh out of training and had no idea how to deal with it other than constant tellings-off. I rebuked them every time they did so, and thought I was doing my best. Then one day I left the room to reprimand a young man for swearing at another, and as I did so I heard a scream. When I rushed back in, she was standing, in tears, screaming at the boys. Down her face dripped an enormous line of spit.

She looked at me like I had betrayed her, and I will never forget the anger in her eyes, the frustration that she was trapped in that room, with those boys, somewhere she should have been safe, and learning. But she was neither. And both were my responsibility. It gives me no pleasure to repeat this, and years later my heart is still heavy with guilt at my failure. But I think it is important to understand the fundamental responsibilities we have, and the sacredness of that.

To educate

Secondly, we must educate them. There are a number of principles that underpin this:

- Everyone wants to matter. *All* children in your classroom are important. Including the ones who are harder to love.
- *You* are important too. We should view every member of the classroom as an individual deserving as much dignity, liberty, esteem and consideration as possible.
- It is not possible for everyone's desires to be met at the same time as everyone else's.
- At times, individual wants will be balanced with the greater good of the community.
- At the same time, the community is composed of individuals who deserve as much individual dignity as we can obtain for them.

A delicate balancing act results – one where we seek to maximise the dignity and learning of as many people as possible, while at the same time not permitting any one student to dominate the others. It is impossible for everyone to behave as they please. The best we can hope for is optimal conditions.

From a behaviour point of view, this means that no student can, under any circumstances, place other students under physical threat. However unsatisfactory the outcomes for the individual student, the needs of the majority massively outweigh the needs or intentions of the one in this context.

For the many and the few

It is very easy, particularly if one is concerned with the welfare of all students, to want to give a violent or abusive student another chance in the class, and then another. You know sending them out will damage their learning, send them further behind, and make it harder for them to catch up. You may have seen their struggle, their progress, and be willing them on to better things.

Stop for a second. Consider the needs of all. The other children are looking to you for protection and safety. They do not understand when we fail to provide this. If we keep a violent or abusive student in the classroom because we want to give them yet another chance to do well, then it is the rest of the class who have to bear the brunt of it. We make them pay for a bill that we run up on their behalf. Their safety precedes all other concerns.

But even when safety itself isn't threatened, no one student should be allowed to set fire to the learning of their peers. Which means there will have to be clear boundaries of acceptable conduct. Where those boundaries are set will depend on the school, class, teacher, context, etc. But there must be a clear point, generally understood by all, beyond which it is not permitted to go. Without a sense of those boundaries, lessons will always be disrupted.

What is good behaviour?

This is not as obvious as it sounds. What do we mean by good behaviour? Here is a simple two-part definition that I find useful.[14]

1. Negative good behaviour. The absence of misbehaviour: *not* throwing chairs around, *not* rolling your eyes at the teacher, not swearing or pushing or fighting. For many teachers, this is a huge achievement, when you can get your class to the point where they aren't doing anything obviously terrible, and all appear to be listening – or at least not talking over you.

---

14. Negative and positive good behaviour deliberately echoes Isaiah Berlin's theory of negative and positive liberty. Freedom is also not as simple a concept as it at first sounds.

Of course, this category of behaviour is not perfect. A class might be behaving very well in this sense, but be utterly passive, or bored, or chronically disengaged, doing the bare minimum.

But this level of behaviour – which we might call passive compliance – is often undervalued by some, when it is actually a very great prize. There are many teachers for whom obtaining this would be a dream come true. If your classroom is chaotic, if fights and arguments are all you know, if you struggle to get all students facing one way and listening, then compliance of this type looks pretty good. In the early days of my career, this was the phase I longed for. It was only once I had achieved an uneasy truce with my classes that I even suspected there was more to behaviour than the absence of misconduct.

Example: *following instructions; being quiet when asked the first time.*

2. Positive good behaviour. This is what might be broadly described as 'habits that help the student to flourish as a learner and as a human'. This is much more than compliance. This is the ability to know how to conduct oneself in a debate; how to argue sensibly; how to behave in an unfamiliar social circumstance; how to forgive someone who has no right to your mercy; how to compose an essay; how to teach oneself a new instrument, and so on. In a classroom, it might be exemplified by how to focus; to follow an argument; to understand another's perspective; to be punctual; to share resources, and so on.

This is much more than just not misbehaving.

Example: ***being punctual*** *is much more than 'not being late'. It involves planning to be on time, getting work done the night before, knowing your journey time to school, checking websites for delays, etc. You can avoid being late by turning up in a mess, unprepared. Being on time takes a web of mature skills, knowledge, habits and aptitudes.*

(2) is frequently held to be the most valuable category of behaviour, perhaps understandably. It represents the higher-order behaviours that promote flourishing, success, and successful communities. But (1) is necessary before (2) is possible. Students must learn to self-regulate, to restrain their own immediate desires and whims, to persevere even when they don't want to, before they can learn more positive habits of independent behaviour.

Both (1) and (2) are important. (2) needs students to be able to do (1), so don't undervalue it. The teacher that aims directly for (2) because it seems so attractive will fail because they need students to be able to get the basics right before they can aim higher. In other words, not only is it not a bad thing to ask children to be able to follow instructions and behave, it is necessary. It is a precondition of building mature habits that children know they should behave, and value that behaviour intrinsically.

I meet many teachers who feel that students need to buy into behaviour systems before we expect them to follow them. But in an average classroom, this strategy means you will constantly be explaining the simplest of instructions, over and over ('But why can't I listen to my music? I'm not hurting anyone!'). Your students need to learn to trust that your instructions are just, efficient, fair and useful. *You must not delegate this responsibility.* If you relinquish decision-making in the classroom, you do not abolish the need to make decisions; you just delegate it to the students. Power is a zero-sum game. It cannot be created or destroyed, only passed around. You need to be the authority in the room, or the students will be. Good luck with that.

CHILDREN MUST BE TAUGHT HOW TO BEHAVE

Being well behaved is not an accident of birth. Students do not create themselves. We are all the products of our circumstances. Students who behave well have been taught these things already. If they have not, the teacher must try to do so.

CHAPTER 2
GOOD AND BAD MODELS

The most common mistake when trying to run the room

After years of watching and teaching lessons, and then teaching people to teach lessons, and then watching that, I can observe that many teachers make the same mistake. It is incredibly common, and at times it almost appears to be the default. The most common mistake teachers make is this:

They wait for misbehaviour to occur and then they react to it.

Why? Usually they often haven't had much training in how to handle behaviour. Teacher preparation in this area is often very light touch (or worse, sometimes impractical), so new teachers can be forgiven for thinking that it isn't important. Who could blame them? If you haven't been shown how to do something, why would you know?. Behaviour management is complex. No one is born good at it. It needs to be taught to you if you don't want to have to figure it out for yourself. And if it isn't taught, you end up with a teacher who has no idea how to direct the behaviour of a group of children, and is therefore forced to wing it, go by gut instinct, or make it up as they go along.

Which is where we find ourselves now.

Hoping it doesn't rain

This results in a strategy I refer to as 'hoping it doesn't rain'. It goes like this:

Day 1 of the new term. The new classroom teacher enters. Students are allowed to take any seat they want, and despite a few token directions and reprimands they ignore the teacher, who gives up and simply begins the lesson.

Perhaps a PowerPoint slide is shown, with an attempt to explain it. Perhaps books are given out in this noisy period of détente, where little is asked of the student, and little is done except by the few. Perhaps there is a spell of silence and the teacher sees her chance to begin. Quickly, one, two, three students start talking over the instruction, or ignore it completely, and tend to their make-up or phones. The teacher then stops the lesson to deal with this. In another part of the room, some other students realise an

43

opportunity has appeared to swap Magic: The Gathering cards. Someone else comments on the first group. Bored students, having lost their focus, find other things to do. The noise level rises again. We are back to square one, but square one is all there is. Driven to despair, the teacher raises her voice a few times, and warns or issues sanctions. The class sneers or ignores her. Repeat, until the merciful bell.

The 'strategy' is to try to teach, and deal with misbehaviour when it occurs. She has walked into a world with dark skies, wearing only a light jacket, and hoped it doesn't rain.

This seems like a reasonable strategy to some extent. If you are a professional who knows a good deal about history or arithmetic but little about running a room (or worse, you don't know that it's a skill set at all), then it's perfectly reasonable to do the thing you are good at, and crucially the thing you believe you are being paid for.

But it is the wrong strategy.

The fire brigade model

Imagine you were the steward of a new high rise, and you wanted to make sure it didn't burn down. But the framework is made of wood, and every apartment runs on a petrol generator. One strategy would be to make sure there was a team of fire engines outside the building, heavy with hydrants and hoses, ready to spring into action the minute flames caught. You *could* do that. But even in the best-case scenario, the building will have already caught fire before your strategy kicks in. You are doomed to always put fires out.

But that's exactly what the teacher in the scenario above is doing. In fact, it's not even that useful, because I've assumed the fire brigade in this story are well trained and equipped to handle fires. Going back to the classroom, most teachers aren't particularly well trained in 'putting out fires' (in this case, dealing with misbehaviour once it's started etc.). Often, teachers have to make it up as they go along. They have no option if no one has shown them any better.

The fire prevention model

It is obvious what the wise steward/architect could have done: design buildings that don't catch fire often or easily: build them out of concrete and iron; partition each floor into inert silos that defy the transmission of heat; demand that all materials used are non-flammable; stipulate a maximum occupancy;

and so on. In short, you reduce fires by making sure they are far less likely to happen and by working out what to do when they occur.

What you don't do is hope fires don't happen, and only think about how to respond when your smoke alarm is shrieking murder at you. The kind of caution that drives health and safety regulations is amongst the dullest but most necessary of human instincts, and as sure an indicator of social and civil flourishing as the invention of language.

It's equally crazy to walk into a classroom without planning for the most common problems that occur. But we do it. It reminds me of a complaint I sometimes hear from people who object to managing behaviour at all. 'I'm paid to teach,' they say, 'not to manage their behaviour.' Brother, are you in the wrong job.

Teaching is not just standing in front of a room and talking at people. That's a poetry recital; that's a YouTube lecture; a eulogy. Teaching is much more than that. It is a relational activity. It is dialogic. It involves directing the behaviour of a group of people to behave civilly with one another and with you. It involves directing not just their academic habits but also their social habits. In short, the teacher, if she wants to teach, has to understand not only her subject with detail and fluidity of recall but also how to run the room.

Why aren't teachers fully prepared to manage behaviour?

Perhaps you are at the start of your career, wondering if you will ever be able to manage a room. At this point, simply the thought of providing enough content to fill the time is overwhelming enough. Or you may be mid-career, a few years in, and wondering when – if ever – behaviour will be good enough. Or maybe you've seen many seasons in many schools and you can feel your career slipping into past tense and you ask, 'Why was behaviour never good enough?' The answer is probably 'Because no one showed you how to manage it.'

My first classes fed me to the Wicker Man. My first classes brayed and shouted at me and asked when the real teacher was turning up. It was awful, truly awful. A few schools later and it was still pretty bad. I used to go home every night, frustrated to the point of tears, and wonder, 'Why can't I do this?' What I should have been asking was, 'Why has no one shown me how to do this?'

Why indeed? Why would a pilot blame herself if she couldn't land a 747 first time? What physician would reprimand a colleague for his ignorance of open-heart surgery if he was a librarian? And why should a training teacher be good at something as complex as managing the behaviour of dozens of recalcitrant children without some kind of structured training in the topic?

We had, and have, a very big problem with behaviour instruction for teachers in the UK. And from what I've seen of the world, many similar countries have a similar problem. High-quality, practical and structured early-career training on how to run a room full of children is very hard to find. There are some providers who deliver good programmes. But at present many teachers lack a basic training in classroom management.

It is still too often assumed that teachers will learn this part of the job on the job; that it forms part of the craft of the classroom, unpacked as you progress. But in no other profession would we applaud ourselves for so recklessly abandoning the crucial phases of career instruction to the vagaries of fate, where you are fortunate if you encounter a wise mentor who is not only good at behaviour management but also adept at training it. And those are two separate things.

The lost art of behaviour

Running the room risks becoming a lost art in many schools. But the good news is that there is a body of knowledge you can learn, and strategies you can learn how to apply. There are things that tend to work well with some children, and strategies that work better with others. There are learnable micro-behaviours that are easy to practise once demonstrated, but hard to discover by oneself. To quote Dylan Wiliam, 'Everything works somewhere, and nothing works everywhere.'[1] Discerning the *when* and the *where* of effective strategies is every teacher's task. When managing behaviour, we can say with reasonable confidence that some things tend to work more reliably than some other strategies, and some things work rarely, if ever.

In short, we do not train teachers half as well as they should be trained in one of the most important skills of their jobs, and that, to my mind, is some kind of tragedy. When I think of the countless hours and careers and futures sacrificed on this altar of ignorance and stubbornness, it drives me into despair. This book is an attempt to address that.

---

1. Wiliam, D. (2018) *Creating the schools our children need: Why what we're doing now won't help much (and what we can do instead)*. West Palm Beach, FL: Learning Sciences International.

Of course you cannot learn a practical craft entirely from a book. You may as well learn to drive by reading The Highway Code. But a book can provide a useful language to think about behaviour and point you towards some of the most effective strategies that others have found before you. A book can provide you with a map across a jungle. You can find your own way, but at least you have the map.

Why is current thinking so wrong?

Sadly, many mistaken approaches are explicitly taught to teachers at the beginning of their careers. For example, I was told that children will behave well if you let them follow their interests, if you make the lessons engaging enough, and if you permit them to express themselves. There is a commonly held view that children naturally want to learn, are innately inclined to learn, and it is the unnatural classroom model that creates friction, conflict and misbehaviour as much as anything else. In other words, *schools and teachers themselves* are responsible for most bad behaviour.

This is obviously nonsense. It is absurd to suggest that children would behave well if only we got out of their way and let their angelic natures self-direct towards the love of knowledge and wisdom and goodness. Children are lovely indeed, but they can be lazy, and kind, and hypocritical, and selfish, and angry, and forgiving, and every other sin and virtue. Which is to say, they are just like us.

Some common behaviour myths:[2]

- **Some people have 'got it'** – the magic touch with children. It's true that some have better interpersonal skills than others, but subscribing too much to this leads us to the sin of essentialism – that teaching is an innate gift rather than something that can be learned.
- **If they misbehave, it's your fault.** Sometimes we can antagonise children, or handle them the wrong way, but if they tell you to get stuffed, it is rarely because your starter activity wasn't engaging enough.
- **Teacher authority is oppressive, because everyone is equally important.** Everyone is important, it's true. But this aphorism is usually mangled to mean 'It's wrong to tell children what to do.' But the teacher needs to be the authority in the room, for very good reasons we'll explore throughout this book.
- **Kids need love, not boundaries.** They need both. Boundaries without love is tyranny, but love without boundaries is indulgence.

---

2. At least, I still hear them.

- **They need to like you.** It's great if they like you but we're not here to be liked. We're here to teach them, and if we make their liking us the aim instead, we will sacrifice their learning for our relationships. The best part is that if you teach them well, they probably will like you.

We're not designed to behave naturally

Classrooms *are* unnatural to some extent, of course, given that they are unique to our species. They are also highly evolved, efficient methods of imparting a lot of knowledge to a lot of people at once. We're not, as yet, in a place where we can afford to privately tutor every child; and until that point, learning will have to be a communal activity. It remains 'groups of people sitting together', learning how to cooperate in ways that would dazzle a less collaborative species or ancestor. In the now-ancient film *Crocodile Dundee*, the titular protagonist, a grizzled Australian bushman from the Outback, comes to America, and the film's high concept rests on his 'fish out of water' character arc. Upon arriving in New York, he looks out of his limousine onto the teeming masses of Fifth Avenue streaming along the pavements, so unlike the lonely desolation of the baking Outback. 'New York City, Mr Dundee,' says Mark Blum. 'Home to 7 million people.' 'That's incredible,' he replies. 'Imagine 7 million people all wanting to live together. Yep, New York must be the friendliest place on earth.'

It wasn't the world's funniest joke even then, but the humour rested on the then well-understood premise that New York was a violent and often dangerous city. At the time, it was famous for its muggings and inner-city unrest. The 'gag' was that New Yorkers were legendarily brittle and cynical.[3]

It's not all about relationships

But in a sense, he was absolutely right. Even just to co-exist in such close quarters, in circumstances of such density, is a massive achievement for any social group. Think of the intense, constant background buzz of accepted norms and tolerance levels, and mutually agreed contracts of forbearance and self-regulation that prevents these people from all selfishly demanding their own needs be placed first. Those who claim that good behaviour is 'all about relationships' need to deal with this problem: how can people behave well in communities where they have no relationship with the majority of their fellow citizens? The answer is, of course, law.

People in large communities do not abide with one another peacefully only because they have a relationship with one another, or with those who enforce

---

3. A stereotype that repeated visits confirm is deeply untrue.

those laws, e.g. police officers and judges. That helps, but most people obey most laws because they prefer to live in a lawful community and because they do not wish to be arrested. Imagine, if you will, what would happen if all laws were suspended, and people could do as they pleased. How long do you think the civility would endure? An hour?[4]

We can find this demonstrated neatly. In 1969 the Montreal police went on strike in protest about pay and conditions. The next day, this was the way the television news described what happened:

> Montreal is in a state of shock. A police officer is dead and 108 people have been arrested following 16 hours of chaos during which police and firefighters refused to work. At first, the strike's impact was limited to more bank robberies than normal. But as night fell, a taxi drivers' union seized upon the police absence to violently protest a competitor's exclusive right to airport pickups. The result, according to this CBC Television special, was a 'night of terror'. Shattered shop windows and a trail of broken glass are evidence of looting that erupted in the downtown core. With no one to stop them, students and separatists joined the rampage. Shop owners, some of them armed, struggled to fend off looters. Restaurants and hotels were also targeted. A corporal with the Quebec provincial police was shot and killed at the garage of the Murray Hill limousine company as taxi drivers tried to burn it down.[5]

For social order to break down, it doesn't even require that *everyone* chooses to ignore rules and laws. It may well be that the majority of people would rub along quite happily under most circumstances. But all it takes is that some of them choose to reject the rules sometimes, where they see advantage in doing so. 'If it be known that there is one thief in a city, all men have reason to shut their doors and lock their chests.'[6]

---

4. On July 13th, 1977 a series of lightning strikes on power substations caused an electrical blackout that affected almost all of New York City. Widespread looting, crime and arson ensued as the police infrastructure struggled to cope with the newly emboldened criminal fraternities. In fairness, similar blackouts in 1965 and 2003 did not lead to these consequences, but this does show how little it can take for social restraint to dissolve.

5. CBC Television News Special, Broadcast Date, Oct. 8, 1969, Host: David Knapp. Retrieved (08/06/20) from CBC Digital Archives: www.bit.ly/3fEeEbM

6. Martinich, A.P. and Battiste, B. (2010) *Thomas Hobbes' Leviathan Part I and II, revised edition.* Broadview Press.

It is easy to become so used to safety, security and civil society that we forget that it is not our natural state. We also forget how good conduct is carefully passed on and perpetuated from one generation to another. It cannot be assumed that our children will simply spontaneously behave well.

Adult behaviour affects student behaviour

Children do not behave well by default, and nor do we. Throughout this book I refer to children's behaviour, but in most of the sections we could easily be talking about the adult behaviour. We, as adults, need to make sure that our conduct is of a high standard, otherwise how can we expect children to change their behaviour?

Classes will not run smoothly unless we think clearly and explicitly about what behaviour we need to succeed, and how to direct the minds of children towards it. The classroom project is a microcosm of the great project of society and civilisation. Because they are both communities. And they both need to be run. Leaders and teachers need to make the weather.

Students need to be taught to behave

It is a matter of urgency that we focus on this; that we start, collectively as a profession, to understand that students need to be taught how to behave. From that principle, another follows: teachers need to be taught how to teach students to behave well. And from that, we can conclude that we need to create a system that trains others to train others to do so. There is a lot of work to be done, and it is all vital that we set ourselves to it if we care about the well-being, education, and sanity of millions of children around the world.

But it starts, first of all, with you.

Summary:

- Students need to be taught to behave.
- Not all students find it easy to behave.
- What we do affects what they do.
- Reacting to behaviour is not enough.

TEACH, DON'T TELL, BEHAVIOUR

Behaviour cannot be modified in the long term by simply telling students to behave. The behaviour curriculum must be taught, similarly to how we would teach an academic or practical subject.

CHAPTER 3
RUNNING THE ROOM

'Running the room' is a phrase I first picked up in nightclubs. The Peter principle[1] states that we are all promoted to the point of incompetence, and rarely has this been so nimbly demonstrated than by my own career. The job was to run the *space*; to see it as a *room*, not a series of tasks or problems one after another. What you did in one part of the room affected the other parts. What you did in the past affected the future. It was an enormous Rubik's Cube; change one square and you change everything else.

It meant taking a step back, anticipating problems and heading them off before they happened. That might be servicing the ice machine before a heat wave, or planning bartender rotas that matched the strongest staff with the toughest shifts. In fact, one of the best indicators that a night had been planned well enough was simply that no problems occurred, or any that did were swiftly dealt with. From the point of view of efficient club management, the best nights were the boring ones.

It definitely also meant having a feel for the atmosphere, the style, the way the staff dealt with punters, the vibe we meant to convey. That meant that you had to think about staff training, shift meetings, menu options, pricing, music, décor, security etiquette, and a hundred other things.

So too with the teacher. They need to *run the room*. That involves managing a complex web of competing desires and needs and trying to bend their actions to your intentions. It is perfectly sensible for people to be a little selfish. Which of us does not want to get what we want, or does not want to do as we please? A room with 30 children and an adult has 31 different ideas about what good behaviour means. The teacher's job is to make sure that their vision of what should happen actually does happen.

The room must be run. If the teacher does not run it, the students will, because power abhors a vacuum. And if you permit students to do as they please, then ask how would you have behaved in such circumstances as a child?

---

1. Peter, L. J. and Hull, R. (1969). *The Peter principle*. New York, NY: Morrow.

We can apply this model to behaviour management. This involves creating conditions where good behaviour is more likely, bad behaviour is less likely, and designing systems to respond to misbehaviour/good behaviour when it occurs.

This can be described in terms of a *proactive* and *reactive* approach to behaviour.

1. Proactive: Creating an environment where students know how they are expected to behave in advance of them having to do so; where they perfectly understand the behaviours you want from them, how to do them, and why they are important.

2. Reactive: Responding to student behaviour when it happens so they understand if what they did was correct, and how to correct it if it was not. Providing external stimuli after the event.

In short, the students should be immersed in a classroom where good conduct is heard, seen, demonstrated, encouraged and expected all the time. They should be surrounded by constant displays of what good behaviour looks like. Like fish, unable to conceive of anything beyond the water in which they float, good behaviour should be the atmosphere they breathe. Ideally, they should find it hard to even imagine misbehaving, because they see it as being an absurd way to behave.

Proactive behaviour management involves what I call 'getting in front' of misbehaviour by establishing what they should be doing *before it happens*. This element of behaviour management is often found in more experienced teachers. As Elliot notes:

> Perhaps the fundamental point to emphasise is that skilled teachers tend not to have to react to problematic situations as often as do novices. Student teachers, for example, often seek to observe expert teachers' reactions to acts of student indiscipline … rather than upon the very subtle, and less perceptible, behaviours that reduce the likelihood of such problems occurring in the first place.[3]

This is a really important point for newer teachers to appreciate: often, if you go to observe a more experienced teacher, it's almost impossible to see what it is

---

3. Elliott, J. G. (2009) 'The nature of teacher authority and teacher expertise', *Support for Learning*, 24 (4), pp.197-203.

they're doing to get good behaviour. It just seems to *happen*. That's because what they're 'doing' was started a long time ago, and is now merely being reinforced.

It's also important to understand that novice learners and expert learners think very differently about material, and that includes novice and expert teachers as well as students.[4] Expert room-runners take in everything that is happening and pick out exactly what they need in order to change the direction of the class behaviour sensibly. Newer teachers drown in all of the information flooding them. They can't discern so easily between relevant and irrelevant data. That's why, when you are new to teaching, you see all the misbehaviour and react to everything as you see it, tearing your lesson to shreds as you jump about from behaviour to behaviour.

As we shall see later on in 'Scripts', most of the problems we face in classrooms are common ones, and we face them over and over. As we get better, we learn the best ways to deal with them, so that the next time we face them we have a better strategy ready to hand rather than having to think what to do. Expert teachers have what we call more advanced schemas (patterns of how we think about something). This means that they learn to deal with problems better *when* they happen but also crucially, *before* they happen.

Reactive strategies involve doing something about what they *have already done*. *Your* behaviour should provide feedback on *their* behaviour. This is where we find the classic sanctions and rewards model of school behaviour management. These strategies are also very important. A school culture can't flourish without them. But by themselves, they are only partially effective; and in many schools, they aren't done very well at all, which, as we'll see, makes them far less useful.

Both proactive and reactive strategies will be dealt with in detail later chapters. For now, remember this: *The most effective teachers use a combination of proactive and reactive strategies. Neither strategy alone is enough to get most children to behave.*

Many teachers are taught very little – if anything – about proactive strategies, and where they are, it is in an unstructured way. More teachers learn a little

---

4. Kirschner, P. A., Sweller, J. & Clark, R. E. (2006) 'Why minimal guidance during instruction does not work: an analysis of the failure of constructivist, discovery, problem-based, experiential, and inquiry-based teaching', *Educational Psychologist*, 41:2, 75-86 at 80.

about reactive strategies, but often badly. We see many teachers being given the school rulebook or teacher planner with a three-page behaviour policy and told, 'Do that.' Then they are expected to just get on with it. That's *not* high-quality training. No wonder these strategies are conducted badly, inconsistently, or with little conviction. Worse, teachers are often expected to use them in schools where the whole-school systems are themselves run badly. What a mess.

Monday and Sunday children

No child invents themselves. Every child is the product of their circumstances. Every student comes to your classroom with factory software preloaded: their set of beliefs, values, expectations, aptitudes and dispositions. And these will often be very different.

Monday's child comes from a home where they were exposed to enormous levels of language, rich in complexity and usage; they might have been exposed to an enormous variety of cultural capital, enrichening experiences or knowledge about the world. They may have been in lots of different social circumstances in a safe and structured way they could learn from. They may have been taught from infancy to be civil; to express themselves with confidence and manners; to know how to share; to wait their turn; to speak up when they need to and listen when they have to. In short, some children come with high levels of literacy, cultural capital, self-regulation and social skills.

Their expectations of you and what you represent may be very positive. They may have been raised, for example, to generally see teachers and adults as authority figures, and moreover, authority figures they can trust. These are the ones who have typically experienced adults treating them in responsible and caring ways. They may also value education, and already have a firm idea that school is a special place, that education is valuable, and that in order for everyone to learn and be happy, everyone has to behave kindly to one another.

These children will typically present as well-behaved students. I say typically, because none of this is destiny. But usually, these students will do better in school, or at least go further than they otherwise would have done. They will be more likely to follow reasonable instructions, to value learning tasks, and to persevere independently.

Sunday's child comes from the other end of this deliberately exaggerated spectrum. These are the less fortunate children, whose lives may have been characterised by lack or little luck. They may have been babysat by a television or immersed in low-language-ability backgrounds (see the Matthew effect, later). They may have been left to their own devices long and often, learning to focus more on their immediate comfort or avoiding threats than delayed gratification with purpose. They may know little about the world beyond their living rooms. They may have been exposed to toxic habits and character traits. They may be neglected in a hundred sad and terrible ways. They may have lived lives of distress or dislocation, devoid of stability or structure.

Perhaps they may have been raised to distrust authority. Perhaps their guardians had poor experiences themselves with it, or particularly with schools. They may see all institutions as hostile, and all teachers their agents. They may not see value in education at all, viewing it as a place to hang out with their friends rather than a place to learn and grow.

Their behaviour might often present as misbehaviour. They may be less able to focus because they have never learned how; they may reject any attempt to direct their behaviour because nobody has bothered before. They may treat all correction as an attack, because verbal abuse or abandonment may have been the principal behaviour modification technique of the home. They may be functionally illiterate and see little point in trying to do well at something they feel foolish at.

And of course, you have every variation in between. There are many hours between Monday and Sunday. None of this, as I mentioned, is destiny. One of the elegant complexities of human nature is that people frequently defy these odds. Some children will succeed despite huge odds against them; some will struggle despite the greatest of early-life advantages. Some children take trauma and turn it into rocket fuel when others might be destroyed by the same experience. But in gambling, the house always wins in the long run, and probability teaches us that children's backgrounds have a huge impact on who they become. Different children and cohorts will have different quantities of these qualities; different geographies and demographics, year groups and social strata will represent a complex rainbow of these factors. And they are all in your classroom.

Summary: *children are all different. Their different backgrounds mean they will all have different beliefs about what good behaviour is. They will also have different capacities to perform the behaviours they will need to succeed in classrooms.*

Not all students are created equal

And yet, there is often an assumption we make that every child in your classroom already knows how to behave; that they are classroom ready; that they somehow all start at the same baseline. This is simply untrue. We would never dream of being so rash as to assume children all started classes with the same level of ability in French or maths, or the piccolo. We would find out what they already knew and could do, and plan our teaching based on that. It is equally foolish to take a class and assume they all have the habits and qualities hardwired into them that they need to behave successfully.

In short, we need to remember that a class is made up of individuals. You're teaching a group, *and* you're teaching people, with different ideas and abilities, to behave. That is both obvious and frustrating because it means that if you start a relationship with a new group assuming 'I can just start teaching them' then you will probably hit the buffers at some point. The wise teacher realises that in order for everyone in the class to succeed, everyone needs to be taught how they should behave.

Takeaway: All students need to be taught how to behave in school. Some need a lot more teaching than others. You need to be the one who teaches it.

Behaviour and the Matthew effect

This simple realisation has powerful and extensive implications for teaching. It means that some of our children are simply not as ready to learn as they could be. It also means some of them are good to go from the minute you meet them. If you simply 'just start teaching them', then the ones who struggle to behave will continue to do so, and the ones who already find behaving easier will do well. This means that the disadvantage gap simply continues to widen. This is called the Matthew effect[5]: 'to those that hath, more shall be given'.[6] This is also called the *law of accumulated advantage*, sometimes summarised as 'The rich get richer; the poor get poorer.' People who already have advantages (like wealth, position, status, abilities) find it easier to acquire new advantages than those with fewer advantages. The job of the teacher is to help students defy this gravity.

---

5. In education, Keith E. Stanovich, Emeritus Professor of Applied Psychology and Human Development, University of Toronto used it to mean that children who begin with good basic literacy skills flourish, and those without do less well.

6. Matthew, 25:29

Behaviour is a curriculum

One of the core duties of the classroom teacher is to consciously, explicitly teach children how to behave. This should be done with as much care and effort as any academic curriculum. Because it is a curriculum: the *conduct curriculum*. It will not be learned automatically and it is not self-taught. The vast majority of children are not autodidacts who, like Buddha, sit under the Bodhi Tree and work out the secrets of the universe. They will not, by themselves, invent civility and self-regulation and manners and determination and kindness. These often have to be deliberately taught in a structured and continuous way by somebody. That means us.

The curse of expertise[7]

Being aware of the curse of expertise is one of the most useful and transformative principles of psychology a teacher should know. The curse of expertise is the well-observed cognitive bias where experts in a field have a tendency to overestimate the competence of others in their subject because they assume everyone possesses the same expertise and background knowledge in the subject that they have. Experts often assume that things that seem easy to them must be easy to others. Informing this fallacy is the fact that the expert no longer notices that much of her reasoning and ability has been built on thousands of hours of practice, involving basics that eventually become automatic and unconscious, e.g. the PhD mathematician who has such instantaneous recall of times tables and number bonds that he can forget how hard these are for children who have never been exposed to them. But at some point, even these basics need to be learned.

Teachers are expert behavers – and that's the problem

Teachers are usually graduates and, by virtue of having held employment in a high-status role, will possess some degree of self-regulation and social skills. This already makes them expert behavers. They already know how to do many of the things that make people good at working and learning in institutions. Thinking about the curse of expertise, we can often forget how difficult some students find it to do things we find easy, like sitting still, taking turns, asking politely, etc. But if you're not used to doing such things then they can seem alien and difficult. How many students see nothing wrong with shouting out because that was always the winning strategy for them at home? Or how many students have little idea what you mean when you say 'try your best' in an essay or exam? When they have never been shown what trying hard looks like and

---

7. Also known as the 'curse of knowledge,' this term was coined in a 1989 *Journal of Political Economy* article by economists Colin Camerer, George Loewenstein, and Martin Weber.

what sustained effort can achieve, you are asking them to imagine something they have not experienced.[8] In summary, it is easy to forget that we know very well how to behave the way they need, and they often do not.

When my daughter was five, she came home from school one day looking glum. I asked her what the matter was, and she said, 'My friend won't let me choose any of the games we play. She says she has to choose them all, and I'm a big silly.'[9] 'So,' I said, 'what did you say to her?' 'Nothing,' she shrugged. And why should she? Why should she know what to say in such an unusual and complex scenario? When your best friend won't let you play, and won't share, and turns it around so that you appear to be the one at fault? A lot of grown-ups might struggle knowing what to do with that scenario.

'OK,' I told her. 'Next time she says that, tell her "that's not nice", and not what good friends do. And that if she won't take turns choosing then you won't play with her.' Nothing ground-breaking, I know. But she listened, and she used it next time, and to the best of my knowledge all was well. We forget, as adults, how difficult it is to know what to say in a circumstance you've never dealt with before. What seems easy to us is hard to the child. Or observe how awful it looks when someone who is painfully shy makes a mess of a public conversation, a recital, a speech, and you watch it thinking, 'My God, just keep talking, say anything.' Or, 'Stop looking at the ground, just smile and nod and ask how they're doing.' But if you're used to public speaking, it's a breeze. If you're not, it's terrifying.

When you've dealt with a situation a thousand times before, you find it easier to deal with it the next time; you have a set of possible solutions you can already draw from. So an adult confronted with public speaking or a difficult colleague can reach for ready-made strategies to cope. But a child, a novice in behaving and learning, might struggle so much they reach for the most readily available mental scripts, even if they aren't very useful. Or a novice teacher, leaning on simplistic solutions to misbehaviour that don't work, but unable to conceive of better ones. While we may be expert behavers, new teachers are novices at running the room. No wonder we make so many mistakes.

---

8. This is the classroom version of *Hume's Fork*: statements are either true by definition (eg all men are male) or by experience (eg water is wet). Underpinning this is the idea that nothing about the world can be understood that has not first been experienced. This is *Strong Empiricism*.

9. The unforgivable curse.

Summary:

- *Not everyone in the room knows what good behaviour means.*
- *Not everyone knows what you mean by good behaviour.*
- *Not everyone has the habits and skills to behave that others do.*

The crucial takeaway? *Students have to be taught how to behave in your class.* This means treating it like any other part of the academic or formal curriculum.

- You have to plan what you want to teach them. That means knowing yourself exactly how you want them to behave, in lots of different circumstances that seem easy or obvious to you.
- You then have to deliver this curriculum. In other words, there needs to a clear process by which the details of 'good behaviour' are transmitted to students. Of course, this is as complex as any other form of teaching. And that means that everything you know about teaching a subject must also be applied to their behaviour. That means:

  - Checking their baseline understanding
  - Delivering an ability-appropriate curriculum
  - Checking for understanding
  - Repeating instructions if necessary
  - Doing this as many times as necessary. Possibly forever…

- You need to encourage them to 'revise' this learning so that it becomes embedded. By all means treat it as an examinable subject. Get them to do refresher courses if they forget any of it.

We'll explore this outline in **Section 2**. For now, it's enough to be aware that this is probably the most important part of managing behaviour: teaching it. To teachers unused to this model, it feels strange and almost revolutionary. But it is what highly successful teachers (and schools) do in real-life classes all over the world. Because they have to. And because children need us to.

NO ONE STRATEGY WILL WORK EQUALLY WITH ALL STUDENTS.

You cannot punish students into behaving. You cannot reward students into good behaviour. You cannot tell, teach, trick, or nudge all students into better behaviour habits. Different people are motivated for different reasons. The wise teacher uses a range of strategies to reach as many students as possible.

CHAPTER 4
MOTIVATION

Why don't students like school? is the provocative title of a seminal book all teachers should read by Professor Daniel Willingham.[1] It asks one of the most apposite questions: why *should* students like school? Here we are, asking them to do so many things, and really, why should they do any of it? Why not just tell us to get stuffed?[2] Willingham locates the answers to his titular question in cognitive psychology and the architecture of the learning mind, especially in the natural barriers between us and thinking hard. Once we appreciate these and incorporate workarounds into the way we teach, we give students – and ourselves – a fighting chance to succeed.

Understanding what motivates students is crucial for teachers. We cannot expect them to instantly do as they are asked. We do not possess mind control. Almost all behaviour management is ultimately persuasion. Students behave this way or that depending on how motivated they feel to do so. Motivation is a complex combination of internal factors (e.g. values, goals, feelings, habits, tastes, personality, etc.) and external ones (e.g. rewards, sanctions, environment, etc.). You *can* motivate by threat or cruelty, but all this is likely to guarantee is rebellion the moment your back is turned.

Crucially, we should not succumb to the sin of the *fallacy of the single cause*. This means assuming that students' behaviour has one obvious cause, or one obvious solution, and is the teacher's equivalent of only possessing a hammer so assuming everything must be a nail.[3] It's easy to assume that all misbehaviour stems from one simple thing, especially if that simple thing is something we have strong feelings about. There are plenty of people who think students only muck around because they are career anarchists; there are others who believe it is all down to their tragic backstories; there are others who attribute misbehaviour to weather, or exams, or the act of setting a sanction. Rousseau

---

1. Willingham, D. T. (2010) *Why don't students like school? A cognitive scientist answers questions about how the mind works and what it means for your classroom.* San Francisco, CA: Jossey-Bass Inc.

2. Obviously many do.

3. I have worked with builders who thought this. Also, teachers.

claimed it was the corrupting influence of society that degraded a child from their natural innocence into sinful sophistication. Freire believed that it is traditional education itself that corrupts and oppresses. Some believe in the influence of stars; others, demonic possession.

None of these offer us a single, universally useful lens through which to consider the reasons for misbehaviour, or, more correctly, 'behaviour'.

An important motivation for behaviour is how much satisfaction someone derives from pursuing an activity. By 'satisfaction' I don't just mean 'pleasure', although it can also mean that. The important meaning here is 'Do they see value in it? Does it give them something they want?' In this context, the 'something' can mean 'meaning, status, peer esteem, self-esteem', and many other similar goods. These are the things we really seek in life. These are the things that matter to us and motivate us. But they can take many forms, and some people are motivated by things that we do not wish them to be motivated by (e.g. taking joy in cruelty, drugs, humiliating others etc.).

School can provide many positive things that students can find motivating. But it is clear that it can also provide stimuli that students undoubtedly find demotivating, and things they do not want.

Why do students misbehave?

When you ask teachers this question, you get the same sensible answers repeatedly: boredom, lack of understating, peer pressure, problems at home, tiredness, mental health issues, and so on. These are all wise and appropriate responses. But these answers also locate the issues in the exact circumstance of that child. Not everyone has a mental health issue, not everyone is anxious about exams, not everyone is bored, and so on. Understanding these issues is important, but extremely hard for any teacher to do, requiring superhuman levels of intuition, empathy, training and perceptiveness each time.

What if we turned the question around 90 degrees and asked (in the style of Willingham), why should people behave at school in general? And why should they enjoy behaving?

Ten reasons students don't enjoy behaving in school

1. We ask them to do what they might not be inclined to do. What average child feels like doing trigonometry or sitting still on a bean bag to be registered on a sunny Friday morning? This is the first behavioural hurdle we have to climb. We are asking them to do what they might not otherwise choose to do. And we must. If we only opened our doors to the willing student, we would teach in almost-empty rooms, 200 days a year.

2. We ask them to think. This is one of Willingham's main points about learning, not behaviour, but it applies here too.[4] Thinking is hard. It's relatively easy to passively let experience and sensation wash over us. It's easy for music to play in the background. It's hard to consider what it means, and what might follow from it. It's hard to stop and listen and ask ourselves, what instrument was that? Why then? What does this mean? *Who am I?*[5]

3. We judge them. Students face a day full of assessments of their character, judgement, knowledge and skills by the staff, their peers, friends and strangers. If a student fears looking stupid or inadequate in some way, it is natural to assume they may not view the school day with joy. Even able students can be made uncomfortable by the dislike of being judged, if they derive more anxiety from the fear of failure than from the joy of success.

But judge them we must. It's probably impossible *not* to judge. Evaluation is intrinsic to understanding how well they are doing. But many find being the subject of evaluation hard. Social anxiety disorders tend to appear around adolescence, but even without looking at pathologies, feeling awkward and anxious while being scrutinised by others is a very common sensation. And in schools, this can become an Olympic sport. One of the ways that some students deal with social anxiety is by avoidance (doing something that will render the 'threat' harmless, like misbehaving to get out of a test) or escape strategies (leaving a room, for example, when asked to read a difficult text).[6]

4. We ask them to focus. How long can you concentrate on something that fascinates you before your mind wanders? You might be able to get lost in a fantastic book or film or song for a short period, but even then, our concentration span withers over hours. Remember the curse of expertise. How long can a child concentrate? On something that doesn't interest them? On something they aren't good at? This is sometimes called *attentional focus*,

---

4. Willingham, D. T. (2010), Ibid

5. Channelling the perpetual perplexity of Derek Zoolander, *Zoolander* (2001).

6. Schneier, F. (2006) 'Social Anxiety Disorder', *The New England Journal of Medicine*, 355 (10), pp.1029–1036.

and we know that children are less good at it than adults.[7] Getting children, especially young ones, to focus is hard work. It isn't easy or natural to be able to choose what to attend to without effort.

Focus is probably a combination of aptitude, temperament, the interest one has in the object, and accrued habit. Some people are naturally better at it than others, and some people learn to manage their focus. Children's attention – especially very young children – is 'diffuse'. They attempt to attend to everything. As adults, we typically only attend to about 1% of the environmental informational available because we are better able to determine salience. And of course, some things are more fascinating than others, but that is highly subjective. You cannot guarantee that everything you say will be gripping. In fact, you can guarantee it won't. Helping students to manage focus in these conditions is a key skill for teachers to build in their students.

Developing an attention span is a reflex that takes time. Children are reading less than ever these days,[8] perhaps thanks to the internet, but crucially they're also reading shorter texts for shorter periods of time. Like any habit, focus can be accrued or lost, and in each direction, it is facilitated by how much or how little practice is put in. At university, I had to read at least one long book per week, plus poems and chapters. At first it was hard, until it became a habit. Then I worked in the service industry for over a decade and lost the habit. Then I had children. Then I bought a smartphone. Now it takes me considerable effort to read over 800 words at a time. Habits can be built *and* dismantled.[9] They only last as long as they are maintained. If I stop going to the gym and start eating KFC for breakfast, I get fat.

Which *doesn't* mean students shouldn't be expected to demonstrate focus. But they can be helped to develop it. And we should appreciate that it's hard for some kids. We should still expect it to happen (indeed, without that expectation, they

---

7. Davidson, M. C., Amso, D., Cruess Anderson, L. and Diamond, A. (2006) 'Development of cognitive control and executive functions from 4 to 13 years: Evidence from manipulations of memory, inhibition, and task switching', *Neuropsychologia*, 44 (11), pp.2037–2078.

8. A survey by the National Literacy Trust in 2019 found just over half (52.5%) of 8-18-year-olds reading for pleasure in 2019, down from 58.8% in 2016, and only a quarter (25.7%) reading daily, compared with 43% in 2015. This was the lowest % since 2005, when the charity first started recording data.

9. Wolf, M. (2018) *Reader, come home: the reading brain in a digital world.* New York, NY: Harper Collins.

won't improve as easily) but they will need help. Create circumstances where students are expected to practise concentrating, even if it's only five minutes of quiet reading, built up, day by day. (And of course that assumes the students can read fluently – if they are one of the estimated 20% of children who haven't mastered decoding, then this alone won't help. Students need to understand what it is they are focusing on.)

5. Distractions are abundant. Of course, there are many things in the classroom that students will always find more interesting, no matter how we plan. Geary suggests we have a *motivational bias* to prefer learning about things like peer interactions, play 'hunting', and exploring our physical environment. Many people claim humans are instinctively curious, and they probably are, but that doesn't mean they're automatically fascinated by trigonometry. Curiosity is not evenly distributed between everything we see. This might explain why children are so easily distracted by one another. People are fascinating to people.

It is also a reckless myth to assume that we can simply 'make' everything fascinating. This false belief is behind the endless, turgid lessons where we attempt to teach Shakespeare through rap, as if every child preferred that to any other musical style, or by injecting learning desperately into some hugely contrived game, where all that the children remember is the game, not the content.

Some things can be made more or less engaging, but ultimately learning must be acquired in ways that will not always delight all students. Learning and behaving are often simply hard work. For some children, a wasp in the classroom, or the dreaded smartphone, will provide ample opportunity for a child to shift the precious real estate of their attention from the Tudors to TikTok.[10]

6. Schools exist to teach biologically secondary skills. Biologically secondary skills are things which evolution has not fitted us to find easy to learn or to feel motivated to learn. Current thinking speculates that we may have evolved to learn some things more instinctively than others.[11] Watch a baby and it's

---

10. I am sensitive to the fact that by the time you read this, TikTok will seem as hip and current as the Charleston. Trying to keep up with youth argot makes Ozymandiases of all adults. Know only, reader from the future, that I tried.

11. Geary, D. C. (2008) 'An evolutionarily informed education science', *Educational Psychologist*, 43(4), pp.179-195. Retrieved from www.bit.ly/310VQ1I

obvious that they are learning about the world, albeit often through activities that don't look much like the kind of studying seen in later childhood.

But every tumble, or smashed rattle, or parent's smile or frown is a learning journey towards apprehending gravity, cause and effect, pain, social interaction and so on. Children acquire this knowledge without deliberate instruction (in the absence of any neurological problems). They acquire verbal language with ease and without classrooms, and the most we can do is provide nurturing environments where this can happen – word-rich interactions etc. They also learn the basics of human interaction, how to get attention, how to make us laugh. Geary called this *folk knowledge*. But much of what we want them to learn at school is what we can call propositional knowledge (such as 'Paris is the capital of France') or procedural knowledge (such as how to do long division). This is much harder to teach. Our brains haven't evolved to learn these things as easily, because things like mathematics and written language etc. have only been with us for a few thousand years – a mere heartbeat in the evolutionary timescale. It requires levels of focus and concentration that our cognitive apparatus does not find easy. Our motivational bias leads our focus away from sums and verb endings, and towards what's happening outside the classroom and what our shoulder partners are whispering about.

I should note that classroom management is also a form of secondary knowledge in this model. It doesn't come naturally just because you put teachers into challenging classrooms. It requires highly skilled teaching in itself.

7. They're not successful. Think how long you persevere on any task that you don't enjoy, or worse, one you completely hate. As an adult, you may persist because you might have some sense of duty to complete, or you may see the task as a means to a more desirable end. But all of us, no matter how committed, will naturally feel less inclined to do something that makes us feel bad. And struggling helplessly with a subject is a powerful deterrent. By 'bad', I mean, 'normally unsuccessful at it'. So, if a student finds something hard, and doesn't succeed, we mustn't be surprised if eventually they give up, or find other things to do. It's a rational decision. Therefore it's essential to provide children with the experience of success through learning and behaving well.

8. They think they aren't supposed to like school, and nobody counteracts this. Many students do not come to school with rosy or sentimental or even particularly positive views of institutions. They may come from homes where school is seen as a necessary evil, an act of state oppression or a pointless waste of time until they reach the age of employability. It is easy for some people to believe that the lessons of school are irrelevant to the real world; most of what we learn there we will never directly use. So why care about it?

Some students come from circumstances where state institutions are mistrusted, or where authority figures are seen as adversaries. This is sometimes even taught deliberately to children by misguided parents who themselves have been the beneficiaries of structured institutional education but believe they are helping their children by teaching them to reject school. Bring that mindset into school – let them continue to believe it – and see the difference it makes to their behaviour.

9. They are happier misbehaving than behaving. Amazingly – and some people find it controversial to hear this – a lot of what we call misbehaviour is mostly just messing around. And messing around is frequently done for fun. Trigonometry, the repeal of the Corn Laws or Julius Caesar are not, for many children, their idea of a good time. A child's idea of a good time might resemble more obviously pleasant past times: making your friends laugh, chatting about nothing, doodling, loafing, relaxing, etc. And don't forget that trying and failing at classwork will make them look and feel stupid. So for many the solution is simple: don't try.

While there are undeniably intangible riches to be found in the pursuit of pure knowledge, they are often pleasures that need to be cracked open with effort like walnuts, rather than gobbled with ease like marshmallows. Even subjects that some might think are naturally 'more fun' – like sport, drama, painting, etc. – are, to some students, a gauntlet of boredom or misery. Misbehaving is frequently much more fun, no matter the subject.

Crucially, students need to know that if they take a risk and try in lessons, they won't be punished socially by the teacher or by their peers. They need to feel that trying will be rewarded rather than stigmatised, no matter how well they do. The teacher can help with this by building up their confidence, congratulating weaker students for small milestones, and patiently explaining and re-explaining things they may find difficult. The teacher also needs to communicate clearly to the whole class that effort is a good thing, and actively dismantle an anti-intellectual or anti-effort classroom culture.

As David Thomas puts it, 'The aim of these lessons [is] not to excite or engage in the popular sense. The aim is to convince all students that if they try, then they will learn.'[12]

Gradually, they can be taught that they can succeed at the work asked of them and start to feel the enjoyment that comes from doing well at something. But only if the teacher makes sure they won't find more enjoyment in not trying at all.

10. They have bigger problems. Students come from every circumstance, from good and ill fortune. Some face abuse, trauma, mental health, want, hunger and every shade of sadness we can conceive of. In the face of such things, number bonds and phonics may fade into the background in terms of their priorities.

All of these issues will be found in your classroom at some point. It is important for a teacher to know if any of these issues affect their students. William Booth, the founder of the Salvation Army, famously realised that there was no point preaching spiritual messages to people if they were too inebriated or harrowed by poverty to care about them, which is why the Army made its mission from the start to tackle social ills before (and alongside) their religious missionary work. There is a lesson there for educators who care about the lives of their students, not only because it matters anyway, but because it matters to their education too.

These issues are complex and often require unique, specialist strategies and support. The classroom teacher cannot be expected to solve these for their students – would that they could. The stitches of children's lives cannot be unpicked so easily. But teachers can be part of the process whereby such children are directed to people and environments that *can* help them – specialists, in-school experts, external agencies and so on.

Once we take all of these into account, perhaps the question we should ask is 'Why on earth would any student behave at school?' 'Because we want them to' is not a good enough reason. Nor is 'Because it's good for them.' If it was, no one would smoke and everyone would have an ideal body mass index, wars would never happen, and everyone would start a pension plan at 18. But we don't. Our actions are only partially rational.

---

12. 'Trying is risky', David Thomas' Blog: www.bit.ly/3eBn0j1

Summary: *don't assume that all students can behave. Assume that many cannot. Yet.*

This brings us back to our earlier point: complex behaviour must be learned, which means it must be taught if children are to have any chance to acquire it. Teachers must teach what evolution has failed to provide: the traditions, conventions, and ritual behaviours of being a successful student and person in a school.

These are reasons, not excuses. None of these ten reasons are *excuses* for students to misbehave. In fact, the danger of treating them all as excuses is that they *excuse*, which means the student has no responsibility any more. If we treat them like that then we inadvertently teach children that it's OK to behave like that because they're bored, they're angry, because they can't help themselves. This is exactly the opposite of what we want. We want to teach them to take responsibility for their actions, and to try to be better than they are already.

But these reasons do provide us with valuable insight into why children may stubbornly resist what we ask them to do, and why we should understand that school is not an easy or natural environment to be a part of. They can change, and they can do better, but they're going to need our help to do it.

How do we motivate children to behave well – and learn?
We need to define 'motivation' carefully. Motivation is sometimes used in teaching and TED talks as a shorthand for inspiration, enthusiasm, or an excitement that drives one to act. It certainly can be. Here, I mean, 'What impulse causes a student to behave in one way and not another?' These are the causes and reasons for actions. We can be motivated by revenge, a headache, or charismatic YouTube Zumba coaches. What motivates students to behave in the classroom? What influences or stimuli make them decide to listen to you or their headphones; to try their hardest or not?

Much of our decision-making is, if not actually irrational, then sub-rational – which is to say it is generated from emotional causes as much as practical ones. Behaviour is very often dictated by our values. To paraphrase Hume, 'Reason is – and should be – the slave of passion.' By that he meant that reason alone cannot decide what to value; our passions dictate that, and then we use reason to obtain the object of these passions sensibly and efficiently. It is not rational to sacrifice our lives for a stranger, but we might do it because it has meaning for us. Many actions are value-driven, not reason-driven.

reasoning, discernment, problem-solving, attention control, working memory, inhibitory control, and so on. This is similar to what we might call self-regulation, or self-control. Can I manage my desires, or am I helpless to resist temptation and impulsivity? Who am I, and what do I actually want from life?

Helping children to behave well is one of the greatest acts of liberation there is. If we permit children to do as they please, we condemn them to the endless succession of their whims and desires. Some children may have excellent self-control, but many children cannot discern between what they want in the moment and what is in their best interest. Unless we prescribe what they can and cannot do, we condemn them not to freedom, but to slavery – the slavery to one's own wants. Who do we consider to be more truly free? The child allowed to do anything, who indulges every desire, however selfish or self-destructive? Or the child who chooses freely *not* to indulge their desires, delays gratification, and achieves some greater end, such as learning a language, or passing an exam?

If you really want to set children free, teach them how to control themselves. Self-regulation (inhibitory control) is frequently referred to as one of the key factors of success in many fields. Few things we value are achieved without dedication, sustained effort and the ability to resist the temptation to give up.

Teaching this is no easy feat. It is not a lesson, a hand-out, or a webinar, although there are plenty of people happy to take your credit card details who want to persuade you it is a commodity they can supply. Self-control appears to share some features with muscles:[17] overuse depletes it, tires it out, but over longer periods, repeated use of it makes it stronger. If you are constantly under pressure to resist temptation, for example, you may eventually succumb. But the more you persist, the better you become at it.

Summary: *we do not liberate students from the classroom, but with the classroom. We teach them how to be free by teaching them how to master their desires and understand the difference between what they need and what they want.*

Why do we behave at all?

Human behaviour is so complex, we might see two people act completely differently but inspired by the same reasoning and goals. Two sisters may want to be famous, but one pursues metallurgy and the other goes writes op-eds for

---

17. Diamond, A. (2013) 'Executive functions', *Annual Review of Psychology*, 64, pp.135–168.

The New York Times. Or we might see two people act identically but inspired by completely different reasons, like two people laughing at different jokes. The factors involved in these are so varied and numerous that it is difficult to see even why we behave the way we do ourselves, let alone identify the motivations of other people.

Students are obviously no different. A student may behave well one day but not the next for the most inscrutable of reasons. Little causes can have unforeseen effects on our minds. In A Christmas Carol, Dickens memorably describes a disbelieving Scrooge ascribing his vision of Marley's revenant to disorders of his stomach: 'You may be an undigested bit of beef, a blot of mustard, a crumb of cheese, a fragment of underdone potato.'[18] A quiet student might be unsettled and argumentative because of snow outside, a fight with a friend over break, or a hundred other reasons, equally inscrutable and unique. Even a fragment of underdone potato.

Certainty is overrated. Probability is more useful

But we mustn't give up hope. Humans are complex, but not infinitely so. We can, with care, make some judgements about how *many* people will *typically* act in most circumstances; we can even make a stab – less certainly of course – about how people might act in unusual circumstances. This is the theory of mind – that we can imagine and predict and infer other people's mental states from an examination of their behaviour and our own internal mental state.

All students are human. And human behaviour and psychology exists within finite limits of probability. There are some things we can say about most people at least some of the time, some people most of the time, and some people some of the time. The greater the number of people we want to discuss, the greater the precision we seek, then the more cautiously we must make our forecasts. People are like weather. We know that it will be – generally – hotter in summer than winter. We know that warm fronts and low atmospheric pressure generally precede rainfall and thunderstorms, but even satellites can't tell us with certainty anything specific beyond a few days out.

We can make reasonably certain, general predictions about human behaviour, and less certain, specific ones. If we bear these caveats in mind, we can start to speak sensibly about human behaviour in the classroom. We should have no time for snake oil salespeople who offer universal predictions, certainty or

---

18. Dickens, C. (1812-1870) *A Christmas Carol and Other Stories*. New York: Modern Library, 1995.

panaceas. Everything works somewhere, nothing works everywhere, and the wise student of the human mind seeks only cautious and contingent truths. The classroom teacher must be guided as best as they can be by the best evidence we possess about the ways humans typically interact and react to one another.

Human motivation is enormously complex, and we might rightly despair of ever being able to understand exactly why students behave the way they do. Indeed, we often only appreciate our own motivations partially and imperfectly. The interior lives of others are often doubly mysterious and inscrutable. But the teacher's role is the art of the possible, not the perfect, and it falls to us to manage behaviour even when we have an imperfect grasp of why people act and react. Besides, were we to only interact with others when we were certain of their reactions and motivations, we would die as hermits. We must act, and direct students. So, these questions remain:

1. What are the biggest influences on student behaviour?
2. Which ones can we meaningfully affect?
3. Which ones should we prioritise?

What do we want?

In 1943, Abraham Maslow published 'A Theory of Human Motivation' in *Psychological Review*.[19] The triangle derived from it will be familiar to anyone who has spent ten seconds in the education sector, as it enjoys enormous ubiquity.[20] Maslow attempted to describe what it was that we all wanted, deep down; what were the things we all sought in life? Wealth, fame, partners, etc. perhaps. But why did we want them? What about people who did not want these things? What was that all about? Maybe we all just wanted completely different things.

He suggested several categories, e.g. survival needs, safety, social needs and self-actualisation. He never intended these to be definitive, and rejected the suggestion that these categories were set in stone as a hierarchy. They are not settled science and we should not consider them to be such. But they do offer us a useful metaphor for the kinds of broad needs and desires we all possess. Because understanding what we all want is a very useful way to understand how to motivate people, including students.

---

19. Maslow, A. H. (1943) 'A theory of human motivation', *Psychological Review*, 50 (4), pp.370–396.

20. Education is addicted to triangular diagrams. Funnily enough an enormous number of them are as useful as a triangular wheel.

I will survive

In the midst of winter, I found there was, within me, an invincible summer. And that makes me happy. For it says that no matter how hard the world pushes against me, within me, there's something stronger – something better, pushing right back.

Albert Camus, *Return to Tipasa* (1954)

One of our greatest goals is **survival**: obtaining air, heat, shelter and so on. These are undoubtedly core desires for almost all of us, and people will do a great deal to achieve them – even kill. A friend of mine who worked as a scuba diver in the Thames police division spent most of his days fishing corpses and firearms out of London's great watery artery. But he noted that in many cases when a desperate soul had flung themselves into the Thames, even they were often overcome with something like Bernard Shaw's 'life force', an overwhelming compulsion to survive. Many of them found a reactivated will to live when confronted with death. We should find solace that even in those dark depths of despair, there is still a light for some.

People will knock down walls with their hands to live. Foxes will gnaw their paws off to escape a trap. Cars may have been lifted by desperate parents to save their children in feats of hysterical strength.[21] Life finds a way. In the classroom, we rarely see students gasping for breath, but we do see them hungry, thirsty, and haunted by home neglect. One of my colleagues once caught a 12-year-old student in the staff room, raiding the fridge. The inclination to set a penalty was immediately dissolved by the discovery that parental neglect meant he hadn't eaten in days. Such stories marble our careers and haunt us.

Another powerful goal is **safety**; we seek not just to survive, but to do so in circumstances of security where we can plan and relax in the knowledge that the world will be stable and safe. The political philosopher Thomas Hobbes rooted his powerful defence of civilisation in this feature of the human experience. As we saw earlier, he noticed that in the absence of laws (the state of nature), humanity's lives were 'nasty, cruel, brutish and short'. In order to escape this

---

21. This phenomenon may be apocryphal; anecdotes are abundant, but strong evidence is scant. Still, adrenaline combined with hysteria could – in theory – produce such events. There is a five-year-old inside me who desperately wishes it to be true, eyes glazed from watching *The Incredible Hulk* on TV.

living hell, we formed communities and agreed to be mutually bound together by laws, conventions and rules. We give up some freedoms in order to be secure, which in turn allows us to be free in greater ways.

Additionally we all have powerful **social needs**. In the absence of immediate threats to our lives, these drive a great deal of everyday human behaviour. The need to be loved; to be recognised by a community of peers; the need to be valued. More on this later.

Finally, many are driven by the need for **self-actualisation**: to realise one's ambitions, and do more than merely survive: to thrive. To become the best versions of ourselves we can be.

What is best in life?

What is flourishing? Aristotle saw it as a constant process of becoming the best one could be in one's *role* – mother, son, lawyer, citizen, gardener, teacher, student, whatever space one found oneself in. Aristotle saw our identities intrinsically linked with these roles. When someone asks, 'Who is Tom Bennett?' (for example), we normally say something like 'Father to Ben and Gabby, brother to Anthony, husband to Anna, behaviour advisor to the DfE', and so on. Our concept of identity is strongly based on our relationships to others.

Once we have worked out what our roles are, Aristotle thought that in order to be a 'good' person we had to try our best to be 'good at these roles'. In Aristotelian ethics, it doesn't make sense to say an action was good or bad without considering who was performing it, and what their role was. Therefore, 'doing the right thing' could mean different things for different people depending on their role. A fireman may be duty-bound to tackle a fire, while a doctor may be doing his part when she stands by with oxygen and medicine ready. And they both flourish when they try their hardest to be the best in their roles. That's what flourishing means.[22]

This required that good people worked hard to build up the qualities needed to flourish in their role. Therefore, a teacher flourishes when they work on their pedagogy, subject knowledge, classroom management abilities, etc. Flourishing is definitely not the same as sensual happiness. The point of life, according to

---

22. Aristotle. *The Nichomachean Ethics*, translated by Martin Oswald (1962). New York: The Bobs-Merrill Company.

Aristotle, is not to be happy in the sense of 'feeling pleasure', but to experience the constant sense of growth (*eudaemonia*) which may often entail temporarily unpleasant experiences. The athlete may not *enjoy* a punishing workout; a teacher may tire of study; a father may not love getting up five times a night to soothe a baby; but these actions are intrinsically connected to their flourishing. These experiences are *valuable*, even when they are not *pleasant*.

Example:

A student's role is to learn, try to get on with their peers, and contribute to the life of the classroom. In order to flourish (do well) at this, they have to work on the qualities of focus, kindness, patience, perseverance, fortitude and many others. In a lesson, this might mean that they are expected to do the reading for the lesson or to have brought in a show–and–tell, take a seat quickly, get to work quietly, ask questions when they don't understand, wait their turn to be called upon, do their best to complete the work and help their table partner when they don't understand. A lot of this might not be pleasant, and some of it will be hard work, or even boring. But by the end of the day, the student will have learned more and will have been a good student. The teacher's role is to guide them through this process and help them to appreciate what they have achieved. This involves another set of qualities that the teacher needs to flourish in their role.

Living your best life[23]

A clear understanding of what we are trying to achieve through education is useful in order to maintain the sense of moral purpose we need to persevere when times get tough – and in teaching, they often do. Teaching will test you and it can quickly become a gauntlet, especially if one loses sight of its importance.

Summary: *the aim of teaching is not just to keep our students safe, but also to support their academic and social flourishing.*

A piece of cake, obviously.

---

23. Contrast this with the answer famously given by the fictional Cimmerian barbarian-philosopher Conan when asked, 'Conan, what is best in life?' His answer referenced Genghis Khan: 'To crush your enemies, see them driven before you, and to hear the lamentation of their women.' *Conan the Barbarian* (1982). Food for thought for us all there.

We do not seek the *happiness* of the student – not directly. Rather, we aim to enrich their lives, minds and abilities in ways that will enable them to flourish independently of our direction, long after we cease to be part of their lives. Thinking that our aim is to make students happy will take us down some unintended and unhelpful paths. We quickly find that happiness can be achieved in many ways that are not useful to the flourishing of the student, academically or socially. Hedonism is fun until it isn't. Many teachers have stepped on the garden rake of seeking to amuse or entertain their students purely as a way to keep a smile on their faces. But finding purpose and meaning is also pleasurable – perhaps more enduringly so.

While we should always hope that students find their time at school pleasant (and some low-learning/fun activities can be justified as a way to leaven all that effort and focus), learning is not – and cannot – always be an unmitigated pleasure. Activities aimed purely at their happiness can become a waste of time if they become the norm. It is good for students to have occasional activities and lessons that are more fun than educational, but the only people who suffer when this becomes the norm are the students – and the least advantaged the most of all. It is easy to allow children to do as they please. But we are here to give them what they need, *not* what they always want.

The irony is that when we give them what they need, we help them to unlock and develop capacities that can lead to greater happiness. Teaching a child to read means that the child unlocks worlds and galaxies of imagination, reflection and the shared cognitive reservoir of humanity and its tapestry of historical narratives. It opens doors to careers, study, communication, and a million unseen or unimagined benefits. The greater good of a child is not always found in the moment but seen holistically over a million moments that connect invisibly to build a better future.

Every aim we might have in teaching is best served by helping children to achieve better habits and conduct in their lives at school. We usher in the next Martin Luther Kings, Marie Curies and Martina Navratilovas when we do so.

How does this help in the classroom?

Being sensitive to what motivates us provides a useful reminder of what people and students really want, deep down. And knowing this unlocks a profound understanding of how to motivate them and direct their behaviour. If we can persuade students that by directing their labours to the tasks we prescribe, and by aligning themselves with the values and habits of the classroom, they will find in these actions the fundamental goods of life we all seek, then we have the world's greatest spur for them to try hard doing the things we need them need to do.

Take survival. Students are – obviously – highly motivated to obtain the material resources that will sustain biological life. Almost everyone will invest enormous energy to do so in all but the most desperate of circumstances. Many of our most inspirational stories are extraordinary narratives of people who struggled to stay alive despite gargantuan odds.

Biology eats culture for breakfast

People are often capable of extraordinary feats of willpower, and we hear of many people who endured hunger or pain to reach some greater goal. But this doesn't disprove that deprivation and lack are powerful behavioural drivers for many students. Hunger harrows their ability to learn and behave. It will surprise no one to remember that we are, as well as glorious, almost magical beings with ambitions and dreams, also wet bags of chemicals held up by sticks, pressure and sentient electricity. The human machine must be fed, watered and kept warm if it is to run smoothly. Like the aforementioned William Booth, who understood that before we are beings of light and spirit, we are flesh; and hungry flesh cannot concentrate. So, he fed the poor, and clothed them, and led them into temperance. There is a saying: 'culture eats strategy for breakfast';[24] but there is an even more primitive principle preceding this: *biology eats culture for breakfast.*

What does this mean practically for teachers? Schools and teachers need to address these following factors, individually and collectively:

- Research suggests that providing universal free breakfasts in high schools not only improves learning, it also decreases behavioural incidents like fights and truancy, as well as improving well-being and test scores.[25]

---

24. Often attributed to Peter Drucker, but this is not substantiated. He certainly used it, and his understood meaning was that focusing on building a company's culture is a better way to ensure its success.

25. Norwood, B. (2010) 'Breakfast of Champions: Universal Free Breakfast and Student Conflict and Test Scores in Texas Schools' (January 2, 2020). Available at: www.bit.ly/2DScTKJ

Schools should watch out for students who are undernourished, and if necessary (and where resources permit), compensate for this deficit. This can mean breakfast clubs, low-cost, nourishing school meals, freely available water, etc. Food should aim primarily at being nourishing and healthy, and empty calories or filling but low-value food avoided. For some students, this may be the only substantial meal of their day, so it has to count.

Malnutrition takes many forms, and many students may have bellies full of junk, with little nutritional worth. Highly caffeinated drinks should be banned; students have their whole lives to acquire adult addictions. Teachers can be foot soldiers in this system of support, but no teacher should have to supplement their students' diets personally, and where malnutrition is suspected, line managers should be enlisted to discuss solutions, e.g. working with the family etc.

- Classrooms should be well ventilated. Rooms saturated with CO2 exacerbate tiredness, reduce the ability to focus and concentrate, and provide an unnecessary drain on that most precious of student resources: attention. Research by Harvard University in 2016 found 'statistically significant declines' in cognitive function scores when CO_2 concentrations were increased to 950 ppm, which is 'common in indoor spaces'.[26] Keep a window open, manufacture a breeze.
- Encourage students to improve their sleep hygiene. Sleep is one of the most overlooked areas of student (and staff) health. It is one of our most basic biological needs, but it is often treated like a luxury. It is not; it is essential. The fact that our minds switch into an almost supernatural state alternating between standby, intense fantasy and meditation should be a constant source of wonder to us; instead, we treat it as a nuisance, a snack, a treat.

---

26. Allen, J. G., MacNaughton, P., Satish, U., Santanam, S., Vallarino, J. and Spengler, J. D. (2015) 'Associations of cognitive function scores with carbon dioxide, ventilation,and volatile organic compound exposures in office workers: a controlled exposure study of green and conventional office environments.' *Environmental Health Perspectives*, 124 (6), pp.805-812.

We now know a little about the multiple processes, physical and mental, that sleep facilitates.[27] It is a restorative draught, a healing time, an update to our cognitive operating systems, and a hundred other things. Its deficit leads to dozens of known health and mental problems, or their increased likelihood. Cancer rates, heart disease, schizophrenia, Alzheimer's and many other perils correlate significantly with its lack.[28]

On a more everyday basis, and more relevant to our aims here, it has an enormous influence on multiple factors associated with classroom success: focus, memory, attention span, irritability, patience, cognitive load and so on. Tired people make mistakes, get ratty, lose their tempers, lack patience, and make poor decisions much more frequently than the same people when rested. Being tired has a massive impact on our ability to regulate our emotions.[29] When we are sleep deprived, we are less emotionally resilient. 'Sleep is the glue that holds human beings together.'[30]

Adolescents throughout the world do not obtain adequate sleep. A recent proliferation of experimental and quasi-experimental studies on teens concur in finding that multiple successive nights of restricted sleep can impair multiple cognitive functions. These effects cumulate over successive nights, may not achieve complete restitution after weekend recovery sleep, and may even be compounded by re-exposure to sleep restriction.[31]

27. Walker, M. (2017) *Why we sleep: the new science of sleep and dreams.* New York, NY: Scriber, an imprint of Simon & Schuster, Inc.

28. Mukherjee, S., Patel, S. R., Kales, S. N., Ayas, N. T., Strohl, K. P., Gozal D. and Malhotra, A; on behalf of the American Thoracic Society ad hoc Committee on Healthy Sleep (2015) 'An Official American Thoracic Society Statement: The Importance of Healthy Sleep. Recommendations and Future Priorities'. https://doi.org/10.1164/rccm.201504-0767ST

29. Owens, J. A., Dearth-Wesley, T., Lewin, L., Gioia, G. and Whitaker, R. C. (2016) 'Self-regulation and sleep duration, sleepiness, and chronotype in adolescents', *Pediatrics*, 138 (6) https://doi.org/10.1542/peds.2016-1406

30. Damour, L. (2020) *Under pressure – confronting the epidemic of stress and anxiety in girls.* London: Atlantic Books.

31. Lo, J. C. and Chee, M. W. L (2020) 'Cognitive effects of multi-night adolescent sleep restriction: current data and future possibilities', *Current Opinion in Behavioural Sciences*, Volume 33, June 2020, pp.34-41.

So, the message is clear: to help children learn, behave and thrive at school, we should encourage them to:

- Get at least seven hours of sleep every night.
- Try to have more regular habits of when they go to bed and when they rise. Regularity improves the quality of sleep.
- Avoid alcohol, caffeine or other stimulants after 5 p.m.
- Avoid screen time within an hour of going to bed.
- Avoid using their beds for multiple purposes. Studies show that sleep efficiency is magnified when the bed/bedroom is seen as a place to sleep, not to game or socialise.
- Avoid having their smartphones in their bedrooms at night, and certainly not in visible modes. Studies show that even the presence of a smartphone in the sleeping room can encourage the habit of checking it or being aware of the light from the screen as it flickers and hums for our attention.

Some of these are easier than others, but they should be an aspiration for all students, and all staff to encourage. It needs to be pointed out that all staff should take this advice too, although in doing so I am aware of the stoniness of the ground on which this seed of an idea will land. But consider: how effective are you when tired? Would the time lost to effective sleep be repaid in increased efficiency, happiness, focus and attention when awake?[32]

Safety
We all need to feel safe, stable, and protected. Like many things we often take for granted, this is more keenly felt when it is absent. The child from an insecure or overcritical background can often carry that anxiety into school, perhaps overreacting to criticism or judgement.

Students who are lacking in this fundamental good will often be motivated to find it and demonstrate this through their behaviour. It is vital that schools and classrooms make students feel safe, otherwise their behaviour will change to obtain it. Students need to feel secure in the classroom. One thing that teachers can do to ensure this is to:

1. Let students know explicitly that they are welcome and wanted in the classroom.

---

32. Those are rhetorical questions, incidentally

2. Teach them that it's OK to make mistakes.
3. Teach them that you want the best for them.
4. Show them that they matter by involving them.
5. Treat them with dignity at all times, even if they test you.
6. Watch the classroom at all times for rudeness, bullying, mocking or discrimination, and banish this things forever.
7. Use structured talk to guarantee that everyone has a chance to be heard.
8. Give take-up time for students to think before they respond.

These, and many more strategies, give students a chance to feel that even if they struggle with the topic, the classroom is a safe space for them. They need to feel like there is something in it for them. They need to feel included. That doesn't mean that we tread softly around them if they misbehave – we look out for all students' interests and well-being – but it does mean that even if we send a student out or reprimand them, we do so in a way that explicitly leads to the hope of their reintegration. We tell students, even if they're in trouble, 'You can do better than this. I believe you can. I can show you how.'

Students need to matter

It's loneliness that's the killer.
'Killer', Adamski and Seal, 1990

Next we all need *esteem*, love and belonging. We need to *matter*. We need to feel that we are valuable and valued. Human beings need to feel that what they do and what they are is of consequence. One of the greatest privations is to be alone, unnoticed, unrecognised. 'The mass of men lead lives of quiet desperation.'[33] I quite agree. Few things are as awful as remoteness from others or pointlessness. Our whole human enterprise can be seen as one enormous quest for meaning, on an individual and a social level. The meaning of life and the meaning of our lives are intertwined.

We seek meaning through a variety of mundane means – what do you want to do when you grow up? What job? Where do you want to live? What are your ambitions? The art we consume, our choice of friends and partners. The search for meaning and identity is not some navel-gazing preserve of poets, but something that echoes in everything we do. Teenagers stare into its abyss

---

33. Thoreau, H. D. (2008) *Walden Civil Disobedience and Other Writings*. London: W. W. Norton & Company.

when they gaze at themselves in the mirror and try to decipher what it means. The elderly seek it in the memory palaces of their minds, retrospectively. We glimpse it in the moments between all the busy tasks that batter us from the moment our eyes open to the moment they close.

Meaning is something that all of us pursue. We need to matter, we need to know that, somehow, we count. Being ignored (for example, as a teacher) is frequently worse than dealing with more straightforward rudeness. I remember my own frustration when students acted not as if you were annoying, but as if you didn't matter at all.

As we age, we might start to find pride in our own actions and the people we have made of ourselves.[34] Maturity brings with it – if we are lucky – the confidence to know what we are, and what we find meaning in.

But that is often difficult for children, who unsurprisingly often look to adults to understand what is important, what is right, what is good. The very young, if they are securely attached to consistent adult role models, will defer happily in such matters to them. As we grow up, we become far more influenced by peer groups, and seek value in our relationships, often to the detriment of our previously secure adult bonds.

Defying gravity

Many teachers will be familiar with the other great pyramid of education, Bloom's taxonomy of thinking objectives (compiled by educational psychologist Benjamin Bloom), used by teachers for decades as a touchstone document in building lesson activities.[35] A phrase you may hear is 'Maslow before Bloom', with the implication that you cannot tackle the learning of a student until you have tackled the basic human needs we all have. And to some extent, this is true.

The problem is that the model implied by this aphorism:

---

34. I remember with awe the zip (and possibly a touch of dementia) of an elderly resident of North West London where I lived. She would drive up Kilburn High Road on her mobility scooter into the oncoming traffic, swearing and flicking the V sign at passers-by with a military confidence. It's not admirable, but it was certainly a fine example of something.

35. It is much disputed for its implied hierarchy of objectives, and the damage this can do to teachers' appreciation of the importance of secure core knowledge bases.

1. Encourages us to think that no useful work can be done until all children are happy and secure.
2. Encourages us to expect, and therefore accept, less from children in difficult circumstances.

The first is a problem because it tacitly makes the same mistake many make with Bloom's taxonomy: it implies that the taxonomy must be a ladder and hierarchy; only once we have the lower rungs satisfied can we satisfy those higher up. But many commentators have criticised this. We seem to be able to fulfil these aims simultaneously. As for the second problem, it is dangerously seductive to lower our expectations for children who may be anxious or insecure. While we absolutely must make accommodations and adjustments to help children in difficult circumstances, there is a danger that when we expect them to be helpless, we can habituate them into helplessness. The danger is that we overcompensate, and expect nothing from them. The child who tells you they didn't do their homework because Mum and Dad are splitting up may very well warrant some form of accommodation. But for how long? Or do we just say, 'OK, we expect no homework from you from now on, forever'? What does that teach the child apart from that it's *OK not to try any more when life gets hard?*

So to answer the Maslow/Bloom question: neither model precedes the other. We do both. We don't wait until perfect learning conditions are achieved in the lives of all of our students, because that will never occur. We teach them, not just the curriculum, but how to cope with life, with all of its mountains and canyons.

Section one: closing thoughts

And it is by being aware of all of these issues – and by understanding that behaviour management will always be an act of persuasion as much as it is one of coercion – that we understand a little more about what it means to be a human, a teacher and a student. It is often said, 'The only person you can truly control is yourself,' on the grounds that ultimately the only body we can command is us; everyone else must be convinced to command *themselves* to act the way we wish.

In section one, we have considered human nature, teaching as a practice, why we're in such a mess with behaviour in schools, and started to think about what behaviour management actually involves.

In section two, we will look at the practical matter of what one actually does in the classroom; how behaviour is taught; how it is monitored and maintained, and how to respond when it goes wrong, which it will – frequently. In this next section, we will look at the three most important vehicles to build better classroom cultures: norms, routines and consequences.

MAKE IT EASY TO BEHAVE AND HARD NOT TO.

Some students find it harder to behave than others. Remove any obstacle you can to them developing better habits. Provide support for them to achieve the expectations you have of them. Challenge low standards every time. Make good behaviour satisfying.

SECTION 2:
CREATING THE CULTURE

Part 1 – Social Norms

Make it normal to do the right thing

Part 2 – Routines

Teach children habits that help them to flourish

Part 3 – Behaviour Feedback

Let them know how they're doing

SECTION 2
PART 1
SOCIAL NORMS

After a while, you could get used to anything.

Albert Camus, 1942, *The Stranger*

In this section, I explore the practical strategies that teachers can use to change the behaviour of the classroom. We begin by exploring the importance of social norms; how they create problems for students and teachers, and how we can use them to everyone's advantage.

CHAPTER 5
THE CULTURE OF THE CLASSROOM

Running a room means being aware that you are directing the behaviour of not just one student at a time, but a group. This simple fact is how we begin to understand how to run a class. The classroom is not an archipelago of inert pebbles, remote from one another. It is a pool. Ripples from one affect all the others, radiating out in complex waves and back again. It is a churning Brownian motion of influences and feedback. Your job is to create order from this, while being part of it. You are no mere observer. You are a participant.

What is a classroom culture?

Culture, expressed simply, means 'the beliefs and values held by a group'. This is commonly used at a geographical level, a national level or a local level (e.g. the French; Glaswegians, etc.). It can also describe a group of people spread out over a wide area, but who share common group beliefs and values (e.g. the Jewish diaspora, the Muslim ummah), or societies united by common interests or appetites, clubs, etc.

I use the term 'classroom culture' to mean the beliefs and values of the classroom. What does the group think is important, and what matters to them? Do they, for example think handing in homework is important or trivial? Is the class normally quiet when they work, or is it normal to chat?

A **social norm** is the accepted behaviour that an individual is expected to conform to in a particular group or culture. These **norms** often serve a useful purpose and create the basis of correct conduct. Social norms allow you to navigate through a culture by knowing what to do in different circumstances.[1]

Every group has different norms. Norms are usually useful to the group (e.g. driving on the same side of the road), but sometimes they can be harmful (e.g. where I grew up in Scotland in the '80s, it was still normal to be offered an ashtray when you entered a house).[2]

---

1. Sunstein, C. R. (2019) *Conformity: the power of social influence*. New York, NY: New York University Press.
2. Your *own personal* ashtray, I might add.

Beliefs and values are hugely important to behaviour in the classroom, because they are a source of a lot of classroom behaviour. If a student comes from a home where they have absorbed their parents' attitudes that education is pointless, or that institutional authority is hostile, then those beliefs are manifested as *not* handing in homework, following simple instructions, or trying very hard to achieve academically.

Conversely, a student who comes from a home where education and authority are seen positively will act quite differently when asked to bring in their show-and-tell or write an essay. A great deal of behaviour flows from our prior beliefs and values.[3]

And students arrive at school, at all ages, preprogrammed with masses of culture. Some of it is helpful to succeeding in school. Some of it is less so.

The classroom culture

Every classroom has its own culture; its own predominant beliefs and values about what matters and what does not, about what is acceptable and valued, and what is scorned or derided. In some classes, hard work is mocked, and those who buck the culture are punished by their peers. I've seen classes where handing in a piece of homework results in death by a thousand sniggers. Other classrooms would be shocked if a student were to sneeze without asking. Some students are so habituated into silent focus, they resemble scribes in an abbey. Sub-cultures (cultures within the broader culture) are always in constant competition, and some may predominate more than others. But whether the teacher likes it or not, these cultures exist. We walk into a soup of their beliefs. And we bring our own stock to the pot.

The three ignoble assumptions of behaviour management

One mistake many teachers make is to expect instant compliance as soon as you issue an instruction. This makes several mistaken assumptions, which I call the three ignoble assumptions:

1. They value the same behaviour you do.
2. They know what they should be doing.
3. They know how to behave the way you want them to.

---

3. Some of it comes from biological demands; some from other external pressures. In this context, I refer to behaviour we can choose to perform, or not, according to our will.

But if your instructions swim against the cultural currents of the classroom, then don't be surprised if the riptide sucks you under. If you teach a room full of children who have already been raised to believe teachers are authority figures, school is important, and they should defer to adult instruction, then even the greenest of teachers might find their every instruction followed with more or less total compliance. The mistake we make as observers of teachers is to assume this person has 'amazing behaviour management skills' when what they actually possess is a very fortunate demographic of children preloaded to behave in the way that matches the teacher's desires. Another mistake which follows from this situation is to think, 'Hey, this is easy. I'm great at getting classes to behave. I will now write a book about how everyone should teach like me.'[4]

When we walk into a classroom, we walk from the cosy living rooms of our own minds, where we possess absolute command, into the weather of other people's will, where authority is not a given. The weather is there before we arrive.

Making the weather

Billy Connolly famously said, 'There's no such thing as bad weather, just the wrong clothing.'[5] Some teachers learn to cope with whatever weather they walk into; they dress sensibly and cope with the wind and the rain of behaviour, basking in sunny spells and wrapping up against gales. It is *possible* to last as a teacher in this model. Many supply teachers learn this kind of adaptive invulnerability, evolving the thickest of skins or the quickest of wits to dance around difficult behaviour or simply survive it. But both tactics extract a high cost in terms of job satisfaction, student attainment, and mental health.

The most effective teachers I have observed do something quite different; they endeavour to make their own weather.[6] They build the classroom culture. For example, they don't let students pile into the classroom at the start of the lesson; they teach them to wait outside in a line. Or they teach children how to ask questions or offer an answer rather than all shouting out at once. These

---

4. This mistake appears to be compulsory dogma in most behaviour management books, teacher training, and on social media. More seriously, it is also a real problem in some schools, where senior staff, with formal authority, light timetables, and lots of power berate harassed, over-worked rookies for not having the magical gift that they imagine themselves to possess.

5. The rest of the line is, '...so get yourself a sexy raincoat and live a little,' but that takes the metaphor to places I don't want to go.

6. I first heard this said by Vic Goddard, the inestimable headteacher of Passmores Academy.

apparently simple behaviours (and many more besides) are the building bricks of the classroom culture.

Creating a culture

Creating a culture is enormously time consuming. It is hard, hard work; it requires constant attention, and maintenance. But it is by far the most effective and enduring of all behaviour management strategies. It involves directing the students' appreciation of what is valuable and important towards those things the teacher knows to be useful or good or valuable. You can slowly get children to value good behaviour as you define it.

If you can *persuade* students to do the right thing, if you can convince them to truly believe this behaviour is desirable, or useful, or *normal*, then classrooms can become places of endeavour, success and wonder.

At its foundation, it requires the teacher to convince the class that:

- Learning is important, individually and personally.
- Everyone in the room matters and is important.
- Good behaviour is the best way everyone can get what they need.

And that requires that the teacher unpicks the tangled knots of 30 students' various attitudes towards leaning and combs it into a harmonious agreement that these things are important. This is the task, and it is not an easy one. These 30 children have 30 different value systems; 30 different perspectives on what good or bad behaviour is; 30 different views on what right and wrong are.

And everyone believes that what they believe is right. We are strongly biased towards ourselves. We very rarely see ourselves as the villains; we very frequently see ourselves as the heroes and heroines in self-penned melodramas, where everyone else is a walk-on part. Research confirms this:

> People often prioritize their own interests, but also like to see themselves as moral. How do individuals resolve this tension? One way to both pursue personal gain and preserve a moral self-image is to misremember the extent of one's selfishness ... people tend to recall being more generous in the past than they actually were ... when people's actions fall short of their

personal standards, they may misremember the extent of their selfishness, thereby potentially warding off threats to their moral self-image.[7]

We are rarely at fault; someone else was. We don't like to see ourselves as the bad guy, so we rationalise what we did as good after it happened. The teacher (and more broadly the school) needs to convince the students that it is in their interest to behave the way you know is right. Behaviour management should always involve more persuasion than coercion.

Building the culture definitely *doesn't* mean telling them that their home cultures are wrong, that their parents are wrong, that their beliefs don't matter. Far from it. We must act respectfully towards the vast plurality of value systems from which our students emerge. But it does mean teaching them to appreciate that the classroom – your classroom – has its own culture, and that here, if nowhere else, these specific values and beliefs should be held, and demonstrated through behaviour. It is specific to the space in which you teach.

This should be as uncontroversial as declaring that a library, a night club, a cinema, have their own implied values. A library culture prizes behaviour like silence and contemplation; a cinema also centres silence but welcomes casual low-light dining. But sitting quietly and eating hot dogs in a busy night club would earn you a trip to the fire exit with the bouncers.[8] Cultures are contextual, and often highly local. This is not hard for students to grasp. Every teacher will be familiar with students who behave impeccably in one room but bounce off the walls like a pinball in another. Children are very quick to grasp what the cultural norms are in different classrooms, with different teachers. Out there, there are different rules. But in here, with me, these rules exist. And they are important.

My room, my rules

In 2010's Oscar-hoovering film *The King's Speech*, Geoffrey Rush plays Lionel Logue, the speech therapist to the future King George VI. While being treated for a stammer, the King lights up a Chesterfield in the manner of a man accustomed to doing as he jolly well pleases. But the upstart Australian Logue forbids it. At once the King starts to splutter in indignant protest, but Logue interrupts him. 'My room, my rules,' he scolds.

---

7. Carlson et. al (2020) 'Motivated misremembering of selfish decisions', *Nature Communications*, 11: www.go.nature.com/2ZKEiWU

8. With the emphasis on 'he tripped'.

Every teacher will encounter this: the clash between the student's expectations about what is permissible and the teacher's. I met many students who, with some innocence, thought that it would be OK for them to leave the room to go to the bathroom when they wanted, or listen to music on headphones as they worked. Often it was deliberate and confrontational – they knew what the expectations were – but sometimes it was simply a genuine belief that such things were normal and allowed. The teacher's duty here is to clarify that there are different expectations to the ones the students assume, and that these expectations are set by the teacher. For everyone's benefit, but definitely set by the teacher. Many teachers feel nervous about being an authority figure, but they need to get over that and accept that they are one. Or at least they need to be.

This demonstrates neatly the dynamic of the teacher in the classroom. The therapist enjoys privileged status in their practice because their expertise confers authority, and also because carrying out their duties privileges certain behaviours in its execution. So too with the teacher in their classroom or space. The teacher's authority and right to establish the culture of the room does not derive from goodness, or power, or anything else. It originates in necessity. The necessity that, in order for children to flourish individually and communally, there must be agreed – or at least observed – consistency in habits, behaviour and beliefs between everyone in that community. It is impossible to expect that a room of 30 individuals will be so mature or charitable to spontaneously agree upon a charter of rules and behaviour aimed at maximising everyone's well-being and education. People disagree. People can be selfish as well as magnificent. We have good days and bad.

And so, as sure as the sun will rise tomorrow, we need the teacher to be the arbiter of not just the curriculum and classroom activities, but social behaviour. My room, my rules indeed.[9]

---

9. This simple axiom sends some into convulsions, distressed by the suggestion that children must be directed at all. My first response is normally to suggest that most of these people have never taught a class of even moderately challenging children with any success or know which way up a child goes. Such people should return to writing long, unreadable (and unread) essays on Freire or Foucault and leave teaching to people prepared to actually do it. And get out of the way.

We are social animals[10]

Humans are, as we know, extremely sociable creatures. We naturally gravitate to one another. We form clans and tribes, clubs and groups, teams and WhatsApp covens. Not all species share this trait – sharks are famously antisocial – but some devote themselves to it, such as ants. Even the most antisocial of humans usually finds succour in some way through other people. The craziest of loners finds other crazy loners and forms a tribe of crazy loners.[11] The internet has facilitated this magnificently. No one need be a hermit today, and the most eccentric recluse can find fellowship, even if they have to find it internationally and anonymously. In schools, students bond together, bound by common interests, goals and beliefs. American teen cinema provides us with some stereotypes: the jocks, the cheerleaders, the preppies, the goths.

These groups are united by culture: beliefs, values, expectations, ethos, what is prized and what is not. Consider also what we know about Maslow's hierarchy of motivation: people seek meaning and esteem. These facts are not unrelated. There are many reasons why we are so social. Adam Smith would point to the economic value that is added to our endeavours through collaboration and security.[12] Anthropologists might say we developed communities as an evolved response to the need to rear our children through an extended infancy that lasts much longer than most animals.[13] Some political philosophers would argue, as Hobbes did, that building social contracts with one another, or compacts and alliances, was a rational, egotistical flight from the state of nature.[14] And psychology might add that one of the reasons we band together is to find esteem, status, meaning and approval from groups with which we surround ourselves. Reasons might vary, but the fact remains: we are highly social animals.

---

10. Aristotle's quote here was actually, 'Man is a social animal,' but I think we can do better than that in the 21st century. And it's rare that you can claim to improve upon Aristotle, after whom Alfred Lord Whitehead said all subsequent philosophy was a footnote. But here I am, correcting him. In a footnote. I told you I'd make something of my life, Mum.

11. And I say this with some authority, having played *Dungeons & Dragons* as a youth.

12. Smith, A. and Cannan, E. (2003)*The Wealth of Nations*. New York, NY: Bantam Classic.

13. Morris, D. (1969) *The Naked Ape: A zoologist's study of the human animal*. London: Corgi Books.

14. Hobbes, T. 1588-1679 (1968) *Leviathan*. Hardmondsworth: Penguin Books.

Few places demonstrate this more obviously than classrooms. Students band together in alliances, bound by perceived common interests. Tribes form, and rivalries and alliances. Some are more sociable than others. Some enjoy high status within their peer group; some vie for that status; and some are happy to be followers. Multiple friendship groups and sub cultures exist within the greater class culture. Some of these alliances are geographical, and only exist in that classroom space; some friendship groups are for the playground, some for the dining hall and some for the walk home.

Social identity theory

Writers like Durkheim[15] started to analyse the powerful, positive benefits to being part of a group. He wrote about 'collective effervescence', the uplifting collective sensation of being part of a large group sharing goals and activities. But something even more interesting was observed by some researchers: that people are more likely to behave in a way appropriate to a group when they feel part of that group; this was called social identity theory. People who feel outside of those communities, do not. In other words, when you feel part of a group, you feel more inclined to act as they do. Given that classes are groups, this feels important. Students who feel secure in their identity as a class member – perhaps they are a form captain or table leader – will more readily do what they think the rules of the class are, because they see them as their rules too. But a student who thinks the whole class are dullards won't feel any need to do what they do. Why would they?

Our identity affects our behaviour. If you identify as a member of the Scouts, you may feel more inclined to do good deeds on bob-a-job week ; if you identify as an alumnus of a university, you may feel more inclined to fund-raise for them and not other universities or institutions. And if you identify as a member of a crowd, you will be more willing to do as they do, to fit in, to conform. If that is a football crowd, you may find it hard to resist cheering when your team scores or taking part in a Mexican wave. I do good deeds for my family because I see myself as a loyal family member, and so on.

This might be because there are many benefits to being in a crowd and doing as they do:

A huge number of studies shows improved mood, reduced loneliness, greater self-esteem and feelings of belonging when we are in a crowd.

15. Durkheim, E. (1912) *The elementary forms of religious life.* New York, NY: Free Press.

Feeling part of something that is bigger than yourself is a major source of well-being. These rewards draw people into crowds, keep them there, and make them want to return in the future.[16]

Students can derive great pleasure from being in a successful group, like the pride they might feel being on the winning team on sports day. They can become incredibly animated and competitive if you set a game up in a lesson that pits one row against another. Communal events like leavers' parties, proms or school discos can provide them with a great deal of fun.

It has been suggested that the reasons for these benefits are probably due to shared attention, i.e. we all focus on one thing, which increases our ability to focus and think about it when others are also doing it. Picture a crowd watching a school football match. The social component of observing everyone's behaviour creates a strong incentive or pressure to do the same as everyone else. And when we do, the emotional intensity is magnified by being part of a group: imagine the roar of the crowd and knowing that everyone around you is feeling the same way. Activities can become synchronised as we observe one another's behaviour, from clapping to tooting our vuvuzelas.[17]

We see this in joyful families in maternity waiting rooms, in friends making memories on a night out, in funeral groups, in congregations, watching a concert with thousands of other fans and in a million circumstances where we share an experience. Emotions felt simultaneously and collectively can be very powerful. This is probably because we can easily imagine how our companions are feeling, and then empathise with them.[18] When a school team wins, its participants can remember the memory forever.

So happy together

Humans have a deep need to belong to groups.[19] As psychologist Chris Merritt says:

16. Merritt, C. (2017) 'Why crowds are good for you', *Medium*, www.bit.ly/30QIofz.

17. Ellamil, M., Berson, J., and Margulies, D. S. (2016) 'Influences on and measures of unintentional group synchrony', *Frontiers in Psychology*, 7, 1744.

18. Páez, D., Rimé, B., Basabe, N., Wlodarczyk, A., and Zumeta, L. (2015) 'Psychosocial effects of perceived emotional synchrony in collective gatherings', *Journal of Personality and Social Psychology*, 108(5), pp.711–729.

19. Baumeister, R. F., and Leary, M. R. (1995) 'The need to belong: desire for interpersonal attachments as a fundamental human motivation', *Psychological Bulletin*, 117(3), pp.497–529.

We seek out social contact, not only because of the life functions it can fulfil, but also because it is inherently rewarding. These neurobiological mechanisms – built around opiate and oxytocin release in the brain – feel great and make us want to socialise more. This process probably developed to foster social bonding for survival advantage – if our ancestors could bond and co-operate, they were more likely to stay alive.[20]

Watch how long it takes a new student to bond with members of a class. If the school has been sensitive and professional, it will have created a structured induction process: a welcome day, a buddy system, a class partner, a series of catch-up meetings, and so on. If it is not, then the student will either wait to be approached if they are shy, or approach others if they are less so. But students invariably find their tribe. There is a natural affinity to one another, especially if they see themselves in one another. Like attracts like. Sporty kids find common purpose with other sporty kids. Quiet, bookish children swap books with other bookworms.

Being in a group helps us stay physically and mentally well and helps us achieve our aims – *and* they make us feel good.[21] Historically some social observers saw crowds negatively, as individuals often abdicate their sense of responsibility and become capable of mob behaviour like witch hunts or lynch gangs – behaviours that can also be seen in more modern contexts such as social media pile-ons.[22] Or in the playground, mobs of boys egging on a beating, or a large group of girls victimising and bullying the new girl in the class.

A *Tik-Tok* video that went viral recently illustrates this in a sweet way. Adrian Urban[23] was filming in a London park after the Pride parade, focused on an older man, sitting by himself, belting out the opening verse of Bon Jovi's 'Living on a Prayer' in an enthusiastic rather than accomplished manner. At first he's a lone voice on the edge of a large park filled with uninterested groups of people minding their own business. Then, as the (unquestionably catchy) verse starts to edge towards the chorus, a few 'first followers'[24] see the fun in joining in. In

20. Merritt, C. (2017) Ibid.

21. Troisi, J. D., and Gabriel, S. (2011) 'Chicken soup really is good for the soul: 'comfort food' fulfils the need to belong', *Psychological Science*, 22(6), pp.747–753.

22. Ronson, J. (2015) *So you've been publicly shamed.* New York, NY: Riverhead Books.

23. https://bit.ly/32yJO0J [retrieved 14/02/20]

24. See later.

seconds, an amazing thing happens: a Mexican wave of unity seizes the park, and everyone – everyone – joins in with the chorus. No one was forced to do so, but everyone did anyway, because for a moment, just a few seconds, they all saw themselves as part of the same tribe. Admittedly, a fleeting, blink-and-you'll-miss-it group identity of 'people singing Bon Jovi lyrics in the park' but no one said alliances or tribal identity were permanent.

This is Stan[25]

This desire to seek companionship and group identity is strong, especially when it is absent. In cases of isolation, people often follow celebrities via the news, or social media – *para-social contact*, when you relate to someone that you don't know personally. For some, this synthetic intimacy feels so real that they forget it isn't reciprocated, and they can react violently to what they perceive as a slight. Or they can immerse themselves in the melodrama of soap operas or fictional worlds in books and films – a phenomenon called *social surrogacy*.[26] Children love a bit of melodrama too, and surrogacy is often seen in the way that students will diligently follow the gossipy narratives of each other's lives as if they were their own.

Some of the benefits associated with being in a group can be obtained in online contexts,[27] which is demonstrated by the popularity of online activism and hobbyism. But the beneficial effects are reduced, which may go some way to explaining why so many teachers and students often report solitary, online, distance learning to be unsatisfying in the long term.

And this leads us to a fact about human nature that we rarely permit ourselves to admit: human beings are, amongst other things, highly conformist.

---

25. Eminem, *Stan* (2000) Echoing 'I'm your number-one fan' from Stephen King's *Misery* (1987)

26. Derrick, J. L., Gabriel, S., and Hugenberg, K. (2009) 'Social surrogacy: How favoured television programs provide the experience of belonging', *Journal of Experimental Social Psychology*, 45, pp.352–362.

27. Garcia, D., Garas, A., and Schweitzer, F. (2017) 'An agent-based modelling framework for online collective emotions', in Holyst, J. A. (Ed.) *Cyberemotions: Collective Emotions in Cyberspace*, pp.187–206. Zurich: Springer.

Conformity[28]

This suggestion at first repels many,[29] with its connotations of robotic, slavish compliance. But all that it means in this context is that most of us possess a strong desire to fit in with our peer groups in order to obtain their approval. That's it. We can still, if we choose, defy the gravity of this equation, and do as we please. But the truth is that we often don't. We very often succumb to its force or choose to allow ourselves to do so. If everyone in the class is clapping, it's very hard not to. You don't *have* to. It's just hard *not* to.

This can come about because of the physical presence of others, and also the imagined expectations of others even if they are not present. People like to fit in. They often don't like to stand out or draw undue attention. I say 'often' because this is not evenly and universally expressed. But it is a powerful current in our behaviour. Some students will happily bite their thumb at convention, and even revel in being counter culture. But most students are happier not sticking out constantly.

Conformity can be described as 'yielding to group pressures'.[30] Group pressure takes many forms: persuasion, praise, bullying, teasing, criticism, admiration etc. Conformity can be brought about by a desire to 'fit in' (normative conformity) or a desire to conform to a social role (identification).[31]

The power of norms

Conformity and norms do strange things to our public behaviour. One of the most famous demonstrations of this is Asche's research into conformity in 1951[32]. He studied the extent to which individuals 'yielded' to majority views, and how much they stuck to their own guns in defiance of them.

28. Sunstein, C. R (2019) *Conformity: the power of social influences.* New York, NY: New York University Press.

29. I can hear the book being dropped from here, flung across studies, or tossed across the Ottomans of a thousand drawing rooms and conservatories.

30. Crutchfield, R. (1955) 'Conformity and Character', *American Psychologist*, 10, pp.191-198.

31. Deutsch, M., and Gerard, H. B. (1955) 'A study of normative and informational social influences upon individual judgment', *The journal of abnormal and social psychology*, 51(3), 629.

32. Asch, S. E. (1951) 'Effects of group pressure on the modification and distortion of judgments', in Guetzkow, H. (Ed.) *Groups, leadership and men*, pp. 177–190. Pittsburgh, PA: Carnegie Press.

Groups of eight volunteers were asked to take part in a simple perceptual test. They were shown a line, and then asked to say which of a subsequent three lines was closest in length to the original line (see below). Easy enough, but it wasn't simply a test about people's ability to correctly guess or compare line length. In reality, all but one of the group were paid participants, who had been instructed to lie publicly about their choice, and select the most obviously wrong line.

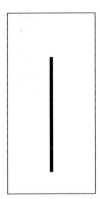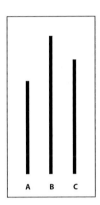

The experiment was to see what effect their choice would have on the one remaining group member, who was unaware of the experiment's real purpose. Would they change their minds and conform to the group norms, or would they resist, using the evidence of their senses as their safety rail?

In the control group, where everyone simply answered as they wanted, there was almost a 100% correct answer rate. But in the experimental conditions, 75% of participants gave at least one incorrect answer out of the 12 trials they took part in. In other words, it seemed that the power of conformity was significant, even in something so apparently straightforward as the evidence of one's senses. Only one in four people consistently defied the norms. But three in four participants deviated at least once in the experiment.

Even those who stuck to their guns and did not change their answer reported feeling doubt and conflict. Of those who conformed to the group norms, some reported that they thought the others must be correct; others reported that they thought they must have made an error in understanding the experiment; and still others reported that they simply didn't want to seem 'out of step' with everyone else.

This experiment is often used to demonstrate the effect of normative social influences, i.e. conforming to a public norm in order to obtain some perceived level of social approval. Others have even argued that it demonstrates that participants genuinely experience perceptual distortion as a result of the influence of others, rather than acting simply to be approved of.[33]

The majority of those involved were not influenced, most of the time. But the influence of other people's beliefs cannot be underestimated. Our behaviour in front of others, our opinions, and perhaps even how we interpret our own perceptions are subject to social influence. Being in a group plays havoc with our intentions. Suddenly we start to strongly consider how we appear to others. Many of us will remember adolescence in particular as a centrifuge of peer pressure, awkwardness, and a graceless white-water ride down a churning social ravine.[34]

Jenness (1932)[35] studied how people frequently changed their minds about issues when they saw what other people were saying, in this case guessing how many beans were in a jar. Participants very frequently changed their own guesses to be closer to the group average, once they knew what it was. This phenomenon is familiar to anyone encountering a controversial but unfamiliar topic in the morning news, and then, uncertain, reading what everyone else is saying about it to form their own opinion. Clothes, music and style also provoke this effect. 'Is this fashionable?' Many students are desperate not to be unfashionable, and one common way in which students show how high status they are is by ridiculing someone else for not being up to date with the latest phone/shoe/bag. I remember one student being shocked when she saw our school librarian's phone, which was perfectly serviceable but by contemporary standards quite basic. (It wasn't even internet-ready.) 'That's so weird,' the students said. 'She acts like she doesn't even care it's a brick.'

---

33. Turner, J. C. (1985) 'Social categorization and the self-concept: A social cognitive theory of group behavior', *Advances in Group Processes: Theory and Research.* Greenwich, CT, pp.77–122.

34. That might have just been me.

35. Jenness, A. (1932) 'The role of discussion in changing opinion regarding a matter of fact', *The Journal of Abnormal and Social Psychology*, 27, pp.279-296.

Kelman[36] defined three categories of conformity:

- **Compliance** – conforming to the group because you're looking for a favourable reaction from them, to avoid sanction, or to achieve a reward. In this form of compliance, the individual goes along with group behaviour even if they don't agree with them. This kind of behaviour change is temporary; when the group is no longer there, there is no pressure to conform. You may pretend to like K-pop when you're with your K-pop-loving line peers, but not at home.
- **Internalisation** – when you genuinely accept group norms, you believe them to be intrinsically rewarding, and you perform the behaviour whether the group is there or not. Teachers should aim for this level of norm adoption from their students – they behave because they want to and believe it to be the right thing to do.
- **Identification** – when you accept group norms because you identify as one of the group, rather than a specific allegiance to the behaviour itself. You may disagree with confiscating mobile phones in classrooms, but you do so because you acknowledge that you are a teacher and it is part of the school policy.

Several factors affect how much individuals conform to group norms: the size of the group, the level of unanimity of the group's opinion, the status of those demonstrating the norms, the commitment of the individual to the behaviour beforehand, and so on. These are all relevant to any teacher who wants to try to build healthy and positive norms in their classroom (as we shall see in the next chapter).

When do we conform?

Some research[37] provides these suggestions:

Normative conformity

- Because the person wants to fit in with the group
- Because they are scared of being rejected

---

36. Kelman, H. C. (1958) 'Compliance, identification, and internalization: three processes of attitude change', *Journal of Conflict Resolution*, 2, pp.51–60.

37. Deutsch, M. and Gerard, H. B. (1955) 'A study of normative and informational social influences upon individual judgment', *The journal of abnormal and social psychology*, 51(3), 629.

Informational conformity

- When the person lacks knowledge about how to behave and looks for it in the group
- When their situation is unclear or ambiguous

Non-conformity

Of course, many people love to stand out, and there are times when we all do; but more often than not, we don't. It's exhausting being the centre of attention, and hard to maintain if that attention is generated solely through disapproval. Of course, there are some who sincerely and doggedly reject any sense of approval from others – for example the authentically psychopathic personality. But this is rare. And even psychopaths sometimes conform in order to get by. Those who endlessly and devoutly bite their thumb at all conventions tend not to last long in society. Or in a classroom. Contrary to popular belief, many of the worst-behaved students are not seen as the coolest or most likeable. Often they are derided and socially excluded by the rest of the class. Very bad behaviour incurs social penalties from those who are negatively affected by it.

There are many factors that affect an individual's desire to conform. Ironically, one of these factors appears to be cultural. Some studies[38] have suggested that people from Western cultures such as America and the UK are more likely to be individualistic when compared to people from East Asiatic countries that value group and community membership more. It is interesting to watch groups with extremely libertarian values and notice how conformity affects even these people. In essence, they conform to the norms of non-conformism. And in schools, even the rebels seek other rebels to bask in their approval.

There is an odd tension at the heart of this: we often admire the rebel, but scold those who rebel in ways we disapprove of. I think this is because we simultaneously understand the value of both conformity and non-conformity. Sometimes fitting in is a good thing: following the herd encourages approval, acceptance, friends, position, status. Sometimes challenging the status quo is the catalyst to better things: we can all admire iconoclasts like Martin Luther King, Nicolaus Copernicus, or Elvis Presley . Neither position is intrinsically good, or always bad. Perhaps we need innovation and conservatism simultaneously. Classes also need to be cauldrons of both: a great deal of conformity to the social

---

38. Smith, P. B. and Bond, M. H. (1993) *Social Psychology Across Cultures: Analysis and Perspectives*. Hemel Hempstead: Harvester Wheatsheaf.

norms that are necessary for mutual flourishing, but also space for students to express themselves artistically and come up with new ideas .

The interesting thing is that it is far easier to achieve classrooms full of the latter when the former is well attended to.

Norms in action

If we have a strong streak of conformity, then what we conform to tends to be the *social norms* of the groups we exist within. We see this effect all the time; we look to one another for clues about how to behave, how to fit in. There was once a kitchen fire in a restaurant I worked in. These are impressive things, as a busy commercial kitchen is essentially a candle, an enormous wick covered in a wax of smoky grease. Smoke billowed out from the kitchens into the dining area front of house, and a dark foggy ceiling started to slowly descend upon the clientele...who all *sat there eating*, looking upwards with unease, but still forking enchiladas into their maws, like the oblivious Muscovites from *War and Peace*, acting as though Napoleon's armies weren't bearing down on them.

None of the customers moved, because no one else was moving. In fact, the presence of other, unconcerned diners seemed to soothe any alarm, and it was only at our insistence that people started to get up and leave. Once inspired to do so, a new conformity rippled throughout the restaurant, and where at first we had to prise them off their seats with crab picks, we soon had to hold them back physically to prevent them mobbing the exits in their haste to depart.[39]

This kind of seemingly irrational conformity brings to mind the behaviour of gazelles in nature documentaries, as one of their unluckier relatives gets picked from the pack by a hungry lion – at which point, the rest of the pack stops running and gets back to eating grass calmly, as cousin Pete gets eviscerated metres away. No one else is panicking. 'Hey, he's not eating me.' What other people do affects what we do.

The social proof model

When we are uncertain of how to behave, we look to other people as a safe guide of what to do. This is called *social proof*, a term coined by Cialdini[40] in 1984. By seeing what others do, we have 'proof' that it is the right thing. It is perfectly

---

39. Of course, they still walked off with their plates.

40. Cialdini, R. (1984) *Influence. The psychology of persuasion*. New York, NY: William Morrow e Company.

nappies on the ground, three metres from a bin. Which most of us would normally never do. But suddenly it's permissible because everyone else is doing it. Students who would never drop a piece of litter will do so if they see piles of it in the school playground. Students who might not otherwise shout in the corridor might do so if they see their peers do in it.

That's the power of social conformity. It prompts behaviours that, alone, you may not have considered. There are many other examples of social influence on our behaviour, some positive, some less so:

The bandwagon effect is a phenomenon where beliefs, values and fashions are adopted at a greater rate the more other people adopt them. So, a new fad or idea may not be popular at first, but if a large number of people publicly support its adoption, the more likely it is that other people will do so, for a variety of reasons: *fear of missing out*, for example. This is how crazes and fashions occur. Some psychologists describe this as an information cascade effect – we stop using our own reason to make choices, and instead rely on information about how others are behaving to inform our choices. This may be another evolved survival trait, watching the behaviour of others and using it as a rough-and-ready guide to how we should behave.[45] How many crazes have I seen flood through a school, only to see them fade away? You can track such things: hula hoops, roller skates, cat's cradles, *Pokémon, Magic cards*, Grolsch bottle tops on your shoestring holes, fidget spinners, cups.... That's why the wise teacher tries to stay permanently five years out of date. Avoid trying to appear cool to the children. You have already failed to do so even before you try. Never use student in-group slang, unless ironically. Its purpose is to signify tribal membership, and you will never trick them into thinking you are 13; and why would you want to?

Crowd psychology (or mob psychology) is the study of how individuals think and behave when they are conscious of being part of a group. One effect of this is to reduce (and sometimes remove) the sense of personal responsibility in group situations, which is itself affected by the size of the group. Herd mentality is the idea that people can be influenced by their peers to act in a certain way, largely based on emotional factors rather than rationally.

---

45. Interestingly, this undermines the normal economic principle of supply and demand, which is based on the premise that people make rational purchasing decisions based on their own needs and their ability to afford the products. We often buy things because they're useful and we have enough money to do so. But bandwagons lead to impulse buys we don't need and can't afford.

Researchers at the University of Leeds conducted an experiment[46] where people were asked to walk around a large hall. A small number of participants had been asked to walk in a fixed pattern, purposefully. In the end it was discovered that it only took 5% of the crowd to influence how the rest of the 95% walked and behaved. The authors stated that 'a minority of informed individuals can lead a naive group'.[47]

This effect has also been studied in online arenas: people asked to vote positively or negatively in online feedback forms are more likely to vote one way or another if the person prior to them has already (and publicly) voted one way or another. 'Prior ratings created significant bias in individual rating behaviour … creating a herding effect.'

Some believe this effect is discernible in elections where the voting takes place over a large distance or a long period of time, such as the US primaries or general elections in the UK. For this reason, election reporting or campaigning in many countries is paused on or around the day of voting itself ('election silence') in order to avoid influencing the result of the outcome. For example, if early polls suggested a strong possibility of party X doing well, it could galvanise undecided or reluctant constituents to cast more votes for party Y later in the day.

A common cliché many teachers use when reprimanding a student for acting as foolishly as their peers is, 'If all your friends jumped off a cliff, would you do it?' Unfortunately the answer is often, 'Yes! OMG have they done it already? What cliff?'

Groupthink is a long-observed phenomenon where people achieve a consensus of opinion due to a desire for harmony and cohesiveness and to minimise conflict. It helps group members avoid controversy. While individual thought processes are suppressed, group goals are prioritised. This can be dangerous, as the creation of an *in-group* (the 'right thinkers') can create a distorted sense of infallibility, where group values are held to be sacred, and dissent is not tolerated. It also creates *out-groups*, who are treated the opposite way. Once a group has decided they don't like someone, it can be very hard for any student to

---

46. Dyer, J. R. G, Ioannou, C. C., Morrell, L. J., Croft, D. P., Couzin, I. D.; Waters, D. A, Krause, J. (2008) 'Consensus decision making in human crowds', *Animal behaviour*, Vol. 75, No. 2, pp.461-470.

47. That quote also being the discarded first draft title of this chapter *winky face emoji*

speak up and try to defend the person who has been cast out. Which is another good reason to have adults moderating the behaviour of the class. We have all had to engineer group tasks to include the unpopular student that no one wants to work with.

This is particularly dangerous in circumstances where ideas need to evolve or adapt. For example, imagine if aircraft engineers felt unable to challenge their line managers when they had a safety concern. Speaking out is discouraged, members of dissenting out-groups are sanctioned, and their views held to be less valuable than they might otherwise be. Members of the in-group can often be persuaded to go along with the actions of the group, even if they would normally consider them immoral. Greater permission to treat out-group members (the 'wrong thinkers') badly is granted, because they are seen to be of low status, and are dehumanised.

This can be seen often in social media, where participants are exposed to a vast array of views and beliefs, and what is acceptable to say is often routinely policed by others. Many find that certain beliefs become harder to express than others within one's own social media group. This can be seen in board rooms, management teams, cults, religious groups, political fringe movements, fascist regimes, fan bases, and countless other circumstances.[48]

Many people tend to conform because it can be easier than making decisions for oneself; because it enables one to be accepted by a group; because they do not wish to be rejected; because there are survival advantages in doing so; for security; and more. None of this is deterministic. Individuals do not have to conform, and very frequently they do not. Even when they do, it doesn't mean they will conform to desirable or socially positive behaviour. Career criminals may conform to the beliefs and values and behaviours of their less law-abiding community than that of their victims, for example. We may have a strong disposition to conform to the behaviour of the group, but what the group values can vary enormously. In the Jonestown massacre of 1978, individuals were so in thrall of their charismatic and domineering leader that most were persuaded to commit mass suicide by self-ingestion of poison dissolved in Kool-Aid. Conformity has sinister as well as beneficial consequences for us.

---

48. Ronson, J. (2015) *So you've been publicly shamed*. New York, NY: Riverhead Books.

Copycat suicide is a well-documented phenomenon also known as the Werther effect,[49] where a publicised suicide can sometimes act as a trigger for further suicides in susceptible people, unless protective steps are taken. These are called suicide clusters, and it is thought that this effect might be caused by providing susceptible people with models of behaviour to emulate, especially where the susceptible person shares age and sex with the original suicide. It is also suggested that there may be the presence of similar mental health issues in these subsequent victims.

Hysterical contagion is when people in groups show signs of similar illnesses even when there is no physical explanation of the ailment, indicating the roots are psychological. People imitate one another's behaviour through the power of suggestion. Many people will be familiar with the power of suggestion to play subtle perceptual pranks on us: if someone talks about itching, crawling or other insect-related horror stories, many of us will start to feel these effects too. The June bug epidemic[50] is a good example of this.

In the Middle Ages, we find reports of mass dancing sicknesses. Dancing mania could last for weeks. Some forms of reported demonic possession probably had their origins in such phenomena,[51] where nuns would exhibit distressing or perverse behaviours, such as speaking in tongues, crudity and exhibitionism. Perhaps it can be found in the Children's Crusades of the early 13th century, which appear to have been characterised by this kind of group religious fervour, driving masses of poor individuals to act with extreme levels of recklessness. In one, thousands of youths, following the self-proclaimed 12-year-old prophet Stephen of Cloyes, left their homes in France and started the long march to recapture Jerusalem peacefully. They believed the sea would part to allow them to cross. Sadly it did not.

School children frequently and sincerely report that they suffer from maladies that their classmates share, even in the absence of any obvious cause ('Oh I have a headache too!'). In fact, it seems that schools are particularly prone to this phenomenon. In 1965 in Blackburn, several girls fainted and swooned, and within a few hours 85 were rushed to hospital with teeth chattering, moaning

---

49. After the novel *The Sorrows of Young Werther* by Johann Wolfgang von Goethe, first published in 1774.

50. Kerchkoff, A. C. and Back, K. W (1968) *The June bug: A study of hysterical contagion.* New York, NY: Appleton Century Crofts.

51. One hopes.

and laboured breathing. No illness was discovered, and it was concluded that the outbreak had been brought about by stress combined by the personality profiles of the 'patients'. In 1999 in Belgium, a large group of school children fell 'ill' after drinking Coca-Cola[52]. In 2009, girls at an Afghan school reported dizziness, fainting and vomiting. And so on.

In more modern contexts, we see mass hysteria and fainting by groupies; the great collective, national supergrief over well-known but non-family figures such as Diana Spencer; the evidence-proof appetite for self-destruction of the millenarianist cults, cursed to wait forever for the spaceship to take them away. The thinking behind mass hysteria may be deeply irrational, but the emotional and social pay-offs for playing along are anything but. Mass shooting contagion is the theory that media coverage of mass shootings increases the likelihood of subsequent shootings, another example of cultural contagion theory. People who perform such copycat shootings are often attracted to the fame, notoriety and attention that the original shooter receives.

And so on. We do not have to look far to understand that the behaviour of others has an enormous influence on our own behaviour, and vice versa. And, from these brief examples, it can be shown that such an influence can be extremely powerful. Not only do social groups offer powerful models of acceptable behaviours (and concomitantly, ways in which recent arrivals may understand how they should act), they also offer powerful influences on behaviour and values. They suggest strong and established norms that a new person is offered not just as a guide of how to behave, but as a guide to how they *should* behave .

Overconformity

A powerful fictional representation of this type of effect is to be found in *Die Welle* (The Wave),[53] a German film that explored the grisly impact of extreme conformity to manufactured and toxic social norms. A young, idealistic and anarchist teacher is given a class of high school children to teach the subject of autocracy. He despises conformity, and after they express the opinion that fascism could never rise again in Germany, decides to demonstrate to his class how dangerous and seductive the lure of fascism is.

He creates a group identity and declares himself the leader of the class. No one can question his orders. He creates a slogan and a uniform, He describes his

---

52. I wouldn't be surprised if Pepsi were behind that one, frankly.

53. *Die Welle* (2008) Constantin Films.

class as better than the other classes and advises them to isolate themselves from other students because they are weak, inferior. Slowly, he starts to create a deep well of in-group conformity with them. In some ways they act positively, standing up for one another and creating a shared identity, self-esteem and belonging. But gradually the darker side of this extremism starts to manifest itself and the film ends tragically. By whipping the students into a fascistic fervour, he demonstrated how easily people can fall into step with one another, despite previous good intentions.

Conformity has a dark and dangerous side. There is a reason why art and literature frequently idealises non-conformity and iconoclasm, even as it creates new icons. Elvis Presley and James Dean were considered revolutionary in their time, and the next generation revered them as agents of innovation and safely edgy rebellion. Conformity provides security and belonging, but it also provides a reason to never change anything – including for the better. Observe the 1984 film *Footloose*, where hep cat Kevin Bacon falls foul of the small-town fun police in the county that banned dance.[54] Observe, too, poor Galileo, imprisoned until death by the Church for the heresy of the Copernican doctrine, the temerity of suggesting that the earth observed a heliocentric orbit rather than the preferred geocentric model of the heavens that some inferred from Genesis.

In an even darker vein, we may still shudder at the infamous Milgram experiments,[55] conducted at Yale University in the '60s, where volunteers were studied to see how willing they would be to administer electric shocks to strangers – even up to the point of injury or death – if they were instructed to do so by an authority figure. In reality, the shocks were fake and the patients were actors, but crucially the volunteers didn't know this. The experiment found a depressingly high number of people who would obey the instruction to inflict harm on another, even though some of them were reluctant. Conformity can be one of our greatest vices when married to unscrupulous authority.

The takeaway for the classroom teacher? To be fair, kind and as just as possible. To never abuse one's authority for selfish purposes, or in order to make us feel important, to make someone else feel small, or to amuse ourselves. This is yet another reason why the teacher's moral compass is a vital component of what we do and who we are.

---

54. *Footloose* (1984) Phoenix Pictures.

55. Milgram, S. (1963) 'Behavioural Study of Obedience', *Journal of Abnormal and Social Psychology*, 67 (4), pp.371–378.

What use is this to us?

Understanding this helps us in two ways in the classroom:

1. It helps us understand why students behave the way they do, and the effect that being part of a group can have on them.
2. It offers us a way to improve matters. If we can engineer changes at a group level, not just an individual level, then we might be able to engineer ways to improve whole-class behaviour in a sustainable way.

The global golden rules?

As a psychological mechanism, social conformity has been with us for a long time. It is a cornerstone of human culture, widely seen as a way to spread and maintain behaviour within a group.

It may have emerged as a behavioural habit that assisted one's survival: we found protection in groups, bound to one another in primitive alliances, perhaps based on the extended families. But once groups get large enough, it becomes harder to guarantee common behaviour codes and rituals or beliefs about right and wrong. The more people in a group, the more likely that they will disagree what the right way to behave is. And of course the more people, the more chances that some will act selfishly, or thoughtlessly, or carelessly. It becomes prudent to write down the codes – in other words, laws and rules – by which we agree to live and try to stick to them. Or more than prudent – probably essential to the survival of any society.

Interestingly, if we look at civilisations throughout history, we can notice that they all seem to share many moral codes in common. In a study from 2019, a team of anthropologists at the University of Oxford determined that there appeared to be seven moral rules that could be said to be universal, across the world and throughout time. Based on a study of ethnographic accounts from 50 societies, they concluded that 'while morality may not necessarily be innate, every single culture analysed seems to be ruled by the same moral precepts'.[56] The authors continued:

---

56. Curry, O. S., Mullins, D. A. and Whitehouse, H. (2019) 'Is it good to cooperate? Testing the theory of morality-as-cooperation in 60 societies', *Current Anthropology*, 60(1).

People everywhere face a similar set of social problems and use a similar set of moral rules to solve them. As predicted, these seven moral rules appear to be universal across cultures. Everyone everywhere shares a common moral code. All agree that cooperating, promoting the common good, is the right thing to do.

The seven moral rules seen in every culture studied ultimately come down to the following:[57]

- Family values – help your immediate relations
- Group loyalty – help the groups you belong to
- Reciprocity – treating others as you would wish to be treated
- Bravery – stand up for your beliefs
- Respect – deferring to agreed hierarchies, accepting authority sources
- Justice – divide up resources fairly
- Property rights – ownership

If we accept that morality may not be innate,[58] that seems to suggest that morality may have emerged to facilitate cooperation. Societies vary a great deal in the interpretation of these concepts, but the prevalence and similarity of the values suggests that they are important to the cohesiveness and continuity of human culture; essential, even. Political philosophers have chewed over various models of how society should be run, but arguably society is impossible if it isn't based on these principles in some way. People from Kropotkin to Marx to Jim Jones have all speculated on alternative utopian models that eschew some parts of these; but annoyingly for the theorists, no examples of these can be seen that are large or long-lived or attractive. Small groups can get by on trust and tacitly

---

57. My summary

58. An assumption that is not undisputed, of course. Many natural qualities appear to have a biological origin as much as a sociological one: sympathy, empathy, attraction, protectiveness to family, and so on, let alone appeals to more spiritual properties such as the conscience.

agreed rituals; large groups can get by for short periods of time. But eventually, law is necessary, or evolution selects cruelly against these experiments.[59]

The Oxford study 'tested the theory that morality evolved to promote cooperation, and that – because there are many types of cooperation – there are many types of morality':

> According to this theory of 'morality as cooperation', kin selection explains why we feel a special duty of care for our families, and why we abhor incest. Mutualism explains why we form groups and coalitions (there is strength and safety in numbers), and hence why we value unity, solidarity, and loyalty. Social exchange explains why we trust others, reciprocate favours, feel guilt and gratitude, make amends, and forgive. And conflict resolution explains why we engage in costly displays of prowess such as bravery and generosity, why we defer to our superiors, why we divide disputed resources fairly, and why we recognise prior possession.[60]

Food for thought indeed, especially when we are designing classrooms to be safe, moral, dignified and supportive spaces. What principles underpin the room you build and run? What do you stand for?

Perhaps without these assumptions and expectations of behaviour, social communities simply aren't possible. Perhaps these kinds of rules (and beliefs about rules) are an essential component of any community that survives. In other words, some level of conformity is essential, for some things, in order for societies to flourish. We may allow ourselves agency in many areas (art, expression, beliefs, worship, etc.) but next to none in others (murder, theft, etc.).

Conformity, while obviously connected to many things we might rightly abhor

---

59. There are considerable sections of the education sector that believe this is not the case, and attempt to replicate their ideological ambitions in school practice. I repeat my earlier comment: such things may appear to work for small groups, or for short periods of time, but never beyond that. I might also mention that these experiments also predominantly occur as a result of the wishes of highly privileged people with little experience of lack. I would suggest that they refrain from treating other peoples' children as guinea pigs for the fairy tales they tell themselves, but in truth I feel that is unfair to imply I would wish it on their children either. Our primary duty towards children is to protect them from harm. That includes witless good intentions.

60. www.bit.ly/2CYR0rZ

– obedience to tyrants, etc. – can also be seen as a positive force, a necessary one, and a cement that binds us to one another. We have already seen that Thomas Hobbes would have argued that without a widespread agreement about how we conduct ourselves with one another in large groups (the social contract), human society is simply impossible.

On the other hand, conformity to healthy and positive norms, aimed at the well-being of the group *and* individual flourishing of all members of the group, is not only an efficient mechanism for the common good, but is also a hugely moral enterprise. It requires that we balance individual rights and group rights with principles of the greatest good for the greatest number. This is not an easy circle to square. But this is an inescapable and essential component of all leadership, all communities, including classrooms. It is not a responsibility that can be shirked. If the teacher chooses not to address what the norms of the classroom should be, then norms will still exist – only this time they won't necessarily be the ideal ones. In fact they are almost certainly going to be much, much worse, unless you believe that children naturally organise themselves into kind and dignified groups without adult direction, which I do not. As Captain Jack Aubrey tells us at the start of this book, 'You've come to the wrong shop for anarchy.'

In the next chapter, we will start to look at how teachers can use norms that can be successfully built into the classroom.

GOOD RELATIONSHIPS ARE BUILT OUT OF STRUCTURES AND HIGH EXPECTATIONS.

The teacher-student relationship is important, but it is built on trust – and trust is built on mutually predictable behaviour. And that requires sincerely executed norms and routines.

But we do not expect students to only behave when they have a strong relationship with all staff. The expectation is that students should behave well because it is the right thing to do.

CHAPTER 6
ESTABLISHING USEFUL CLASSROOM NORMS

It is essential that teachers build safe, calm, dignified classrooms by teaching students how to behave and that is it normal to do so. The teacher needs to design and teach these norms to the students in order for everyone to be on the same page:

> It is just not possible for a teacher to conduct instruction or for students to work productively if they have no guidelines for how to behave or when to move about the room, or if they frequently interrupt the teacher, or one another.[1]

This leaves us with an interesting challenge. Students frequently conform to group behaviour, but not everyone, not always and not equally. Some actively seek *not* to conform. But even when they do, they still gravitate to like-minded peers. They want to fit in, not because they are mindless followers, but because we all seek approval and recognition, and one of the easiest ways to achieve this is by performing in a way that a group approves of. Any group, in fact, that will provide us with the motivational goods we want in order to feel valuable, valued, and important.

Children pick up on norms fast. It is easy to see what the normal, acceptable behaviour actually is, and it is often *not* what the teacher would want the norm to be. Norms are demonstrated by actions; not our hopes. They are not the rules on the classroom wall. They are what happens, not what we wish to happen. They are what we see and hear and touch.

The golden rule of behaviour: make it easy for them to behave and hard for them not to.
We need to make behaving as easy as possible for children by removing as many obstacles to them getting it right as we possibly can. At the same time, we put up small, often visible (sometimes highly visible) tripwires and impediments that guide them away from getting it wrong. Road signs not only point out

---

1. Evertson, C. M., Emmer, E. T., and Worsham, M. E. (2003) *Classroom management for elementary teachers (6th ed.).* Boston: Allyn and Bacon.

limits (e.g. speed limits) but also steer drivers into the right behaviour with speed bumps and cat's eyes. This is much more than 'carrots and sticks'. This is designing a curriculum for brilliant behaviour.

How do we build positive social norms?

The know – teach – maintain model

First of all, we need to *know* what norms we want to build. What values do you want to see demonstrated? What will they actually look like in practice?

Next you need to *teach* the norms to the students, not tell them.

Finally, you *maintain* those norms.

DEFINE NORMAL FOR THEM

When establishing a norm, be clear about what it means.

Imagine you want children to not shout in your lessons; you want a calm space. But what is 'calm'? It can mean a lot of things to different people. For some people, 'calm' can imply calm talking, calm moving around the class; for others it means quiet or silence. What does it actually look and sound like not only in general, but when doing tasks? When reading a book? When conducting a debate?

For you as much as the students, it is important to define 'quiet', and what it should seem like normally.

Example:

> The teacher wants the students to be quiet generally and avoid shouting. But instead of assuming they already know this, or just telling them to 'be quiet', the teacher teaches them what *normal* volume sounds like in different circumstances:
>
> • Silent voice – a voice in your head only you can hear
> • Partner voice – a voice only your partner can hear
> • Table voice – a voice only your table can hear
> • Class voice – a voice the whole class can hear

Then the teacher asks the class to try it out, and moderates it, so the class can hear as a group what normal volume means, rather than just imagining it:

- 'Everyone let's begin, and I only want to hear table voices! Go!'
- 'That was well done but some of the table voices were class voices. Who can tell me why that's important?'[2]

One of the best sectors in education I've seen for unpacking norms is the early years/kindergarten, because they deal every day with children who may not yet grasp what you mean by 'be kind' or 'be patient'. They understand children cannot easily grasp what we might take for granted.

One of my favourite posters I see in early years environments is this classic:

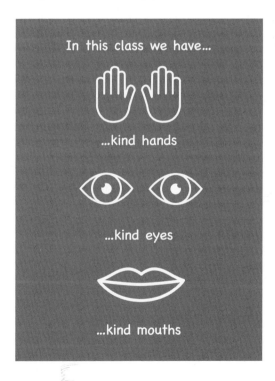

---

2. Perry, G. (2019) 'Your behaviour policy is rubbish', *FutureBehaviour*, www.bit. ly/2CQhNa2 [retrieved 25/02/20]

This isn't really there for the children – they can't read. It's there as a prompt for early years professionals to use as a visual prop for conversations about what kindness means in different contexts. Remember, very small children haven't learned all there is to know about altruism, sharing, forbearance. Someone needs to teach them. We teach them through talking about it, insisting upon it, and getting them to practice it. No one will ever be as kind and understanding to children as teachers (apart from parents), so school becomes a training ground where mistakes can be made safely as practice for the often difficult realities of life after school.

Good early years practitioners know that they have to unpack and explain sometimes even the most obvious of behaviours. When little Ryan in kindergarten clobbers someone with Megatron, the teacher could do one of two things:

1.   Tell him off. 'Don't hit him!'
2.   Sit down with him and ask, 'Was that kind hands?' and see what the response is. Then suggest what kind hands might look like, and then get another class member to demonstrate it. Then Ryan is asked to try it out, and then discuss it. And then they have a conversation about what to do next time they feel like, e.g. clobbering someone with Megatron.

In this way, behaviour is demonstrated clearly in a way that Ryan can grasp, rather than simply as an instruction not to do something. That, fundamentally, is how you teach good behaviour and habits, not just by sanctioning against incorrect behaviour (although often, that too, especially if you believe the behaviour is deliberate). Practitioners in specialist behavioural settings also know this, realising that older children often also need this level of boutique, targeted support to help them learn healthy values and behaviour.

Communicate the norms

We can communicate what normal should be in many ways. We need to clearly and explicitly define, demonstrate and model what normal behaviour is and what values underpin or justify it. The real beauty of this is that you are welcome to decide what values and behaviours you think should be the classroom norm (within reason). Are you trying to promote kindness? Hard work? Forgiveness? Determinedness? Work that out first, and then teach it to the students.

Example:

At the **Michaela Community School** in North West London, one of the classroom values is *gratitude*. They want students to understand that there is always something to be grateful for. They believe people who are grateful tend to be happier. Thinking of who you should be grateful to forces you to step outside of your own selfishness and consider others. It's a motivation for students to do the right thing.

In order to encourage this value as a norm, the teachers have to **teach** gratitude. This means lots of discussion with children about what gratitude is, what it means, and why it is important. But it also means *expecting* them to be grateful. Talking and thinking about it are important but they are only the first step. The next step is to do something, otherwise it's just empty gestures.[3]

So students are taught from the first day in a classroom to perform acts of gratitude in their normal everyday interactions. They teach them to say thank you as they leave lessons. They are reminded to be grateful of the fact that their school cares about them and are encouraged to acknowledge the effort of staff to teach and look after them. They reprimand students who don't show gratitude – for example to dining staff, for serving them. And every lunch time, after lunch, the whole year group spends time publicly affirming gratitude for any person in their life who has helped them.

Example:

A nother of the school norms is *community*; students need to understand that they are valued members of the school community, and also members of their neighbourhood community more broadly. To do this, they remind them that 'you never get a second chance to make a first impression'. They teach the students the kinds of behaviour they mustn't do in the community – pushing, shouting, fighting – and encourage them to think of themselves as better people than that, and to take pride in how they look and behave towards others, even if they are strangers.

They're told not to gather in large groups in the area, to use simple rituals like please and thank you in local shops, and to consider the reputation

---

3. Birbalsingh, K. (2020) *The Power of Culture*. Woodbridge: John Catt.

Student ambassadors

Consider creating roles for students in your class that offer opportunities for model character and abilities to be platformed. Students are heavily influenced by their peer groups, so rather than do all the heavy lifting yourself, create opportunities where exemplary students are given the spotlight, and held up as an example to emulate, such as class monitor, prefect, leader of the table, queue leader, etc.

Example:

> A student hands in a piece of homework where the aim was to record what they did at the weekend. In this instance, they have made a huge effort, and drawn a whole cartoon strip about volunteering in a charity shop. The piece has been edited several times for language choice, spelling and accuracy. The teacher, in addition to marking or grading it, might take a minute to hold it up to the class, congratulate the student for the piece, and specifically discuss the **effort** required, the **compassionate** nature of the activity, and the **precision** of the redrafting. Any student in doubt about what constituted 'good' homework (and many are) will have been given a lesson in how they can do the same. The social proof has been provided by the teacher, explicitly and clearly, with examples.

This kind of platforming should be seen as a privilege and an honour – it must be students who really deserve the spotlight, not merely popular ones, or ones who think it's their 'turn' to be noticed. If students think that praise is distributed like a bill being split after a meal, then they are less likely to try any harder than they would normally, or change their behaviour.

The teacher sets the standard for the class

Teachers need to live and breathe the school values. If teachers act in a way that suggests they think the school values are stupid, irrelevant or tedious, the students might think you are cool, or they might think you are odd. But you will have definitely contributed to the weakening of something the school is trying to achieve. It's an easy path to take, frequently inspired by the mistaken belief that students will like you more. But it's unprofessional and destructive.

Example:

> At parents' evening, Ryan's father expresses frustration with the school. 'You're OK, but that science teacher Mr Harrison is a waste of space. He

But if we do this for others, then we create an atmosphere where children know that sometimes their behaviour will be tolerated and sometimes it will not. What they need to see and feel is a kind of immersive environment, where the norms are everywhere, all the time, and they grow to expect them. They need to learn to trust that the norms abide and remain as always. Norms must be normal.

Zero tolerance – a slogan, not a strategy?

On the other hand, it is unrealistic to expect perfection. Life is never perfect, and there will always be moments or circumstances when things will need to *not* be normal.

Example:

> The classroom norm for students might be to remain in their chairs and in the room unless they ask permission to move. But what if the room catches fire? Or someone is going to be sick on the carpet? It would be strange and cruel to still expect everyone to follow the norm, which wasn't designed for such circumstances.

This is why the phrase 'zero tolerance' is really a slogan rather than a workable policy. I have never been to a zero-tolerance school, although I have been to many that claim to be. When I ask them, 'Would you sanction a student for not submitting homework if they'd been hit by a bus that weekend?' Obviously they say, 'Of course not,' and then we see that 'zero' does not actually mean zero – it means a very, very small amount. There will always be exceptions, in which case we do not have zero tolerance at all. We have 'very low tolerance' for misbehaviour. Which is fine, and all that's left to do is work out where we draw the line, rather than pretend we can abolish it. When you make claims of zero tolerance, you open the door for criticism; when you draw your line on a high bar and commit to it, students' behaviour improves.

The important messages we can take from the zero-tolerance approach are:

- **Exceptions must be exceptional and logically consistent.** They must be seen as extremely unusual but understandable.
- **Reasons are not always excuses.** It is possible to have a zero-tolerance attitude to the act but have a more nuanced and tailored approach to the response. We always want to encourage students to take responsibility for their actions, otherwise we teach them they are not

responsible for them . Which then leads to further misbehaviour as the student won't try to control themselves.

Example:

A teacher has a rule: all lateness without a note will result in a detention. Five students come in late one day. Two of them have a note and three do not. Of the three, two were horsing around in the gym between lessons. But one was held up waiting to get into the toilet at the end of break. That sounds like a better reason, but still not a great one. The three are all asked to return for a short detention, but the last student is told how to manage their time better rather than scolded for being tardy.

Example:

Two students are caught swearing at each other during an open evening for parents. The teacher calls them both to separate meetings after school. It turns out that one was the antagonist and one was responding, having been royally wound up. It is tempting to let the latter off completely, but what would that teach them? It's OK to swear in front of people if you're feeling mad? The first boy was clearly more at fault, and his consequence should reflect that. But unless we instil in all students the need to attempt to exercise self-control, we give them licence to behave as their moods seize them. And that doesn't help them learn to self-regulate. So there might very well be a difference in the responses to both students, but there should still be a punitive deterrent for both.

Knowing how to have exceptions but also make them consistent is something we will look at later when we discuss consequences.

Consistency of norms creates norms. You must have a very high level of consistency or the norms evaporate. But don't beat yourself up if you can't achieve *perfect* consistency. For something to appear normal, it must be the normal thing to happen, not the *only* thing that ever happens. It is normal for summer to be warmer than winter. But that doesn't mean that the warmest day in winter can't be hotter than the coldest day in summer. If that were to happen, we wouldn't fret that the world had gone crazy, that summer was now winter and we should wear bikinis on Christmas Day.[6] We would simply accept the unusualness of the situation.[7]

For the best behaviour, a teacher needs to have very high standards. This is easier to say than to do. One problem is that everyone imagines their standards are quite high. Very few people think they have low standards. One reason for this is that we are often comparing ourselves with very little – we rarely see other teachers teach. Also, we are quite heavily biased towards thinking we're doing better than we are.

Genuinely high standards means, for example, accepting almost no excuse for homework being late or not handed in, or reacting with extreme consistency if someone swears at someone etc. It is *extremely* important to have very high standards, and your responses must be highly consistent, or they normalise inconsistency. As has been said by many, 'You may have to fight a battle more than once to win it.'[8]

Why is consistency so important to norms?

This is because the way we normally understand how the physical world works is based not on certainties, but on probabilities. We observe what has happened in the past (e.g. the sun has always risen in the morning) and then form an opinion on what will happen in the future (the sun will rise tomorrow) . Because the sun has risen so many times in the past, we have a very strong belief that the sun will rise again. Or every time your alarm goes off, you believe it's time to go to work. But this will only ever be a high probability rather than a certainty. The process we use to judge probable futures is called *inductive inference* – we infer from the evidence that we have. We may accept deep down that it may not be certain, but it's as near to certainty as we need in order to get by. Everything we know about the world is based on inductive inference. All we have is experience, and probability.

---

6. I am, of course, assuming a Northern Hemisphere climate. Norms are context-specific. Feel free to wear what you like.

7. Some research even seems to support the claim that zero tolerance is, as a literal practice, unnecessary, and that schools that instead have very high standards/very low tolerance for misbehaviour are 'safer, more secure, as indicated by lower rates of student victimisation by aggression or theft. The authoritative schools also [have] a more welcoming and less hostile peer culture, as perceived by both teachers and students.' (Marzano, Marzano and Pickering, 2003)

8. Possibly Margaret Thatcher, although it may have earlier provenance.

Exceptions must be exceptional

Therefore children need to believe that certain behaviours and values will be upheld in order for norms to develop. Exceptions can occur, but they must be exceptional. And if they are, then the norms aren't destroyed, merely strained a little. Teachers must aim for 'universally the norm'. But they must also be honest with themselves that they actually have attempted to normalise the desired behaviour as much as possible, as clearly as possible, with as much emphasis as possible, and upheld it as often as possible. If we have managed this, then we can say that we have done our best, and nothing else can be expected of us.[9]

Summary: *norms must be maintained as much as humanly possible. Otherwise they are not norms, and the impact is lost.*

Monitoring norms

If you want to maintain your norms, you have to monitor them. It is very, very easy to start to let things slide. Consistency and excellence are hard. It is the easiest thing in the world to cut corners. There are a million other pressures and demands on your time and standards, and it often feels the right thing to do in the moment to lower them.

Teachers often start classes with high expectations and notice every misbehaviour. But after time, they start to get used to it, day by day, drop by drop, until what was once intolerable is very tolerable indeed, at which point it becomes unnoticeable. As Camus said, 'You can get used to anything.' And by that point it has become the new normal. And when we reach the stage that we never challenge a norm, it endures, with no pressure to change. Drip, drip, drip. That's how it happens, and I can understand why teachers allow it to happen. Sometimes it's a response to the stress of the role: if I am upset by trying to challenge misbehaviour, one way I can deal with it is to stop caring.

Defying gravity

Teachers need to build in a mechanism by which they can monitor the norms of the classroom in order to avoid letting them slip. This can be done in several ways:

1. Establish a clear, explicit standard of behaviour, and write it down. As we mentioned, we start by making it clear in the first place what is expected, and then we exemplify it to make sure our students know what it means. So, it might

---

9. Apart from your line manager, of course, who invariably demands pictures of Spider-Man by yesterday, banging his fist on the desk as he does so.

be something like turning up on time, handing in homework, having the right equipment and so on.

A useful thing about unambiguous expectations like these is that they are easier to track. If rules are vague, it's harder to know when standards are slipping. But this also means that the teacher must diligently record things like lateness, sanctions, etc. If he or she does not, then the standards can shift like quicksand, and 'normal' simply becomes 'whatever is happening now'.

2. Schedule time in your calendar to revisit norms explicitly with your students, so that they are discussed and explained frequently, periodically and unambiguously. That way, both the teacher *and* the students are reminded of what is expected. This is as important as reminding the children. The standard bearer must also keep revisiting their own standards to maintain them.

Example:

> *Every* few weeks, take five minutes to go through the whole-class rules and routines with the students. I can guarantee that in a room of 30 people, half will say, 'Yeah we know'; a quarter will think, 'Oh, I wasn't sure'; and a quarter will gape like goldfish and think, 'Oh, there are rules?' To paraphrase Snow, doing this is 'helpful for all children, harmful for none, and crucial for some'.[10]

3. External accountability: ask to be observed once every so often, possibly by a line manager, in a very low stakes observation (i.e. it mustn't be used to evaluate your performance formally) and have feedback given by the observer to see if what you *say* are the classroom values and norms *really are* the classroom values and norms. Filming yourself teaching is also an excruciating but powerful way to see what you actually demonstrate.

4. Survey. One way of tracking students' attitudes to behaviour in their own context is to survey them. Best done anonymously, there are many platforms where this can be easily set up online, such as SurveyMonkey, but a paper copy

---

10. Snow, C. E. and Juel, C. (2005) 'Teaching children to read: what do we know about how to do it?', in Snowling, M. J. and Hulme, C. (Eds.) *Blackwell handbooks of developmental psychology. The science of reading: A handbook*, pp.501–520). Oxford: Blackwell Publishing. From a paper on phonics, this statement applies equally well to class reminders.

might work as well. Ask them simple questions about what the class norms are and if they feel they are happening. *Are people actually expected to be kind?* etc. This isn't hard data, but attitudinal information can be useful to reflect upon when deciding if the class norms are holding.

Correct behaviour when it's going well

If you want students to understand the norms of the room, they have to hear and see them happening constantly. When is the best time to remind them? After they misbehave? Certainly then. But one of the most underused strategies in teaching is to reinforce norms *when they are happening*.

Fences are better than ambulances

This surprises some people. The best time to issue a behaviour instruction is when students are behaving. We are more disposed to issue reminders when things are going wrong – and we still should. But this misses an important opportunity. When students are calm, that is when they are most likely to be receptive to behavioural instructions. If we always wait until they misbehave, then we will forever be fighting their emotional states, and trying to cut through whatever hyperactive head space they find themselves in. No, the best time to talk about behaviour is when students are calm, quiet and settled.

Example:

> Every so often, when students are entering as they should, iterate what it is that they are doing well. When they have sat down, quiz the class about why the entry was so good, and what that meant for their learning and safety. Ask them how they will do it even better next time. The key thing is that the discussion takes place when things are happening as they should, not when they are broken.

> If they *do* start to misbehave, this is the second most important time to remind them what the behaviour should be. We call this reactive cueing – prompting them to remember what they should be doing when they begin to do the opposite. It gives them a chance to change direction. This is done in order to:

- Reinforce the correct behaviour.
- Catch it as soon as it starts to slide rather than when it becomes an avalanche.

Many teachers think that if they see a negative behaviour they should wait to see if it fixes itself. This is wrong, because:

- Usually it doesn't.
- If it gets worse, you now need a larger intervention to fix it – which is usually more disruptive, and calls students' attention to the disruption.
- Even if it does get better, students know you saw it, and quietly start to think you're OK with it.

As Charlie Taylor, ex-behaviour advisor to the Department for Education, said, 'Teachers need to be thinking about improving behaviour when things are going well, not only when there are problems to fix.' Catch troubles early with a small fix rather than waiting and necessitating a larger fix. Prevention is better than cure. As David Clegg says, 'A fence at the top of a cliff is preferable to an ambulance at the bottom.'[11]

Following up and following through

Finally, we make sure norms embed by enforcing them. It is not enough just to tell, demonstrate and model norms. There must be some form of consequence for upholding or upending the classroom norms. If students can defy the classroom norms easily, then some might still adhere to them because they want to, but some will not, if the chance presents itself.

There must be some reaction, some official response, to signify that a norm has been transgressed. We'll look at consequences later on, but for now I want to emphasise this one idea: when norms are broken or ignored, it must be challenged. When norms are broken without challenge, it normalises the misbehaviour. It isn't enough to tut inside one's head and say, 'I'll deal with that if she does it again.' Once is enough to create uncertainty. Twice will create a pattern, and three times and people start to think the transgression is the rule.

Norms that are not enforced are not norms, and you may as well not bother pretending you have them. In fact, it is essential that you are painfully honest with yourself. What are my *real* norms, as opposed to the ones I wish I had, or I find pleasant to imagine that I do? Because the illusion you create for yourself may be preventing you from accepting that you're not quite as consistent or highly expectant as you think you are. That's a dangerous fantasy to indulge in.

---

11. Quoted from Twitter, Dec 18, 2018 @davieclegg

Example:

> A teacher repeatedly tells the class that homework is incredibly important. But when it is time to hand it in, she often forgets to collect it . When homework is late, she accepts any excuse for it, and never chases up students who fail to hand it in. It isn't returned promptly, and sometimes books are returned with no response from the teacher about the homework. Low-quality work is marked as 'Great!' with a smiley face, the same as genuinely great work. Students quickly learn that homework is not very important to that teacher. As a result, they do not prioritise completing it, or completing it to any high degree of quality, or handing it in at all. Nevertheless, every time she sets homework, she tells them it is important. But her actions are speaking louder than her words.

Norms and belonging: the importance of feeling included in the group

Classroom cultures do not exist in the abstract; they are generated by people who feel themselves to be part of that culture, consciously or unconsciously. And being part of that culture means identifying with it to some extent. They have to feel part of it – it is you, and you are it.

Consider how some people feel about their families (while obviously remembering that mileage varies enormously in this area). They *believe* that they are members of the family; they are part of it. They share certain beliefs and values with other members; they show loyalty to one another, even to the exclusion of other groups who are not in the family. Crucially, they feel that there is benefit or value in being a member of that family. Or at least, the benefits outweigh the downsides.

This relationship works both ways. We see ourselves as members of a group because we share their values, and we share their values because we see ourselves as members of that group. We find value in this relationship. But if we perceive the group as being hostile to us, or providing more upset that comfort, it is hard to see ourselves as a member of the group , and we might just want to leave.

Most children will belong to a group but it might be an out-group – a group which sets its values in opposition to the in-group (your group). If an out-group becomes large or active enough, it can make behaviour toxic.

In other words, if we want people to identify with the right group values, we need to make sure that they perceive a benefit of some form in them being a member of that group. In the classroom this normally takes the form of them feeling valued, respected, and supported. Students who come to lessons and feel undermined, unwanted, ridiculed, reviled or abused are not likely to be willing members of that community, or to identify as a member of it. They may be physically present, but they are tourists. And in these circumstances, it is less likely that they will feel that they should conform to its values and morals.[12]

The upshot is that students need to feel that they are valued. This is not some fuzzy, feel-good exhortation to synthetically praise students. But it is a recognition that all students, if we want them to remain, belong, and grow as a member of the class group, need to feel valued in some way. They must be treated with dignity, and they need to know that the teacher has high expectations of them – but also that the teacher believes they can reach these expectations and will show them in some way how to do so.

Students who feel like they are stupid or disliked will resolve the conflict of their situation by pursuing a counter-culture strategy: rather than sit and simmer and feel stupid, they will construct a scenario where they may be unpopular, but they are unpopular because the class is in the wrong. The teacher picks on them. The lesson is pointless. Those who behave are swots or kiss-asses, and so on.

All students, if we want them to participate in classroom norms, must feel that these norms are there for their benefit, and that membership of the class club is valuable. This can be achieved by the following actions :

- Explain clearly *why* the classroom has to run on structure and routines, and what the collective and individual benefits will be. This has the advantage of helping students understand why you set boundaries, and avoids the misapprehension that you are doing so out of spite or retribution.

---

12. I remember wandering into an Irish pub in London that, unbeknownst to me, was for IRA sympathisers. As I stood at the bar, the bartender came up to me and passed me a coffin-shaped tin with a coin slot on the top. 'Would you like to donate to *the cause?*' he said, presumably meaning terrorism. 'I don't get involved in that kind of thing,' I said. 'Well you'd better fuck off before you have an accident,' he said. I left for a pub where they didn't threaten to knock your teeth out.

- In one-to-one conversations, constantly reiterate that the student is a valued member of the class, and that the teacher wants him or her to succeed.
- Flood the students with the normative message that they can succeed, that you want them to succeed, and that you will show them how to succeed.
- Simultaneously remind students that no matter what their aptitude, interests, or previous achievements, they can get better, and that effort and relative outcome will be valued as well as overall outcomes.
- Focus on the behaviour more than the person. Avoid absolutist language of condemnation like 'You are a bad person,' and try to focus on, 'This is bad behaviour.' Use language that encourages students to see deviation from healthy behaviour as an aberration, a disappointment, rather than a sin (caveat: this is not to completely reject such language. If students commit acts of great brutality, cruelty, malice or abuse, it is sometimes inappropriate *not* to use language of condemnation, in case it reduces the seriousness with which such actions are held).
- If students need to be removed from the class, or sanctioned, emphasise that you want them to do better, and that they are being removed or sanctioned for the behaviour, not as some form of retribution. Tell them there is a way back.
- Use praise appropriately (see later, when we discuss consequences).

Remember that one of the overriding goals of establishing a classroom culture is to create a set of behavioural and attitudinal cues that students fall into easily and habitually, with a minimum of resistance. One of the most important ways that this is achieved is by creating a sense of intrinsic motivation to want to be there and to participate, and ultimately to learn and grow. This means that all students need to know that participating within the classroom norms means they will be:

- Safe from physical harm, or the threat of harm
- A valued member of the class
- Able to learn useful or valuable lessons (and possibly both)
- Listened to
- Treated with dignity

This is not a one-way contract of course. The classroom contract insists that all of its participants are treated in this way, which means that they all have to learn to expect this treatment, be shown how to treat others in the same way and have those norms insisted upon. This is the essence of social contract theory, but in the classroom. We escape from the chaotic classroom where no one is truly free or safe, and flee instead, willingly, into the arms of our neighbours, binding ourselves to one another by agreements to support and sustain one another.

In the classroom, the agreements are the rules, but much more than just that: they are the norms, the expectations, the routines (see the next chapter) and the habits cultivated in order to be successful members of the classroom. And the teacher is the sovereign in this scenario, defining the expectations, upholding them, insisting upon them, and holding those who do not meet them accountable by a number of means.

If we do not attempt to create a sense of group identity, then we aren't helping students to fit in. That's fine for some of them, because they already identify with the school, or the class, or the subject, or they have their own motivations and pre-programmed ideas about how they behave at school. But many students do not feel so bound to school. For them, school may seem like a hostile place, full of sinister adult authority, rules that do not apply to them, or learning that is difficult or remote or makes them feel bad about themselves. In such circumstances, it is more natural for these students not to conform, because who among us would conform to the rules of a group that we didn't feel comfortable in?

Cognitive dissonance – it's not me, it's you

Cognitive dissonance is the stress felt by an individual experiencing conflicting beliefs, behaviour or attitudes. For example, if you're forced to do a job you think is morally wrong. One way some people resolve this stress is by changing their belief about the job – 'it's not that wrong'.

Classroom example:

    a.   I'm bad at maths.
    b.   I don't like feeling bad at something.

A student might cope with this tension by believing something else that resolves the dilemma.

Example:

    c.   Maths is pointless.

This is an effect often associated with people who choose to ignore information that contradicts closely cherished beliefs (e.g. in religion, climate change, politics) because it causes them discomfort. In this way, people can merrily live with themselves and their misbehaviour.

Examples:

- We got drunk (getting drunk is bad; I'm not a bad person) – but it wasn't that much.
- I'm drunk, and I shouldn't drive (drunk drivers are bad; I'm not a bad person) – but I'm a good driver, I'm safe.
- I cheated on my diet (that's weak willed; I don't want to be weak willed) – but I deserved it because I've been so good.
- I punched him (that's violent; I'm not violent) – but it was because he was being rude to me.
- I cheated on my partner (I'm unfaithful; how could anyone do that?) – but it was because he has been neglecting me.

And so on. Students frequently justify their own actions, either retrospectively, or proactively. *I'm doing it, so it can't be that bad.*

The problem this causes is that it can often lead to students behaving badly, and rationalising that it wasn't so bad, which tends to externalise their responsibility, outsourcing it to others in order to avoid blame.

Examples:

- I told the teacher to fuck off, *but* he's been picking on me.
- I lashed out with a chair, *but* I've had a bad day.

Part of the teacher's job is to teach children not to instinctively make these excuses too easily, or to at least recognise when they are doing so. This can be partially achieved by pre-empting such behaviour, and teaching students that some actions have no justification, no matter how angry/sad/tired they are. This makes it easier to have discussions about these matters when the misbehaviour does occur. Easier, but not easy.

Normalise responsibility

This is why teaching children the norm of taking responsibility for their own actions is important. It is one of the fundamental principles of ethics. If you never accept responsibility then you can do anything. Obviously young children – and some older children – may genuinely struggle with controlling themselves. But the more we can encourage students to see that they are the ones most in control of themselves, the more we teach them not to be helpless, and to see that sometimes they need to improve. It is the beginning of helping students understand how to grow and mature.

Desire paths

People will often act in a way that they think will get them the things they want and avoid the things they do not. That may sound a little obvious, but it is not so simple. When faced with a straight choice between two things, we tend to pick the option that leads to our greatest satisfaction. It is rare that we deliberately pick something that we know will lead to us being unhappier or getting less of what we want.

We might think there are exceptions to this: people who make poor choices, or destructive ones such as smoking or gambling. But we do not make decisions over months; we make them in seconds, and our frames of reference are often very short. If, in the moment before we lit a cigarette, we thought, 'Hmm, this may ultimately contribute to chronic illness and death,' then you would think a rational agent would see the matter ended there and then. But instead, in that instant we weigh up the remoteness of the danger and the uncertainty of the outcome, against the certainty of the pleasure that a cigarette gains us at that moment. But no one said we were entirely rational or good at reasoning.

In Ian Fleming's short story 'Quantum of Solace', the libertine assassin James Bond spends an evening at a friend's house in Nassau. His friend, a governor, tells him a story about a cuckolded civil servant who lived in a state of permanent humiliation with his wife due to her open and scandalous infidelity. But, despite his disgrace, he remains publicly loyal to her. Bond, in what must be a rare moment of emotional introspection, ponders this, and wonders what keeps him in such an unhappy circumstance. The governor narrator explains that even in such an apparently dismal arrangement, the man found some fig leaf of consolation – the *quantum of solace* – in the relationship, something that made it more bearable than its alternative. And when the quantum of solace falls to zero, 'humanity and consideration of one human for another is gone and the relationship is finished'.[13]

---

13. Fleming, I. (1960) 'A quantum of solace' from *For your eyes only*. An odd departure from the character's normal long-form 'boy's own' adventures, Fleming wrote it as a tribute to one of his favourite authors, W. Somerset Maugham.

People usually think they act in a way that pursues their aims, goals and desires, but we are imperfect strategists in this respect, mixing up long-term goals with short-term ones, and mistaking that which is desirable for that which is good. As Bentham says, 'Nature has placed man under two sovereign masters: pain and pleasure.' People try to do what they like best. Frequently that will mean pleasure. And frequently that will mean pursuing actions that have pleasant ends, rather than arduous and testing ones. Water finds the path of least resistance to its descent.

This is relevant because the kind of behaviour we need from children in order that they may flourish is frequently less easy to perform than its alternatives. It is harder to focus than to daydream. It is harder to write than to relax. It is harder to wait your turn than to take your turn when you feel like it, and so on. It takes some time for children to become used to not doing these things, and to a large extent, this book is about teaching children to do so. Behaviour often flows like water, down the easiest path, unless energy is invested in an alternative.

You are the pump

In architecture we find the concept of the desire path. This is a simple and useful principle of human behaviour to think about when considering how objects are designed to be used, and how individuals desire to actually use them. They are frequently very different, and if people desire to do something the designer hadn't intended, then we have a problem. Failing to consider this in the planning process leads to dramatic differences between designed and actual use. The diagram below is an example of how people actually use a public park.

We see this principle every day when we see low hedges with footpaths worn through them where people prefer to cross; rubbish in streets near houses even when bins are nearby. Urban planners have to take such things into account when designing new roads; architects and programmers and engineers take care to consider this by beta testing products before releasing them into the wild.

When we are in the business of influencing student behaviour, we need to take this into account: people do not want to do what they do not want to do. They will attempt to follow their perceived, immediate desires, and the paths these take them down, rather than the ones other people say they should. The prison break from German POW camp Stalag Luft III, immortalised in the 1963 film *The Great Escape*, neatly illustrates this. You can build as many boundaries around a person as you like, but while you sleep, they will be digging a tunnel under your fences and right under your nose – in the most challenging of conditions. In *The Shawshank Redemption*, jailbird lifer Andy Dufresne tip-taps his way to freedom with a geologist's hammer, tenacity, and time. Humans are ingenious; and when they are not ingenious they are persistent; and when they are not persistent they are good at borrowing the ideas of those who are.

The workaround through this enormous obstacle to directing the behaviour of others is to create circumstances where they either

    a.   want to do what you want because they think it valuable
    or
    b.   want to do what you want because it will obtain something that they want

a) can be achieved in many ways. Most of this book has been devoted to this. Persuade them that the behaviour you describe is the best one. b) is an instrumentalist approach – 'If you work hard, you will get a cookie/good grade/job.' Either is fine; I recommend using both.

The trick is to make the desired behaviour (the one *you* desire) as easy as possible for them. Remove any obstacles you can to encourage it. This takeaway is profoundly important to how we view behaviour management, and deserves to be written in golden plates and displayed in assembly halls and village greens:

Make it easy to behave well, and hard to get it wrong.

This book has been written with this principle etched into its DNA. Remove all the obstacles you can from their path to getting behaviour right. And put obstacles in the way of them getting it wrong. Channel their desires into a new path by persuasion, by education, and by boundaries. 'Come this way,' your new path says. 'This is how to follow the path; here is why this is a great path for you.' And remember to put up some walls around it.

- Teach the behaviour you want to see.
- Reteach it as often as you can or need to. In fact, teach it even when you don't need to.
- If students fail to behave the way you want, use a selection of responses to change that: ask if they understand; get them to practise it; sanctions and rewards; encouragements; challenges etc.

These are the main ways in which we make things easier for them. We make it:

1. Obvious, because we are clear and explicit.
2. Desirable, because we explain why they are useful and helpful behaviours.
3. Habitual, because we get them to do it so often it becomes normal, and therefore the default behaviour.

It is vital that you attend to these most fundamental basics. Other ways to achieve this include:

- **Seating plan and classroom geography:** Are students facing each other, and therefore encouraged to interact socially when they should be focusing? Perhaps face tables and desks towards the action of the classroom and make your base the main focal point.
- **Equipment:** Have systems in place to quickly deal with students who lack equipment, or teach them how to obtain it themselves.
- **Homework:** Teach a routine about when homework is due, what to do if it's going to be late, and how to hand it in.
- **Teaching:** Are your lessons too 'busy', i.e. do you drown students in unnecessary information? If so, have a think about how you can strip down your instructions so that they are clear and focused. If you use PowerPoint slides, are they laden with unnecessary imagery that distracts? When you plan lessons, how much of your methodology is aimed at the entertainment of students? Think about such things as Rosenshine's 'Principles of Instruction'[14], whatever the age of your students.
- **Pace:** Do your lessons begin slowly and in pieces, or promptly and quickly? If you leave children with idle hands in classroom, don't be surprised if the devil finds work for them to do. This especially applies to lesson starts – make sure you have a defined start time with enough for everyone to do. Always have work available for everyone, so that those who finish early (or think they do) are occupied. At the lesson end, make sure you have taught them how to pack away, what 'tidy' looks like, when they are dismissed and how.
- **Tech:** What access to smartphone, tech or other distractions are you permitting them? Does this task *need* to be done on the computer or are you only stipulating that to amuse them, or to pretend you are teaching them more innovatively?

---

14. Rosenshine, B. (2012) 'Principles of Instruction', *American Educator*, Spring 2012.

Always be thinking, 'Have I designed this to be clear or confusing? Have I put an unnecessary temptation to give up or misbehave in their way?'

This chapter has demonstrated the importance of norms. Now we can take a look in more detail how these norms can be built practically in the classroom using routines.

PART 2
ROUTINES

Perhaps the single most powerful way to bring efficiency, focus and rigor to a classroom is by installing strong procedures and routines. You define a right way to do recurring tasks; you practice doing them with students so they roll like clockwork.

Doug Lemov[1]

---

1. Lemov, D. (2019) 'A case study in the power of academic procedures and routines.' Doug Lemov's Field Notes, August 5, 2019, www.bit.ly/2EahyY3

CHAPTER 7
ROUTINES

What is a routine?

A routine is a sequence of behaviour that you need to use frequently in order to achieve a goal. An example would be the routine you have for brushing your teeth, or how you make buttered toast. Routines are a recipe, a sequence of 'do this, then do this, then do this'. Routines are similar to norms in that they can both embody the expectations of the group, although what makes routines special is that they are usually:

- Much more specific
- Normally in a set sequence
- Much easier to teach because they are more clearly defined
- A 'packet' of behaviours that are important for the group to function civilly and efficiently

A norm can be broad or specific, like 'being kind' or 'trying one's best'. A routine would be much more explicit and defined, such as:

- Entry to the classroom
- Leaving the classroom
- Transitioning between activities
- Answering a question in class

And so on.

Building habits, not just behaviour

Studies have suggested that a good deal of our behaviour is automatic or habitual. The advantage of building strong habits in the classroom is that they become easy, automatic, more likely to be observed, and students don't have to think about them so much. This is the teacher's Holy Grail. Better, this is the *students'* Holy Grail. Getting children into healthy classroom habits is exactly what we are looking for.[1] We don't want to just change behaviour, one-off. We want to change their habits. We're not trying to encourage them to eat one healthy dinner; we're trying to build a healthy diet and lifestyle. That's a lot harder.

---

1. Wood, W., Quinn J. M. and Kashy, D. A. (2002) 'Habits in everyday life: thought, emotion and action', *Journal of Personality and Social Psychology*, 83, 6, pp.1281–1297.

And that's why focusing on routines can be so useful. They create an atmosphere of behavioural nudges[2] – prompts to behave in a certain way, without relying on constant explicit direction from the teacher. If they are used to how they should behave then that habit will help them make the right choice.

Here's an example of a simple entry-to-class routine:

1. Arrive to the lesson promptly.
2. Line up outside the room.
3. Check and correct uniform.
4. Get out student planner, ready for teacher check.
5. Walk directly to the desk.
6. Remove outside clothing, hang over seat.
7. Get out lesson equipment and stationery only.
8. Bag on the floor next to the desk.
9. Open book at the end of the previous lesson's work.
10. Draw a line.
11. Write lesson, title, and date.
12. Start the work written on the board.

Note how specific these actions all are. Some teachers might look at that and think how drearily precise they are, how unnecessary they are to teach. After all, what student can't grasp this intuitively? I hope I have shown that for many students, none of this is intuitive or obvious. A lesson can be started in thousands of ways, and none of it is obvious if you don't know. For example, it might also be:

1. Arrive to the lesson as soon as you can (with allowances made for toilet stops etc.).
2. Enter the classroom immediately without waiting.
3. Self-register.
4. Wear whatever suits you.
5. Wait until the whole class is present before starting any work.
6. Self-quiz the previous lesson's learning in the meantime.

And so on. And there's nothing intrinsically wrong with either, or a hundred different routines. One of the things I found by visiting hundreds of schools was that classes could run in very different ways and still be terrific environments in which to learn. Some things are essential for classes to run (e.g. the assumption

---

2. Damgaard, M. and Nielsen, H. (2018) 'Nudging in education', *Economics of Education Review*. doi.org/10.1016/j.econedurev.2018.03.008.

that we will all speak in a certain order) and some things are a matter of taste (e.g. what side of the corridor to walk on).

What matters is that the routines are very well known, very well taught, and very well maintained, just like classroom norms. Some lessons begin with a handshake, some with a spelling test, and what seems to set successful classes apart from others is how well the routines are understood, demonstrated and insisted upon by the teacher.

Summary: *routines are the building blocks of the classroom culture. Routine behaviour must be **taught** not **told**.*

Like social norms, routines are not known intuitively or innately. We are not born knowing them. They must be learned, which means someone has to teach them. Even your best-behaved students have learned these routines somewhere else, which means when you ask them to repeat these routines in your class, they can quickly draw upon their previous learning to remember what the behaviour is.

But many students have little idea what routines are expected, or the wrong idea, until you help them to understand. And as we have also seen, helping someone to understand behaviour is very similar to helping them to understand anything, however academic: it is a matter of teaching the routines rather than telling the routines. One cannot simply tell someone to perform a behaviour and expect 100% compliance. Skills must be learned, practised and reinforced in order to be learned.

The availability heuristic

This may also take advantage of a well-known phenomenon called the availability heuristic.[3] This is a mental shortcut we often take when we are making a decision, and we tend to rely on easily available examples to make a judgement. For example, if asked how much crime there is in our area, we might base our answer on a few vivid news stories we've seen recently about burglaries and think that it's high, even if the number is actually very low. The vivid examples have a strong influence on how much crime we think there is, which affects our decisions about going out at night, buying locks and so on. We make our decision based on information that is easily available to us, or easy to recall, because it is recent and vivid.

---

3. www.bit.ly/39l8sU0

This is why we teach routines. We are asking students to make lots of decisions throughout the day. If we want them to make the right decision, then it is important that they have quick, readily available examples of how to behave and what the right thing to do is. That way, they don't have to struggle every time working it out for themselves based on some distant assembly they half remember several months before.

In other words, by providing students with clear sequences of modelled behaviour, either by ourselves or by watching others, **it becomes easier for them to decide how to behave**.

Benefits of a routine

Routines are incredibly useful for any teacher to help children behave:

- They save an enormous amount of time repeating yourself. If a student learns the routine as a habit, they are far more likely to perform it. Do you find yourself repeating the same instructions at the same time, over and over? You probably need to teach it as a routine.
- They reassure the class that there is consistency, justice, structure and sense to the lesson. Students need to feel that the room is being run, not just occupied. They need to feel the safety and security of being in a place governed by boundaries and rules.
- They pre-empt poor behaviour by getting in front of it. They demonstrate what students should do rather than let them stumble into what they shouldn't.
- They demonstrate your high expectations. If you say students should behave in a certain way, it implies that they can. And if they think they can, they are more likely to try. Some students will have been told all their lives they can do nothing. You have shown them how to look up and see themselves as you see them.
- They teach students good habits, which become part of their character. You have changed them by changing their behaviour.
- They free up thinking space for better things. I don't want my students thinking about where their bags go, and what to do if they're late. I want that all to be habitual. I want to free up the limited thinking space they have for greater things – for art and numbers and words and history and music and every other wonderful thing we aspire to teach them. What I don't want is for them to be wondering where to hang their jacket.

- They make future misbehaviour less likely, reducing the need
  to patrol and respond to transgressions, use sanctions, and let
  misdemeanours blossom into felonies.

What routines do I need?

There are many that are probably reasonably universal, and many that are
highly subject and stage specific. One way to approach this question is to ask
two things:

- What behaviour do you want or need to see? Fast entry? Sharper
  transitions between activities? Better manners between classmates?
  Create and teach routines to focus on that.
- What problem behaviour do you want to solve? Lateness? Squabbling?
  Low homework return rate? Create and teach routines that push
  students to do the right thing instead.[4] Give them something to think
  about, and give them something to do.

If you have an existing class, or you have taken over a new one, you will
already be able to see clearly what behaviours are sub optimal – which ones are
impeding learning instead of supporting it.

It is very hard to give a definitive list of essential routines. Some schools have
routines for public areas, and others none. Some have strict uniform routines
and others treat this as irrelevant. To some extent, the school culture you
occupy will help dictate the routines you need.

Some routines are always useful to define clearly:

- Entry to classrooms
- Exit from classroom
- Answering/asking questions
- Transitions from one activity to another
- Toilet breaks
- Getting attention
- Collecting or distributing equipment
- What to do when you need help

---

4. In the 1987 film *RoboCop*, the eponymous cyborg hero is asked by a breathless
   reporter, 'Robo, any special message for the kids watching at home?' Robocop, a
   violent and merciless walking tank of a man turns to camera and deadpans: 'Stay out of
   trouble.' It's good advice, but we can probably do better than that. We tell them what to
   do, rather than just (pretty vaguely) indicate what not to do.

Your school culture will often determine how minutely or broadly you plan routines. Some schools prefer behaviour to be systematised down to a very minute level of detail, practically to the blink rate or the heartbeat. Others are more laissez-faire. Wonderfully, this is absolutely fine. One major revelation I uncovered as I investigated successful schools was that they could come in many shapes and sizes and still be successful. In other words, there is no one perfect school model that all schools should aspire to. When you have children who already have many of the routines you want, you can focus on the ones that they don't possess yet.

There were many, many features that the good classrooms all seemed to have in common, but these were often thematic rather than specific. In other words, **your routine can be quite different from other schools, as long as everyone knows what the routine is and you demand it constantly.**

The great thing about this is that it means that schools can be very different and have a wide range of styles and still be successful. And the same goes for teachers. You can be tall or short, loud or quiet, funny or stern, and there is scope for all of these categories to succeed. One warning: your routines cannot go against the school routines. Even if you disagree with them, follow them, otherwise the school system falls apart, and schools take that seriously.

The routines you *need* to have will also be affected by the children you have.

Younger children will need simpler routines they can grasp; routines that deal with sharing, taking turns, toilet visits, feeling upset, and more. Older children might have more complex and stringent routines about using tech, working independently, how to conduct a debate etc.

Some routines are subject- and age- or phase-specific. It is interesting that in early years education, we see far more developmental milestones that are social *and* academic in nature. This kind of benchmarking is used far more at the infant-toddler-child end of the age spectrum than at later stages. You very rarely see a mainstream school curriculum for older children that mentions their social skills as an assessment criterion, apart from exceptionally challenging children on some kind of school report system. In schooling for the very young, we often refer to their ability to play in parallel with one another, for example, or the ability to grip a pen correctly, to blend phonemes and describe simple number bond relationships alongside the ability to share, wait their turn, or visit the toilet independently.

In some schools where smartphones are an issue, there may need to be strict rules on their possession and use.[5] In some schools, corridor conduct is rough and intimidating, and that needs to be systematised quite strictly. But in other schools, students may wander between lessons promptly and civilly without dispute or clamour, in which case this area doesn't need to be taught so systematically. Context matters a lot.

But with all children, it can be very useful to think about these questions: What behaviour do they need to exhibit? What do they need to know how to do? Teach them how to do it until it becomes easy, fluid and natural.

That said, be careful not to take good behaviour for granted. It may be going well now, but make sure you build a training regime into the behaviour curriculum even for areas that are working. They may go off the boil, so be vigilant.

Example:

> Students in class A are generally very well behaved when it comes to using the desktop computers. But in order that this isn't taken for granted, the teacher still spends a little time every week or so reiterating the parameters about what sites may be accessed, and what to do if they encounter any IT issues.[6] That way, they never forget what they should be doing.

Some important routines

There are certain things you will probably need students to do, but they are often so obvious that we forget to make sure they can do them well:

Talking – everyone knows how to talk, don't they? Maybe, but they don't know how *you* want them to talk. Teach them the signal to begin talking (so they don't just start halfway through your instructions), the signal to finish talking, and how they are supposed to talk during the task. Emphasise the need to stay on task, to avoid irrelevance, deviation, repetition, trivia. If you like, teach them to look at one another, to turn physically. Teach them to take turns. Teach them to summarise each other's points to show understanding. Teach them to take notes if you want. Teach them how to conduct a formal debate. Teach them how to say hello to a visitor. Talking is not just opening your mouth and saying whatever

---

5. I'll add that they should be heavily restricted in any case, up to the point of a ban. See later chapters.

6. I say 'if' as if it weren't a stone-cold, cast-iron, money-back-guaranteed certainty.

you think of. Teach them the expectation of effort, that everyone is supposed to be involved in a discussion if it's a whole-class activity – no abstentions!

Not talking (or listening) – also overlooked. Listening is more than 'not talking'. As with talking, show them the cue to begin listening, and show them what they should physically do to aid this: turn to the front, pens down, books closed, for example. Teach them the routine for how quickly this is achieved. Teach them to take summary notes. Teach them to paraphrase.

Focusing on the teacher – one of the most important routines to teach any student. It creates and maintains class pace, saves acres of time, and conveys urgency and attention and relevance. So much time is wasted on waiting for patches of the classroom to pay attention. Again: have a clear signal, and teach them how fast they have to respond. Where do pens go? Books closed or open? Hands folded or on the desk? All chair legs on the ground? Facing the front? And keep emphasising the time it takes to do this. It should take seconds. That level of response can be taught.

Answering a question – teach them how to answer a question. Do you pick a hand-up, or do you pounce on any pupil any time ('cold-call')[7]? Teach them what to expect. Cold-calling is useful because it means that every pupil knows they might be asked, so it whets the attention and prevents dropping out. But many students like to put their hands up, and it conveys enthusiasm and engagement with the lesson. So I use a combination of both – hands-up and cold-calling – to get the best of both worlds. Students can put their hands up, and I can pick who I please, no exceptions. Teach them to express themselves in full sentences, and model good language choice. Model good answer sentence structures. Teach them they can think by allowing them a little wait time; teach them that you will sometimes probe deeper into what they have just said. Teach them good listening by creating an expectation that you might ask anyone in the class to answer a follow-up question based on another student's answer.

Transitioning from one activity to the next. Another perennial bugbear, students can lose a million dollars of change down the back of this particular sofa. Teach them the cue to change activity. Teach them the acceptable timing, and where things go, and what they have to do with the last activity. You often see even diligent children ignoring the instruction to begin a new task because they are so focused on completing the last one. Teach them that you are serious

---

7. Lemov, D. (2010) *Teach like a champion: 49 techniques that put students on the path to college*. San Francisco, CA: Jossey-Bass Inc.

about moving on, so you don't have to repeat yourself twice, and everyone doesn't have to wait as you wait for them. Time them transitioning and mention it; then challenge them to do better next time.

Writing. Create strong, clear routines for how pages are formatted, how books are filled, how essays are structured, how sentences are formed, how evidence is given, how working is shown. One of the worst assumptions we make is that they know how to write in the structured way we expect. But it is not obvious. Assume they all need to be taught these things. Even university students doing master's courses are frequently given training in how to write a master's-level essay.

There are many more. Think of routines as building bricks. Some of them seem painfully mundane and obvious. Chopping an onion is mundane. No one wins any prizes for adroit onion dicing. But that, and a thousand other micro-routines, is how great cheffing is achieved.

How do you teach a routine?

Once you've established *what* routines, it's time to think of *how* to teach them. Without a careful strategy of teaching them, we simply fall back to telling them. And when we simply tell a group of children what to do, this happens:

- Some understand fully and comply fully.
- Some understand fully and comply to some degree.
- Some understand fully and comply a little.
- Some understand fully and don't comply.

And that's the *best-case* scenario. This also happens:

- Some understand partially and comply as fully as they can (i.e. partially).
- Some understand partially and comply partially (i.e. even less than the above).
- Some understand partially but simply don't comply.

And worst of all:

- Some don't understand but comply accidentally or intuitively a little if you're lucky.
- Some don't understand and don't comply.

Looking at this, it's obvious that only the first group is anything close to being able to behave to a high standard. Everything else is left to chance. But if you ensure that routines are taught and not merely told, then you maximise the likelihood of them doing it.

Teach – don't tell – behaviour

1. Identify the routines you want to see.
2. Communicate in detail your expectations.
3. Practise the routines until everyone can do them.
4. Reinforce, maintain and patrol the routines constantly.

Example:

You want them to line up before a lesson, so you can check uniform/planners etc. as they enter.

- **Decide** for yourself exactly how this will look (In silence? Planners in hand? In pairs?).
- **Frontload** your behaviour expectations – tell them clearly, right at the start. 'This is what a line looks like.'
- **Practise** doing it until it's perfect. 'That's a great line. But how can we make it better?'
- **Remind** them constantly; either verbally, or by consequences (see later). 'Who can remember how we normally line up?'

Rosenshine's 'Principles of Instruction'

In 2012, Barak Rosenshine published an article in *American Educator* that would send an earthquake through the educational crust.[8] A history teacher turned educational psychologist, he studied one of the most fundamental problems in education: how to teach material in order for it to be learned, understood and retained as best as possible. Looking at a combination of research in cognitive psychology, classroom practice, and cognitive support to help students learn complex tasks, he came up with a set of principles that are enormously useful to anyone whose role involves communicating information and skills to others. They have been described as the 'ten commandments of teaching'.

---

8. Rosenshine, B. (2012) 'Principles of Instruction', *American Educator*, Spring 2012.

1. **Begin the lesson with a review of previous learning** – Rosenshine suggests each lesson should start with five to eight minutes of reviewing material from the previous lesson. This checks understanding and retention and strengthens the connection between ideas in each lesson.[9]

2. **Present new material in small steps** – students should not be swamped with new content in large inedible chunks; instead, they should be fed it piece by digestible piece. This reduces the cognitive load on their working memory and allows them to process new information more easily.[10]

3. **Ask a large number of questions (and to all students)** – questions force students to recall previous information, which creates a retrieval effect. This means that facts held in the long-term memory are retrieved, which embeds them more deeply in the memory, consolidating their retention. This is sometimes called the testing effect and is one of the most powerful things a teacher can do to facilitate learning. Questions also challenge misconceptions and provoke thinking.[11]

4. **Provide models and worked examples** – teachers should link what they are learning with what they already know in order to establish connections between ideas rather than teaching knowledge as free-floating islands of information. Knowledge is retained much more successfully when it forms part of a greater web – or curriculum – of knowledge, especially for more conceptual knowledge, such as subatomic physics or numbers.[12]

---

9. Miller, G. A. (1956) 'The magical number seven, plus or minus two: some limits on our capacity for processing information,' *Psychological Review*, 63, no. 2, pp.81–97.

10. Evertson, C. M., Anderson, C. W., Anderson, L. M. and Brophy, J. E. (1980) 'Relationships between classroom behaviors and student outcomes in junior high mathematics and english classes,' *American Educational Research Journal*, 17, no. 1, pp.43–60.

11. King, A. (1994) 'Guiding knowledge construction in the classroom: effects of teaching children how to question and how to explain,' *American Educational Research Journal* 31, no. 2, pp.338–368.

12. Sweller, J. (1994) 'Cognitive load theory, learning difficulty, and instructional design,' *Learning and Instruction*, 4, pp.295–312.

5. **Practise using the new material** – practice makes perfect. Students need more practice to achieve mastery than experts in the same field. Students process the material over and over, correcting errors and making it harder to forget content. The more practice, the better.[13]

6. **Check for understanding frequently and correct errors** – instead of asking open questions like 'do you understand?', teachers should use targeted questions frequently to really drill into understanding and do something about it if errors are found. This then aids the correction of common misconceptions.[14]

7. **Obtain a high success rate** – make sure that students have an extremely good grasp of material covered before moving on to new content. This enables them to understand the next topics more securely and ensures that some students aren't left behind by fundamental errors in their understanding that can take years to uncover and fix.[15]

8. **Provide scaffolds for difficult tasks** – when material is complex, use scaffolds such as writing frames to make it easier for students to access the material.[16]

9. **Independent practice** – at some point the training wheels have to come off, and the student has to try things for themselves, and also has to make mistakes. Students should be competent before being allowed to do this. Practising independently allows what Rosenshine describes as 'over learning'.[17]

---

13. Kirschner, P. A., Sweller, J. & Clark, R. E. (2006) 'Why minimal guidance during instruction does not work: an analysis of the failure of constructivist, discovery, problem-based, experiential, and inquiry-based teaching', *Educational Psychologist*, 41:2, 75-86.

14. Fisher, D. and Frey, N. (2007) *Checking for Understanding: Formative Assessment Techniques for Your Classroom*. Alexandria, VA: Association for Supervision and Curriculum Development.

15. Frederiksen, N. (1984) 'Implications of cognitive theory for instruction in problem solving', *Review of Educational Research*, 54, no. 3, pp.363–407.

16. Rosenshine, B. and Meister, C. (1992) 'The use of scaffolds for teaching higher-level cognitive strategies', *Educational Leadership*, 49, no. 7, pp.26–33.

17. Rosenshine, B. (2009) 'The empirical support for direct instruction', in Tobias, S. and Duffy, T. M. (Eds.) *Constructivist Instruction: Success or Failure?* New York, NY: Routledge. pp.201–220

10. **Monthly and weekly reviews** – Building on the first principle, students should review material at regular mid- to long-term intervals to consolidate older material more fully and to defy the degradation of the learning curve.[18]

These techniques represent a superb summary of what good teachers have done for centuries but may not do so consciously. A good deal of teacher practice is learned gradually, intuitively or partially. Many see this list and think it utterly basic and obvious. But while it may be sporadically in common use, in its totality it is very rare to see all of its principles executed thoroughly.

Rosenshine's principles and the behaviour curriculum.

We have already seen how closely the skills, knowledge, habits and aptitudes of behaving well in a classroom resemble any other organised body of knowledge or curriculum. By extension, this means that we would be very well advised to employ Rosenshine's principles when it comes to teaching students the behaviour curriculum in a similar way. This avoids two main pitfalls:

Telling, not teaching, behaviour. Simply passing the rules to a student and getting them to stick them in an exercise book has as much to do with learning as eating a medical dictionary has to being a surgeon. You may as well bark instructions at them in Ancient Greek.

- Treating behaviour as something obvious to all, clearly understood, and easy to grasp – and therefore in no need of being taught. Instead, we treat well-behaved students as morally superior beings rather than the fortunate recipients of more nourished circumstances.

So, using Rosenshine's principles, we can establish some useful techniques to employ when teaching routines:

1. **Begin the lesson with a review of previous learning** – every lesson, summarise the routines you discussed in the previous learning; get them to demonstrate the behaviour to show understanding.
2. **Present new material in small steps** – every time a new routine is introduced, think carefully about how you might break it up into

---

18. Good, T. and Grouws, D. (1979) 'The Missouri Mathematics Effectiveness Project'; and Kulik, J. A. and Kulik, C. (1979) 'College teaching', in Peterson, P. L. and Walberg, H. J. (Eds.) *Research on Teaching: Concepts, Findings, and Implications.* Berkeley, CA: McCutchan.

254 days, depending on the individual and the context. This tells us that some people can pick up habits very quickly, and some excruciatingly slowly. Another study[20] looked at how long it took new gym members to pick up a gym habit. What seemed to matter was that they persisted – at least four times a week. If they did, then it took them about six weeks to develop the habit of doing so. While this is only suggestive, it chimes with my experience of schooling; it takes (on average) most students about half a term to form at least some of the habits they need to flourish. Not all – *most* of them.

When do we start new habits?

There is some evidence that when routines are broken by some natural means, such as the end of term or moving into a new building, people become more receptive to changing their habits.[21] We might be able to embed new habits more easily when students are at the beginning of an obvious annual or term landmark, such as the start of a new academic year or immediately after a term break. Of course, you may not have the luxury to do so. The good news is that you can start to change habits any time you want.

Make habit changes concrete

We can also use the power of implementation intentions. We know that people often struggle to stick to commitments, even publicly stated ones. 'I'm going to give up smoking' was one I struggled with for years. It was sincere, but being heartfelt wasn't enough to kick the habit. We all struggle with self-regulation, and sometimes willpower seems a very finite resource. We find it hard to begin and persist with resolutions. And if we struggle, you can imagine how much a child will struggle.

One thing that can help is an implementation intention;[22] if we can make the intention more specific and concrete then that has a positive impact on our ability to do so. Rather than say 'One day I'll give up smoking…' (with the 'dot-dot-dot' indicating 'some magical time in the future known only to God'), turn that into 'I will only smoke after a meal, starting from Monday,' and you start to see some results. Deadlines help.

20. Kaushal, N. and Rhodes, R. E. (2015) 'Exercise habit formation in new gym members: a longitudinal study', *Journal of Behavioral Medicine,* 38 (4), pp.652-663.

21. Thompson, S., Michaelson, J., Abdallah, S., Johnson, V., Morris, D., Riley, K., and Simms, A. (2011) 'Moments of change' as opportunities for influencing behaviour: A report to the Department for Environment, Food and Rural Affairs. London: Defra.

22. Gollwitzer, P. and Sheeran, P. (2006) 'Implementation intentions and goal achievement: a meta-analysis of effects and processes, *Advances in experimental social psychology,* 38. https://doi.org/10.1016/S0065-2601(06)38002-1

This can help students if we make routines as specific as possible, set timelines on when they are achieved, and make it easier for them to behave by taking some of the thinking out of it. Instead of 'You should behave today', tell them what behaviour looks like. Instead of saying 'Hand your homework in', tell them when and where, and how, and what to do if there's a problem. It is possible to inadvertently teach them routines that make them more – not less – helpless.

Fletcher-Wood identified three main factors in changing habits:[23]

- Repetition – Students need to repeat the action many times.
- Cues – Students need clear reminders to perform the behaviour, which has been pre-trained. This could be a hand in the air, a finger on the lips, a hand on the head, a bugle, whatever takes your fancy. SLANT and STAR are examples of these.
- Rewards – Students need extrinsic rewards such as prizes etc., but also (or especially) intrinsic rewards where we encourage the student to value the action for itself, or unpack the good things they are doing through targeted praise.

Academic and social routines

Most of the routines I discuss in this book are social; they deal directly with how we interact with one another. But behaviour, as I've argued, is a much bigger concept. It encompasses every action a student can take at school. It therefore includes not only e.g. walking along a corridor and dining-hall etiquette but also how we behave when working or learning.

We can call this 'learning behaviour', and it is just as important (ultimately) for the success of the learner.

Examples:

- How we structure essays
- What to do when a problem is too hard
- How to construct an argument
- How to debate
- How to hand in homework
- How to do homework

---

23. Fletcher-Wood, H. (2019) 'The 3 Principles to helping students form new habits', *Schools Week*, September 16, 2019, www.bit.ly/2OLm01o [retrieved 22/02/20]

but mainly to deter deliberate misbehaviour, not for improving practice. If students don't get behaviour right, it might simply need reteaching. Or more practice…

Example:

> At Dixons Music Primary in Bradford, staff ensure all students practise routines to a very high standard by making it as clear as possible what they have to do. When students are about to transition from one task to another, teachers teach them the pre-transition routine for attracting attention to the fact that they are about to transition: the teacher raises their hand. Children see this, raise their hand, and track the teacher. As the noise goes down, other students quickly notice and do the same. The teacher reinforces compliance with a thumbs-up, and no talking. The teacher waits for silence. All conversations must stop immediately when the student notices the hand up. In early years key stage 1 classrooms, the rhyme '1,2,3, eyes on me' might be used.

> And this is the routine taught to all students and used by all staff. That is important. As students progress through year groups, they expect the same routines, and have it imprinted again and again by repetition, until it becomes easy and natural.

> There is a separate routine for transitioning between activities. This is also taught, and used repeatedly.

Do routines infantilise students?

Not if you're doing it right, In fact exactly the opposite, they are designed to liberate. Does teaching someone the routines to drive a car or to cook oppress or liberate them? We teach them routines so they can do things for themselves. Learning routines frees up working memory – the space they have available to them to think with. Practice doesn't make them helpless. It makes them more powerful than they could possibly imagine. The following routines are good examples of how we can teach children to be independent, rather than just cutting them loose and hoping they cope – which is the default for any system that doesn't focus on consciously taught routines:

Examples:

- How to tie their shoelaces
- How to go the toilet independently
- How to deal with an insult
- What to do when they get lost

- How to cope with being stuck
- Who to ask if they need to report something private and important
- How to use a dictionary
- How to log in
- How to use the internet to research safely
- How to exercise and eat healthily

And so on. Teaching children how to do things they could not do before opens the world up to them, and not just the world of learning.

The process is simple to understand and hard to do. We teach them how to perform a routine. Then we expect them to do it. Then we hold them to account for it and expect them to do it for themselves. Then we monitor that they are doing it right. And we do that forever.

Can we have a fun lesson?[27]

Who doesn't love fun? But while fun is great, not everything we value is fun. Getting good at something isn't always fun. It takes practice. And practice is often not fun. But it leads us to something valuable, i.e. expertise and the greater aptitudes and freedoms that this entails. Practice can be hard work; it can even be a bit boring. But we can't habituate students into thinking that they can give up every time something isn't incredibly interesting. Among the best norms to create in your classroom is the sense that perseverance is valuable; that if things get tough, you should persist; and that not everything needs to be fun. These norms will help them to build the routines they need.

As Hattie tells us, the hard work of learning 'is not always pleasurable and easy; it requires over-learning at certain points, spiralling up and down the knowledge continuum, building a working relationship with others in grappling with challenging tasks … This is the power of deliberate practice and concentration.'[28]

Also, from Didau, 'Kids that quickly throw in the towel at school are willing to persevere at *Call of Duty* until they overcome their limitations. Why do they do it? Because they want to win. Being killed endlessly is all kinds of frustrating; the pleasure comes from mastery.' [29]

---

27. 'No, we may not' or 'All my lessons are fun' are the only answers that are canon.

28. Hattie, J. (2012) *Visible learning for teachers*. Abingdon: Routledge.

29. Didau, D. (2013) 'Teaching Sequence for Developing Independence', The Learning Spy blog, July 4, 2013, www.bit.ly/3jwWafQ [retrieved 18/04/20]

Here are some examples:

- Get to lesson on time, preferably a minute early when possible.
- Get their uniform in order/make themselves tidy and neat.
- Line up outside calmly.
- Walk into the classroom.
- Hang their outside clothes up.
- Put their bag somewhere.
- Get out the equipment they need.
- Find their textbooks/exercise books.
- Hand them out.
- Lay out the new work on a page of their books.
- Ask questions.
- Answer questions.
- Discuss things with a shoulder partner.
- Go from the desk to the carpet, and vice versa.
- Take a space on the carpet.
- Get a reading book.
- Read quietly.
- Use a dictionary.
- Ask for help.
- Ask to go to the toilet.
- Visit the toilet.
- Log on to a desktop computer.
- Use a laptop or tablet.
- Collect in pencils or materials.
- Hand out team tabards.
- Tune an instrument.
- Check headphones are working.

And so on. These micro behaviours will vary by age, by subject, by school rules, by your classroom standards, and so on. Some of the above won't apply to your context; some will. A million things are not on that list that could be.

These are the small behaviours that make up the big idea of 'good behaviour'. And crucially, these must be taught. Because although many of these appear to be absurdly obvious, they are only obvious to us. A moment's reflection helps us realise that most of these mini-tasks can be carried out in lots of different ways.

Example:

Lay out a new piece of work. Title? Date? Underlined? New page? Coloured pen? Pencil?

Get a reading book. Can they bring their own? Does it have to be from the classroom library? Does it have to follow a reading programme? Can they keep it? Does it have to be a book? Is a magazine a book? Can they read on their phone?[30]

Visit the toilet. How long is too long? Do they have to go directly? Is there a special route? Do they need a pass? How often is too often? Do they have to wait for set times?

CLEAR MESSAGING

Questions follow every behavioural instruction, however simple. If you want to maximise the compliance of students, make your direction as *clear* and *specific* as possible. It may seem pointlessly pedantic, but it is vital. Clarity will simplify and streamline behaviour every time you ask students to behave.

Children might take their seats a dozen times a day. If you don't tell them clearly what that looks like, then you have (12 × 30 kids) opportunities to be dragged into turgid conversations where you remind students how to sit their backsides down. Countless teachers have said, 'How many times have I told you to line up!', worn down with exasperation. But if they have not invested the time to make it clear what a line looks like, or why it is important (or not), then they *can expect students to interpret vague directions broadly*. When you tighten up the direction, the outcomes tighten up too.

Routines can be about specific actions (how to sharpen a pencil) or more complex sequences of actions (how to begin a lesson or day). The only difference is in their detail.

To teach sequences, we teach:

- The individual actions
- The order in which they must be performed

---

30. No.

Break big behaviours into smaller behaviours.

Example:

> To learn how to drive, we learn to adjust our seat, to position the mirror, to check for petrol, to hold a wheel, to turn the ignition, to select a gear and use the clutch…and so on, until we have a sequence of behaviours practised, memorised and internalised. Once each is acquired, we practise using them simultaneously.

A pianist starts with single notes, then melodies, then chords, two hands, pedals, pace and so on. A reader starts with letters, then sounds, then meaning, then sentences, then stories, and so on. We build competence in the basics, and then progress to greater competencies.

WHAT ROUTINES DOES THE SCHOOL EXPECT?

Some of the routines you teach will be given to you from above, as whole-school expectations. For a new teacher, this is a good thing, as they will be able to lean on practices and rituals that already exist. The better the school, the more practised and communally accepted (and performed) the routines are. Sadly, many schools don't focus sufficiently on this aspect, and students make up their own behaviour as it pleases them. As we have already mentioned, that may be fine in a school serving communities of well-brought-up, privileged children, but less successful in schools where students are not as used to the types of behaviour that a school asks of them.

The best advice for any new teacher joining a school is to find out exactly what the whole-school routines expected of students are, and to stick to them as closely as possible. In this way, the teacher leans on the community norms and routines, and reinforces them, and has their own behaviour reinforced in turn.

WHAT IF THE SCHOOL'S ROUTINES ARE TOO WEAK?

A difficulty arises when the teacher's expectations are higher, or less flexible than the school's routines. This may not be a bad thing; the teacher may have expectations that are unreasonable. But commonly the reverse is true, and the teacher finds herself struggling against a school system that places less value on consistency than it should.

The best advice in this circumstance is to remember that as long as your norms and routines don't contradict the school routines, you are normally free to add your own classroom norms and procedures on top of the whole-school routine.

Example:

> A teacher joins a school where uniform and equipment expectations are stringent, but there are no clear rules about the consequences of not handing in homework. As long as the school rules don't specifically mention it, then the teacher is free to call home, set sanctions, use reminders, reward compliance, or any other strategy they see fit.

HOW DEEP DO YOU WANT TO GO?

This design phase is crucial. If you skip it, you condemn the students to playing a career-long game of 'Guess what's in my head!' or worse, 'Guess how the capricious warlord is feeling today!' You need to be clear what behaviour you want to see in order for them to be clear about what behaviour to perform. If you're not clear in your own mind what behaviour you want, then you'll make things up on the spot. Good luck with that.

Describe

HOW WILL YOU MAKE SURE THAT THE STUDENTS KNOW WHAT ROUTINES YOU HAVE DECIDED?

Now that you have a clear, coherent and preferably written record of what behaviour you want them to perform, you need a plan of how you will tell them. This is best done at the beginning of a relationship. It should be explained and unpacked so that they understand not just what they are but why they're important. Convincing students that a behaviour is important will go an enormous way to persuading them to actually perform it. We attend much more closely to things that matter to us than things that don't. Telling students 'Just do it because I say so' isn't entirely without merit (after all, there might be plenty of circumstances when you want exactly that, and it is the eventual goal of all this routine building) but as a sole strategy it has limited effectiveness. Try to persuade as you instruct, as long as you remember that you're doing so as a tool, not because the classroom is a democracy. It is not. Your room, your rules.

SELL THE BEHAVIOUR

Not everyone will buy it, but some is better than none. You won't convince everyone that the behaviour is valuable, but you don't need to. The goal of every different strategy isn't to completely win, but to partially win. Enough wins, and you start to win the whole thing. For the non-customers, you'll use other strategies:

Repetition – tell them over and over.

- **What's in it for me?** – try different arguments showing why the behaviour matters to them and their goals.
- **Reteaching** – show them how to do it, or get them to do it again.
- **Consequences** – challenge them every time the routines aren't met.
- **Normalisation** – always treat the routines as if they are utterly standard, not some exceptional ask of them.

TEACHING ROUTINES LIKE A CURRICULUM

Be upfront about what behaviour they need to do. Run through it clearly. Ask questions to *check for understanding*. Get them to tell you what you just said. Get them to discuss it in groups. Get them to demonstrate it. Congratulate their efforts or success. Reteach where necessary. Evaluate their understanding continually. Move on when you are confident they've processed the routines properly.

Suggestions:
- A verbal lecture/lesson on the routines
- A handout to include in their folders or books
- Wall posters
- Role-playing the behaviours
- Whole-class discussion

Or a combination of any of these. The important thing is to make them important, make them known, and make them happen.

HOW WILL YOU MAKE SURE THEY ALL UNDERSTAND THE ROUTINES?

Understanding can be checked in a variety of ways. For example:

- Verbal interrogation. Frequently ask them what the behaviour standards are. Weave it into your general conversations about content.
- Quizzing. Make their understanding part of the curriculum by setting short quizzes.
- Demonstration. Ask them to show you how to do X.

And so on. The important thing is that it is not left to chance. It is not left to their imagination. It is not left to them to decide, or interpret, what the standards of the room are. This is not an exercise in seeing which child can flourish without assistance and which ones will falter. They all deserve the scaffolding of high standards, clearly expressed, carefully taught, and rigorously nurtured. This is an act of gardening, and gardens need effort, love, and persistence. Unless you're happy with wild gardens, or forests. But forests are not kind places for the weak, the lost or the uncertain. Be the gardener, not Lord of the Jungle.

HOW WILL YOU MAKE SURE THAT NEW MEMBERS OF THE CLASS KNOW THEM?

One last consideration: don't forget about new students, mid-year joiners, temporary transfers and similar. They need to understand the class culture too. Remember that it is confusing and challenging enough for new students all beginning at the same time, but for someone from another school, class, or country, it can be terrifying. If your class routines are strong and explicit, then chances are a new student will pick up the good habits fast. But why leave it to chance? Why take a gamble with someone who already is probably feeling a little lost? There are lots of things to make it easier for them.

- Assign a class buddy, a mentor, or a friend. They should be responsible, and a great role model of the kind of behaviour you want to see. They should be naturally friendly and kind, and they should be trained to some degree to be a buddy. This means making it clear what their duties are on a daily, weekly and ongoing basis. You should check in with them regularly, to see how the new inductee is doing. You should ask pointed questions to discern any concerns.
- Design some way to explicitly communicate the class norms and routines to them. Perhaps a short extra-class induction session where you talk about the basic outline of the class norms. This should be a pep talk as much as a lesson. Understandably, not many teachers have a lot of time to do this (hence the mentor approach) but it is an essential investment to at least attempt. There must be a formal threshold experience for the student where they feel welcomed to the class, and given clear instructions about how to succeed. The student should leave feeling like a valued member of the group.
- Create a schedule to check in on their progress. Don't just ask them 'How are you doing?' and accept a vague wave and smile. When will you speak to them? What will you ask them? What are their progress targets, behaviourally? And what will you do if they don't meet them? Reteach? When?

189

This is one of those circumstances where it takes a little more time and effort to get it right, but the difference can be a dividend of great behaviour, learning and acceptance for the rest of the student's career, or its opposite. It is an investment well worth making, however you achieve it.[31]

Remember: Always make it easier for kids to behave than misbehave.

Demonstrate

One of the best ways to help children understand an expectation is to get them to do it. Doing it makes it concrete rather than theoretical. Doing it makes them think about it, which means they have to process it mentally rather than just immediately forget about it. So, once we have explained the routine in painstaking detail, get active.

Get them to practise it until they feel comfortable doing it, and until you are convinced they can get it right every time.

Example: lining up; hands up; equipment checks; transition from group to paired work; lesson beginnings; lesson ends.

Don't be afraid to repeat this until you are happy with it. This is the calculus of embedding routines: the more time you invest in getting them right, the more time you save over the long term. And keep selling the benefit. Let the students know why these routines are important. The language behind this is important. Something that appears to be dreary (e.g. practising lesson transitions) can be energised by imbuing it with importance.

Let them know why what they are doing is a good thing. You can be as entertaining or as straight as you wish with this. Everyone has their own style. I've seen teachers turn moving from the floor to the desk after carpet time into a competitive sport, stopwatches and all. I've seen teachers turn dismissal from lessons into a game of musical statues. Whatever works for you. But teach it by doing it.

---

31. I remember with horror the young girl I once encountered in my lessons, a transfer from a Spanish school. She'd been in my class for three weeks, when I asked her how she was getting on. She said she had some great friends, but she wasn't too keen on the school. When I probed why, she told me that she was still waiting for a timetable. In its absence, she had just latched onto a (thankfully) kind peer and followed her into all her lessons. Can you imagine how she must have felt? Thrown to the wolves.

Demand

In some ways, this is the hardest part, and where most teachers start to slide. Making sure the students have to perform these routines all this time is hard work. If you don't demand it, their behaviour will slide. It is not natural to maintain high standards for long. It is hard to build them up in the first place without someone insisting that they happen. This is crucial for the phase where these are becoming habits. Monitoring and maintaining behaviour is:

- Tiring
- Repetitive
- Time consuming
- *Essential*

Prioritise routine setting at all times. Make it something that you plan into your schedule for teaching. Think in great detail about when you will do so. Build up a vocabulary of phrases you can use to remind, prompt, nudge or cue students back into behaviour that they are starting to slip away from.

Example:

Rather than constantly asking the class to be quiet and pay attention to you, use a cue, like a word or hand signal, to indicate that they need to perform a sequence of pre-taught actions. Some teachers might use SLANT or STAR,[32] or clap once, or raise their hand silently.

MASTER SIMPLE BEHAVIOUR FIRST

Students should be encouraged to become proficient in basic behaviours before they learn to do other, more complex ones. And that means the teacher must demand them, because students will not collectively agree to act in a way that maximises the benefit for all. That is one of the essential roles of the teacher and adult in the room: to insist; to demand what happens. It's not merely to suggest or request (although it also both of these). It is to demand that certain behaviour occurs. It requires a good deal of willpower and resolve from the teacher. This is not easy.

---

32. Two techniques from Doug Lemov's *Teach like a champion*: STAR (Sit up, Track the speaker, Ask and answer like a scholar, and Respect those around you) and SLANT (Sit up, Listen, Ask and answer, Nod your head, and Track the speaker).

THE MORAL COMPASS

Ah, but a man's reach should exceed his grasp
Or what's a heaven for?
Robert Browning, 'Andrea del Sarto'

One of the best motivators I can suggest for a teacher is to remember how important this all is. If you do *not* do this, then the job is so much harder, learning deteriorates, safety evaporates, and no one flourishes as they might have done, including the teacher. I call this the moral compass of teaching. It is hard to be resolute about something you do not believe in. But if you believe in education and what it can do, if you believe in your subject, if you believe that knowledge and learning are transformative powers in children's lives, if you know in your heart that education is one of the jewels of human accomplishment – if you believe all this, then you get out of bed in the morning and you punch in and you do your best even when you don't feel like it. Because it matters. It matters more than anything else I have ever done. You matter.

So, *demand*. Demand that they try. Demand that they reach out to what is possible. Demand because it matters if they do, and it matters if they don't. Wage war on ignorance and swear an oath to their futures. Hannah Arendt used to write about what she called the banality of evil, the fact that some of the greatest horrors were committed by the most ordinary of people doing the most ordinary things.[33] I think this also applies to goodness. We save the world one lesson at a time, atom by atom. Teachers are not saviours or messiahs. They are tiny but vital links in the chain of a child's life. But what an honour. What a responsibility. Go to bed and think about *that* every night, not the fact that Ryan in 9F called you names, or that the class didn't listen. Your job isn't to pull perfect lessons from your perfect hat with perfect children every time like a machine; your job is to hack and slash away at the vines and grasses of ignorance. Slash away for as long as you can.

Do the same small good thing for a very long time.

THE BEST WAY TO DEMAND

- Front-load the student/staff relationship with routines – show how important they are by teaching them right at the start, from the first moment you meet.

---

33. Arendt, H. (1994) *Eichmann in Jerusalem: A Report on the Banality of Evil.* New York, NY: Penguin Books.

- Repeat them constantly – make them into mantras and catchphrases.
- Follow up every time; *never* let things slide.
- *Never* allow students or staff to ignore a routine.
- Revisit your expectations of them in behaviour conversations. And every conversation.
- If necessary, stop other activities to reinforce them.
- Tactical ignorance, tactical follow-up. This means that you can – at times – ignore misbehaviour *if* the greater good is served by doing so *and* you follow up publicly later on.

Just do your best. You can only do what is possible. You can't follow up with everything, Follow up when you can, as much as you can. You'll never catch every misbehaviour; just do your best to let as little slide as possible. Prioritise the big-ticket misbehaviour first, then work down to the smaller stuff.

And as Lemov puts it: 'Doing it over again is the best response to insufficient execution of a routine.'

If a student or a class doesn't do what you've asked as well as you want, one of the best things you can do is make them do it all over again. Not as a punishment, but as a chance to get it right the next time. It's laborious, but then so is reminding students to do the right thing 100 times a day.

When my kids were little, I would ask them to say please and thank you. Every time they didn't, I would say, 'What do we say?' and they would add please or thank you as required. But this kept happening. So I changed my request. Every time they forgot to say it, I would get them to say the whole sentence out again, with please or thank you added at the end. This took longer. But it was obvious to them that it would be easier just to get it right the first time. I had turned off the snooze alarm. They knew they had to get up/get it right the first time.

One last thing – 'professional warmth' goes a lot further with a lot more students than aggression, so when you demand, this has nothing to do with being abrupt or blunt (although you may need this tonal arrow in your quiver at times) and everything to do with talking to students as if they deserve to be treated with dignity, but they have a job to do that must be done.

Disengage

Now give them a chance to actually try out the routines. Although students need to hear a constant stream of behaviour cues and corrections, if you want to see if they are learning to behave, you need to take the training wheels off a little and see if they behave without you asking them to. Otherwise you could create the expectation that you'll correct everything.

- Reinforce good performers with targeted praise. Make this the new normal. Show that their behaviour is a cue for others, and other staff/students should follow them.
- Can you take down the fence? What happens if you don't remind them all the time? Watch carefully to see who forgets and who is trying to ignore the routine.
- Intervene when the routines aren't being adhered to sufficiently. Take stock and feed back to students at the end of the lesson or session.

Top tip: Occasionally revisit the routines explicitly *even when* they are happening. Draw attention to the process so it stays fresh in their minds. 'We're all lining up now, that's good…and I can see everyone has their uniform right… just a few people still need to get their bags off their shoulders…great stuff.'

And never forget you can only take your eye off a routine for so long. They will need you to check on their behaviour from time to time. The minute you forget this, behaviour starts to slide because you have taken it for granted.

'People don't do what you expect, but what you inspect.'
Lou Gerstner Jnr[34]

That doesn't mean students will only behave if you watch them constantly; far from it. But it does mean you need a healthy balance of trusting them to do the right thing and never trusting them too much. Not because they are untrustworthy, but because they are human – and more importantly because they are a group of individuals with different tolerance levels, willpower and patience. They need an adult to keep them on track. That's the teacher.

FIRST IMPRESSIONS COUNT

Early routines – i.e. those that happen early in your first meeting with students and thus set expectations for the rest of your time together – are especially important. This is doubly so when turning around a challenging classroom culture that already exists. What you communicate to them right at the start is

---

34. Gerstner Jnr, L. (2002) *Who says elephants can't dance?* New York, NY: HarperCollins.

a powerful signal to them. If you change that communication afterwards, you'll confuse them or make them think your expectations are variable.

EXAMPLES OF ROUTINES

- Start of lessons:
  Lining up outside/going straight into the room; uniform – ready before entering/checked when entering/checked when sat down; equipment – checked at door/during lesson/at end of lesson; bags and jackets – at desks/on floor/in cupboard/in locker/in tray; classroom materials – in bag/on desk/in tray/brought by oneself/handed out by a classroom monitor, who is designated every day/week/month/scheduled; starting tasks – settling tasks/self-register/work on board/revise previous lesson/silent reading/allowed to chat/news video/quiz/etc.; how/where to sit – at designated seat or table/posture cues.

- Transitioning between activities:
  When a new activity begins and the previous one ends, students stop immediately and listen; pens down, eyes tracking teacher; the teacher times how long it takes to move from floor to table etc.; turning to face the front, hands folded, hand in the air.

- End of lessons:
  Books away in bags, in trays; jackets back on/held in hands; standing behind desks/in chairs; facing front, silently/allowed to talk quietly; recap task in last minute; quick quiz; self-quizzing; who puts equipment away; dismiss by rows columns/by behaviour etc.

- Beginning of lessons:
  Do students answer a quick quiz at the start of each lesson about the previous lesson? Is there a cold-calling activity to begin? Is there a task that requires knowledge of previous lessons? Is homework expected, in order to show understanding of previous work?

- Tests and assessments:
  Clearly understood guidelines about how to ask for help (if allowed); how to ask for permission to go to the toilet; what level of effort is required; what will happen if enough effort isn't demonstrated; what to do if finished; what to do if unwell etc.

Many teachers also find it useful if they think about what routines their students should follow in the following circumstances:

- **When the work is difficult** – teach them a process to help them get themselves out of it and to show them not only that they can do this but also that it is expected of them. Some students feel the struggle and see it as a perfectly good excuse to stop.
- **When the work is finished** – as above – students should know that if they are finished before others, there are still things for them to do. They could check their work; edit for grammar or presentation; pick an extension activity; select a reading book; ask for feedback; help a peer; etc.
- **When they have to hand in homework** – when it is issued; where to find it if they missed the lesson; what a suitable effort looks like; how and where to present it; what to do if it's going to be late; where to hand it in; and so on. Teaching these routines will cut your problems getting it back in half.
- **Duties in class** – do students have to hand out books, collect equipment, distribute pens, open a window, act as a scribe or spokesperson, relay messages, help a supply teacher?[35] Some classes have a designated greeter for visitors; younger kids especially love it, and it creates a fantastic, positive atmosphere for guests.
- **In the corridor** – leaving the class doesn't mean leaving the culture. You can teach students what you expect about how quickly they get to your lesson; how they should conduct themselves on the way; where they are not supposed to stop; how they line or enter; how they prepare themselves.

There are dozens, hundreds of scenarios like this. You do not need to teach them all explicitly, and you cannot. But you pick the ones you need the most and you start there, in the most detail, with the most energy and focus. Then you work down your list, bearing in mind the need to revisit the previous ones from time to time to reinforce them.

---

35. Teaching a student to be a designated host/point of contact for a supply teacher is what heroic teachers do, because the main benefit is for someone else, although ultimately everyone benefits. The supply teacher will sing your name in Valhalla. Teach a student to let them know what the seating plan is, what work has been done, what work has been left, collect and store work done etc.

Routines and character

Excellence then, is not an act, but a habit.
Will Durant[36]

When routines are successfully communicated, implemented and practised repeatedly, they become *habits*. A habit is 'the way we tend to act in a particular situation', e.g. *When I wake up, I always have a coffee* or *When I sit at my desk, I check my emails before starting work* etc. You don't really think about it anymore; you just do it, sometimes without noticing. Once a habit has been acquired, it becomes part of your character. The person has changed, not just the behaviour, because what is character if not the disposition to habitually act in a certain way?

Example:

As a teenager, I slept late whenever I could...until I got a job. It was a struggle at first, but I got used to it, and changed my habit. Later on when I had my own kids, I had to get up three times a night to soothe them. It was a struggle at first, but I got used to it – and also to getting up when they woke up properly at 6 a.m. Now I struggle to sleep past 6 a.m. I'm working on it. My habits have become me. To change me, I change my habits.

We can help children to develop character traits by encouraging, teaching, insisting and reminding students to behave in certain ways. This is an extrinsic approach to building character. The intrinsic approach is to try to persuade them that certain character traits and values are valuable and convince them that striving to develop them is desirable, but it all eventually comes back to practising the behaviours associated with the trait. You cannot become braver unless you are exposed to circumstances where you need to be brave and are taught ways to think and act that neutralise or at least deal with the fear of that moment. You can teach punctuality, compassion, tenacity and hundred other things if you demonstrate what they look like and expect them enough from a student. One day, they do it out of habit, and they are no longer the same person they were when they first stepped into your class.

---

36. Durant wrote this in *The Story of Philosophy: The Lives and Opinions of the World's Greatest Philosophers*. Although he was writing about Aristotle, and the line is often attributed to the Athenian, the words are Durant's. 'This is an example of the way that provocative words tend to gravitate toward famous mouths' – Frank Herron. Or was it Gandhi?

Routines and consistency

Consistency is key to culture. Exceptions to the routine are possible (and sometimes desirable) but they must be exceptional *and* logically consistent with other exceptions. Failure to invest in consistency dooms progress. You'll need big, annual, hypervisible reboots of routines. Support these with the drip-drip-drip of plate-spinning and constant daily reminders throughout your relationship.

Maintaining routines

To revisit a principle from a previous chapter, routines need to be reinforced as often as necessary, and probably far more than you think. And as we mentioned earlier, *fix things when they are going well, don't wait for them to break*. **Make checking your routines part of your routine.**

WHO WATCHES THE WATCHMEN?

Many people find it hard to maintain routines. This is sometimes because they are not used to sticking to behaviour over a long period of time. We are probably all familiar with big, grand attempts to change our ways – e.g. a new diet or exercise regime – only to see it dissipate after a few days or weeks. Gyms are rammed in January and empty in February. There are more unused exercise bicycles gathering dust in people's spare rooms than there are sardines in the ocean. If only we could invent a machine that made routines easier to sustain. One thing that can help teachers to maintain their routines further than their enthusiasm can throw a stone is to build another routine that checks the routines are happening.

In other words: a schedule.

THE BEAUTIFICATION SCHEDULE

I used to work in a major American dinertainment restaurant chain, and one of the least appreciated parts of the daily routine was a process that was named, with clumsy magnificence, 'beautification'. Before you could open to the punters, there was cleaning to be done. But it was a big place, and the list of areas that could be cleaned was enormous: from high-level Americana, fake memorabilia, table wobbles, bus stands, coffee machines, ceiling fans, menu boxes, and so on. A restaurant has thousands of fixed parts, and they all get absolutely *filthy*. So they had to be cleaned.

The problem was that even if everyone who worked there was averagely clean and tidy, it would be easy to:

- Only clean what you see
- Clean some things twice and other things never
- Only clean the things you like to clean
- Clean things the wrong way

And that's assuming you have a body of people who are all disposed to clean as diligently as possible. And that also ignores the fact that everyone has very different standards of what 'clean' even means. Plus who would keep track of what had been cleaned with so many people involved in the process? So how did the great architects of cocktail-hour dining solve this?

The *beautification schedule*. Someone, at some point, made a list of *everything that needed to be cleaned*. Then they estimated *how long* each thing would take to clean. Then they weighed up *how frequently*, on average, everything really needed a clean. Then they worked out what needed a light clean, and what needed a deep clean, and when.

Then, they *divided it all up* into a 365-day schedule, with daily, weekly and monthly tasks factored in. It even included guidance about what materials to use. So, every day, the front of house shift leader and manager would open the schedule and divide it up further between the on-duty staff. Finally, once it had been completed, it was then checked off by the shift leader (head waiter). And only when he or she was satisfied were the duty staff allowed to finish their shift and go home. And after *that*, the duty manager would check out the shift leader, and only when they were satisfied, could they go home in turn. So they also had an incentive to check people out thoroughly.

The next morning, the next manager on duty would check out the check-out from the night before and note down any problems. The general manager would inspect that this whole process was happening over all, and held to account any manager who failed to do so.

What I've just described may seem incredibly simple or pedantic, but it absolutely made sure things got done. And you can imagine how, without this level of simple bureaucracy, it would be as easy as breathing to let things slide. Because things rarely get worse all at once. They get worse by degrees. Dirt builds up. You can skip a clean for a day but wait a week and see what happens to your bins.

of the surgeon Atul Gawande, who devised a simple checklist for surgeons in the operating theatre. He did this because he noticed even very experienced surgeons forgetting to follow some of the most basic procedures, such as failing to account for all swabs used in a procedure. But by using a simple checklist, surgeons saw a significant decrease in post-operative complications or fatalities.

Taylor's simple checklist for teachers is as follows:

Classroom
- Know the names and roles of any adults in class.
- Meet and greet pupils when they come into the classroom.
- Display rules in the class – and ensure that the pupils and staff know what they are.
- Display the tariff of sanctions in class.
- Have a system in place to follow through with all sanctions.
- Display the tariff of rewards in class.
- Have a system in place to follow through with all rewards.
- Have a visual timetable on the wall.
- Follow the school behaviour policy.

Pupils
- Know the names of children.
- Have a plan for children who are likely to misbehave.
- Ensure other adults in the class know the plan.
- Understand pupils' special needs.

Teaching
- Ensure that all resources are prepared in advance.
- Praise the behaviour you want to see more of.
- Praise children doing the right thing more than criticising those who are doing the wrong thing (parallel praise).
- Differentiate.
- Stay calm.
- Have clear routines for transitions and for stopping the class.
- Teach children the class routines.

Parents
- Give feedback to parents about their child's behaviour – let them know about the good days as well as the bad ones.

By following a list such as this, even more experienced teachers can avoid making simple errors in procedure. Plus, it helps when memory is under pressure or time is tight.

Example:

> A teacher has decided that their focus is going to be uniform. In their planner they write down 'Monday, check uniform.' They also write down 'Friday, remind class of uniform standards, and tell them to be ready for Monday check.' Then when Sunday comes, they see their planner included 'Uniform check' so they remember to build a little extra time into their form or class time. Come Monday, the check happens, because they wrote it down. Because they told the students in advance, more get it right than would have normally (why catch them out? Isn't the objective to get them wearing the right uniform?).
>
> Then they write down 'check uniform' on Tuesday through to Friday, the same time each day. Then the same reminder for the following Monday… then Wednesday (not Tuesday), then Friday (not Thursday). Then the following Monday…then Friday. And so on. The frequency is not so important at this point as the fact that they have a schedule that tells them to do something. And as a result, the teacher doesn't need to remember it all the time. It's there in print. A plan.

You're far more likely to follow a long-term plan if you actually plan it. You're more likely to remember what each piece of the plan is if you break it down into chunks and allocate a completion date for each part. Maybe there are some people out there who can do all this in their head. I can't. So write down what you need to do until it becomes a habit and you don't need it.

TEACHER ROUTINES GENERATE STUDENT ROUTINES

If you want children to build routines, you will need to develop your own routines.

When the teacher builds routine-checking into their everyday habits, it builds habits for others, because the students become so used to being held accountable for their actions that they grow to expect it.

So, to get the students to change their habits, the teacher needs to change his or her habits. They cannot rely on students just following instructions perfectly forever after a single telling. They need the framework your behaviour provides as a scaffold for their behaviour. This is tough work. It takes constant effort and vigilance from you.

So why don't we see them all the time?

1. We don't like to think that we would have low expectations, so it is uncomfortable to admit that we don't. Therefore we *must* have high expectations. Whatever our expectations we have, they are high ones. This is cognitive dissonance in action again.
2. High expectations are highly subjective. This is because most of us live in a world of extreme subjectivity, especially morally. In our worlds, our own tastes and beliefs are wise and good and right, whatever they actually entail. People who vary too much from us are seen as eccentric, weird, or – if extreme enough – unreasonable, unpleasant, wrong, even evil.

Example:

If you drive, you'll be aware that anyone who drives slower than you is an over-cautious incontinent snail who should retake their driving test if they can't handle driving at a sensible speed. And anyone who overtakes you is a psychopathic kamikaze pilot with no care for your or anyone else's safety.

The volume you like to listen to music at; the temperature of the bath; the level of wine in your glass; these are all matters in which our personal taste is the North Star, and anyone else's preference is a deviation.

When you think you have high standards, but you don't

If I ask everyone to hand in a piece of homework by tomorrow, I may pre-emptively congratulate myself on my high expectations. But then the next day comes and I find that ten students haven't handed their work in. Three of them have an excellent excuse. Three of them 'left it on the bus'. Four of them didn't do it but were comic in their apologies. I let them all off and ask for it to be handed in the next day. I congratulate myself for being wise and kind. I still regard myself as having high expectations, because most of it came in, and I monitored and reacted to what did not.

The next day comes and I get five more pieces, but they are somewhat half-arsed.[40] Five more pieces are not forthcoming. I give two of them a second deadline extension because they were really, *really* sorry, and set a detention for two because they were cheeky when I rebuked them for tardiness.

---

40. Perhaps humanity's factory setting.

The two pirates fail to show up. But I'm busy, and when I see them the next day, they hand in two pieces of work that could charitably be described as tatty: two-minute jobs on the bus in, using each other's backs as a desk. I shake a finger at them…but accept the pieces. My standards are still high, though. I got all the work in…

But standards could have been *much* higher in this scenario. Missing the deadline the first time should have resulted in some kind of sanction. Because one person's perception of high standards may not be the same as another's. It is very easy to imagine that we are kind albeit adamant taskmasters, but it is just not true in many cases. Frequently when I ask teachers to describe their classroom management style, they describe it as 'firm – but fair'. Coincidently, that is what almost everyone says. (Who would wish to be 'soft – and unjust'?) But they cannot all be right. Often, we fool ourselves.

How to have sincerely high standards

This is why, if you sincerely want to embody high expectations and communicate them to your classes, you should:

- Have a clear, verbalised, explicit grasp of what your standards actually are. This is the beginning of it all. If your standards aren't clear to *you*, then they'll be positively cryptic for everyone else.
- Watch other teachers a lot. A *lot*. It's important to calibrate your own expectations against those of people around you, to get a sense of whether you are strict or not, kind or not, generous or not. It may be that you are the easiest teacher in your whole school, although you may imagine yourself to be somewhere between Miss Jean Brodie and Severus Snape.
- Challenge any and all behaviour that crosses your boundaries. This is much harder than we think. We let things slide all the time, and we adjust our expectations rapidly – usually downwards.
- Check in on your own behaviour from time to time. Am I letting things slide that I used to jump on? Or am I jumping on things I used to let slide? What did I ask them to do at the start of the year? Are they still doing it? If not, how am I responding? Have I taught them to misbehave? You can do this by asking some of the mature children what they think of your teaching now as opposed to then. Or watch yourself teach.

What do you expect from a kid like that? The dark deal we often make with challenging children

One of the easiest errors for a teacher to make is to give up and settle for misbehaviour from the worst behaved children because, well...what do you expect from a kid like that? Written so boldly, it sounds so cruel, and it can be. But it is a sentiment that can come from the kindest of intentions. I think most teachers would recoil from the suggestion that we would expect less good behaviour from someone because of their background etc., but in practice that is what many do. It is easy to say, 'I have high expectations for all,' but if you let things slide with some kids more than others for no good reason, then you don't.

We may have different expectations for children because they:

- Come from difficult circumstances
- Are new to the school
- Are a boy/girl
- Have misbehaved frequently in previous schools

And many more reasons. Sometimes, differences do matter. I would not expect a student with weak English language skills to tackle a complex text without huge levels of scaffolding, translation, etc. In this case, you *should* calibrate your expectations to suit that. But what if the difference isn't that relevant? I have frequently seen teachers make the following Devil's bargain with challenging students: 'If you behave quietly, I won't ask much from you. Just sit there like inert material.'

Of course, no one says this, but this is what happens. Usually, it is the most difficult student in the class. Some days, getting them to simply sit still is a win. So, instead of asking them to join in, or participate, or behave, or complete tasks, teachers frequently give them busy work, and keep them in a holding pattern until the bell rings. Sometimes this busy work is simply chatting with the TA or teacher. They do nothing, produce nothing, achieve nothing – but at least the class weren't disturbed, and the lessons can proceed.

I can *understand* this sentiment; I can sympathise with it even as I disagree with it. It's often a strategy born of desperation, when a student is so difficult that it seems like the best outcome from an impossible situation.

Or you may teach a student who is so brittle, so abusive, so combative, that to push them too hard is to court disaster. So how do you cope? You cut a wide berth around them. I have seen teachers paralysed by this affliction, completely ignoring loud outbursts from students like this, but who will pepper the rest of

208

the class with sanctions for misdemeanours. Usually it is the most inoffensive who suffer most in this scenario. This is entirely wrong and unfair. And the students know it.

Or perhaps a student is having a hard time at home – maybe Mum and Dad are splitting up. You might let them do less in a lesson out of sympathy. And perhaps you might be right once, or briefly, if the student is struggling to process their personal circumstances. But two lessons? All day? A week? Forever? In an attempt to be kind, it is possible to make so many allowances for their difficulty that we undermine any chance they have of flourishing.

We condemn them to weeks of missed learning time because we found it easier to lower our standards for them rather than say, 'I sympathise – you're having a hard time. I know that. I also don't want to see you fall further behind and have a harder time catching up with everyone. So, here's the deal. I need you to…and to help you do this we can…'

We offer support and sincere sympathy, simultaneously. But treating students in all circumstances of distress as helpless is a good way to reinforce their helplessness. Indeed, the task we face as educators is, wherever possible, to help students learn to be independent thinkers and doers, resourceful, and able to cope with difficulty.

This doesn't mean ignoring their distress – quite the opposite; we must do what we can and what is reasonable for our role, understanding our limits as well as our capabilities. It means trying to help children deal with difficulty and for them to learn that they do not have to let adversity crush them.

It's a living demonstration of the Serenity Prayer:

> Grant me the serenity to accept the things I cannot change,
> courage to change the things I can,
> and wisdom to know the difference.[41]

It's a hard lesson to teach, and it's a hard thing to do as a teacher, especially when your natural instinct is to protect as well as educate. It is not an exact science. There will be times that kids will need huge accommodations made as they deal with difficulties you or I can barely imagine. And there will be times that they

---

41. Written by the American theologian Ronald Niebuhr in 1932–33, this has been adapted many times, and a form of it is used by Alcoholics Anonymous and many 12-step recovery programmes. It could easily serve as a prayer for teachers, and all people facing impossible odds.

will need – and I choose that word carefully – *need* someone, a grown-up, to say, 'This is awful. Let me help you learn to deal with this, and other awful things that will happen to you *when I am no longer there.*'

So, embody ambitions for everyone, not just the ones for whom it is easy.

High standards show you care

John D'Abbro, former CEO of the outstanding New Rush Hall schools for challenging children in London, always told me, 'The ones who are hardest to love are often the ones who need your love the most.' And sometimes we show that love by holding them to a high standard. And demonstrate through your actions and words the belief that progress is not only possible but also expected. One of the biggest compliments you can give a student is to say, 'I think you can do it.' When you have high expectations, you treat them with dignity, and you show them that you care.

This is, for some, a surprising way to look at it, but to my mind it is the best way to understand high expectations. When you reprimand a student, you do so because they need to hear that what they have done is less than what they can do. This message must be conveyed: 'You are better than this. You are capable of wonders and marvels. I am disappointed because you could be incredible.'

SHOW AND TELL

But that also isn't enough. Don't just tell them they can do it. Show them *how* to do it. Perhaps they don't understand the work, or the behaviour you've asked them to do. Perhaps they're not used to working like that. Help them through it rather than always only saying 'Do it.' Challenge any difficulties they have with material. Be ruthless in your forensic investigation of what might be blocking their progress, pedagogically or behaviourally. 'I believe you can do it' must be married to 'And here's *how* you can do it.' Once you are satisfied that they do know, then you can confidently expect them to do it, and insist upon it.

LEAN ON THE SCHOOL STANDARDS

The school ethos, its vision, and the strategies used to achieve it must be consistent and consistently demonstrated. You are part of a greater whole. If you lean on the school values, and everyone else does too, the effect on students is profound. If you make it clear that you are an island, and that your rules are personal, they will know that the school will not be on your side, because you are not on its side. So make it clear that you uphold what the school asks, and make sure you know what that actually means – read the policy, the handbooks, and ask for clarification if you are unsure. Just like a good teacher, a good school should teach its values and routines, not just tell them to new staff.

REINFORCE EXPECTATIONS CONSTANTLY

Consistently high expectations are the only high expectations that have long-term impact.

Students learn quickly the difference between what boundaries are supposed to exist and which ones actually do exist. Take time to build them into your day-to-day teaching, but also reinforce them on every occasion you interact with students – on school trips, in assemblies, in form time, at parents' evening, on playground duty. They need to get a sense of who you are, of what you are about; they need to learn about you. Which means you need to know who you are. If you stand for anything, then you stand for nothing.

So what do you stand for?

Summary:

- Routines are the building blocks of class culture.
- Routines must be taught, not told.
- The clearer and firmer they are, the more they embed in student behaviour.
- Your personal behaviour must be consistent in order for the students to adopt consistent routines.
- Checklists can play an important part in making sure you maintain your routines.
- Routines require constant maintenance, or they start to fade away. However, if they are built consistently and clearly, eventually you can maintain them less regularly for the same effect.

CHAPTER 8
RULES AND ROUTINES

All rules are routines; but not all routines are formal rules. A rule is usually a short instruction that everyone is expected to memorise and refer to. They frequently come in short packets and should be memorable and concise. People often ask, 'What should my classroom rules be?' There is no simple answer to this, but roughly they should be no more than ten must-dos that you need students to understand and perform in order for the class to function; ones you cannot do without.

Example:

- No shouting out
- Put your hand up to contribute or ask a question
- Bring all of your equipment
- Always try your best
- Be on time
- Be kind to one another
- Never leave the room without permission

And so on. None of these are complicated, break the Geneva Convention, or should surprise anyone. You could write them on the back of a napkin in five minutes. Were I to ask 100 teachers to make up their own rules (and I have done), we'd get about 90% overlap between them all. This is probably because, like the seven moral rules from the Oxford study (see p. 123), there are probably some conventions and shared behaviours that a community *must* have in order to endure. If you lack any of these, or you allow them to be ignored routinely, then you risk the ability of the group to function healthily as a classroom and a community. You can have varieties of these (e.g. 'no hands up' etc.) as long as there is an agreed and understood convention to direct answers.

Some commentators like Sunstein[1] have suggested that rules and laws are best seen as an expression or signal about good behaviour, rather than a series of mousetraps to avoid. They 'make statements'. In this context, a rule about 'not shouting out' is really a rule about being polite, being patient, and so on. This is

---

1. Sunstein, C. R (2019) *Conformity: the power of social influences.* New York, NY: New York University Press.

a good example of rules being used as *confounding examples*: what you want is manners, politeness etc., but you frame it as an example of what you don't want.

Sunstein also suggests that laws and rules are likely to be more effective if consequence-breaking is publicly challenged, highly visibly, so that onlookers are deterred. Finally, Sunstein notes that rules are far less likely to be effective if offenders are 'part of a deviant subcommunity that rewards noncompliance'. In other words, if students are part of a group at school with a strong enough subculture, they may be unimpressed with the school's rules.

Of course, a simple list of rules cannot cover every circumstance, which is why teachers also need to carefully explain what these rules mean in practice, possible exceptions, consequences for breaking them, and all the other routines, norms and conventions of the classroom. A list of rules is a simple way to keep students focused on the main, big-ticket behaviours they need to grasp. It is not meant to be exhaustive. It never could be. If your students think that the rules are the only things they have to follow, then they will start looking for loopholes and get-out clauses, or things not covered by the letter of the law. A strictly legalistic approach to good behaviour can be useful, but is only ever part of what it takes to get great behaviour from people.

Keep it simple

But a list of rules should be as simple and as short as possible. If they are too complicated or long or hard to remember, they simply won't be followed. Students will give up thinking hard about them. Remember: make good behaviour easy to do. Have the fewest number of rules and make sure they are easy to follow.

Example:

> During the lockdown of 2020, when people were given strict instructions to only leave the house for exercise, you started to see people travelling to beauty spots for picnics on the grounds that 'walking to their picnic site was exercise'. This is what happens when people see rules as a set of tripwires to avoid triggering rather than something underpinned by a set of moral principles and values.

So explain why the rules are there and what they are supposed to help with. Explain why they matter and why they are important. Explain that your laws have both a letter and a spirit.

Example 1:

'The rule is "no shouting out". This is because everyone in the class has a valuable opinion, and we want to hear everyone, not just the loudest or the boldest. Everyone matters. What you think matters. Which is why we take turns to speak.'

Example 2:

In the '80s sitcom *The Young Ones*, we followed the lives of four hapless early-adulthood counter-culture goons living in a grimy semi-detached house in London. In one episode, Vyvyan the punk and Mike 'The Cool Person' are consulting the instruction booklet of their new video recorder, trying to work out where they went wrong in setting it up. When Mike wonders whether Vyvyan really ought to have poured washing-up liquid into it in order to clean it, Vyvyan explains, 'It doesn't say "Ensure the machine ISN'T full of washing-up liquid"!'

Sometimes rules aren't enough.

But formal rules are useful ways to focus student/staff behaviour on a series of non-negotiables. They are a tool, like other tools, you use to get better behaviour. They are not the complete solution to this challenge, but nothing is. This is something we see time and time again when modifying behaviour. No one approach is sufficient, but this doesn't mean that any one approach is inadequate. They are all different tools to build the engine of your classroom.

Making rules clear

In philosophy, the principle of charity challenges us to interpret any statement in the most positive way possible, where there is ambiguity. That way, we avoid being biased negatively simply because we do not like the speaker. For example, if someone says, 'This schoolbag weighs a ton,' we shouldn't mock them for being unaware how heavy a real ton is – we would understand that they meant it figuratively.[2] In public discourse, we often see the opposite: I call it the principle of uncharitableness, where we decide to misinterpret a statement in the worst possible way.

When you write a rule, you can guarantee that someone will read it differently to the way you intended. This might be accidental or intentional. Either way, if your rules have ambiguity baked in, you need to do something about it if you want to make it as easy to behave as possible.

---

2. The literal mind frequently struggles to understand the metaphorical one.

Once you have written your class rules, pick any one and try to interpret it differently. How might someone misinterpret it, either deliberately or accidentally? Most statements contain ambiguity. This is usually unavoidable. The key thing is to either:

1. Rewrite it so it reduces uncertainty; or
2. 'Teach around it' so people understand what you mean more clearly.

Number 1 is a matter of editing well.

Example:

'Be on time' means many different things to different people.

'Be in the classroom within one minute of the bell' is tighter.

The second case is more concrete and easier to observe, or to notice clearly when it has not happened.

Number 2 is a matter of teaching what it means, and then referring back to the rule as an easy way to recall the principle.

Examples:

- *'Be polite' is concise, but can be interpreted very differently. Instead, you could teach the 'be polite' rule and then have a class discussion about what it could mean. Then you focus in on what you mean and give examples. Examples are very useful. They help people to focus on what you mean and what you do not mean. Then in class you use the direction 'Be polite' as a way to cue the behaviour you discussed.*
- *'Let's practise six-inch voices.' This is one from Doug Lemov. It needs a lot of explanation, of course; but once explained, it can be used as a quick cue. It relies on them knowing what it means in the first place.[3]*
- *'So, by "polite" I mean "Say please and thank you. Always hold doors open. Never interrupt someone. Never insult someone." What else could it mean?'*

Stress-test your rules

To stress-test something means to see how much pressure you can put on it before it breaks. In any design process, this is done long before a product gets

---

3. 'Speak as if you were six inches away from me.'

to the customer, because manufacturers want to see how strong or robust something is before they get sued. It is equally wise to stress-test your rules before they break in the wild (the classroom). You can do this by:

- Asking different people what the rule is, and what it means.
- Giving people hypothetical examples and asking them if they think each one is breaking a class rule or not. If there is broad disagreement, then you need to clarify for the class what you mean before they break them in real life, thinking they are staying within the rules.

The point is to try to interpret them as wildly and uncharitably as possible. Imagine, for example, you put out an opinion on social media. What is the maddest, laziest take someone could make of it?[4]

In order to minimise this:

- Rules need to be as clearly defined as possible.
- They need to be illustrated with clear, relatable examples.

Example:

'Be quiet' – too vague.
'No shouting out' – better, but negative framing. What do you want them to do?
'Put your hand up to speak' – clear and concrete.
'Being quiet means raising your hand and waiting in silence to be asked to speak' – better.

Replacing old behaviour with new

When you prohibit a behaviour, try to come up with a behaviour to replace it. This is because it's hard to 'not do' something. Even just thinking about the thing you mustn't do means you are thinking about doing it. This is not unlike the old adage 'Don't think of a lemon!' I guarantee that every time you read that, you are thinking of a lemon. Apologies.

When I gave up smoking, the hardest times were when I would normally embrace the chance for a cigarette: after a meal, with a drink, after a stressful conversation, and so on. The difficulty was being conscious that I was supposed to be 'not smoking'. The absence felt like a phantom limb.

---

4. Social media is a very good place to find out exactly that. Me: 'I really like salads.' Anonymous crazy person online: 'Oh you like salads, do you? YOUR SILENCE ON CLIMATE CHANGE IS DEAFENING.'

The best thing to do is to fill that gap with something else. Come up with a replacement behaviour. After a meal, I did the dishes. What to do while drinking a glass of wine was harder, but I found *more wine* to be a useful compensation. After a stressful situation, I would go cycling. Distractions are very useful when changing an old habit.

So when you tell students to stop doing something, help to think about what they could do instead. This scaffolds behaviour choices for students who need to know 'what to do with their hands'.

Example:

'Stop talking' is OK but 'Back to quiet and get started on the task' is better.

Making rules real

Actions speak louder than words. If you say 'Do X' but then allow Y, then Y is the real rule, not X. This is famously summed up in the phrase 'You promote what you permit'.[5] This is a common mistake many teachers make: they think that merely telling students what to do is enough to make them do it. Then when they don't do it, the teacher lets it slide for whatever reason, and the students learn what the real rules are.

Example:

'The school rule is that uniform must be worn correctly at all times.' Reality: The teacher routinely ignores incorrect uniform in classes. This teaches everyone that the real rule is 'There isn't really a uniform; wear what you like.'

In other words, the teacher needs to live their own rules, and challenge everyone to live the rules too, holding them to account when they do not.

Making rules important

If you want students to feel that rules are important, then show them they are. These factors are helpful to consider:

- **WHEN** they learn them – if you teach them at the start of your relationship with them, you show that you have prioritised them. What you say first must be important.
- **HOW** they learn them – if the rules are carefully explained, in detail, it is far more likely students will understand them and take them seriously.

---

5. Lemov, D, (2010) Ibid

- **WHY** they learn them – if you 'sell the benefits' of the rules, i.e. explain why they are important, then the students are more likely to buy into them.
- **WHERE** they see them – if rules are seen all the time, demonstrated, lived all around them, then they become the norm.
- **HOW OFTEN** they bump into them – if they see them happening frequently, constantly throughout the lesson, this also helps to normalise them.

STUDENTS ARE SOCIAL BEINGS

No man (or woman) is an island. Our behaviour is strongly influenced by other people. Other people and their opinions matter to us. If you teach a class, you teach a group, and group dynamics are not the same as solo or pair behaviour.

CHAPTER 9
SCRIPTS

Teachers are often faced with complex situations, with lots of moving parts, in highly charged, emotional circumstances. Often, they have to deal with people they don't know well or with whom they have no strong pre-existing relationship. This makes good communication harder and misunderstanding even more likely.

When I started to teach, I often found myself wondering what I should say and do, many times throughout the average day. I'm not shy, and I'm fairly chatty. But it's hard to prepare yourself for the kind of exchanges that you typically have in classrooms. On any given day I would be forced to think how to respond when:

- A student came in late
- A parent phoned up to complain that their son was being bullied
- A pupil tried to excuse their lack of homework
- A senior member of staff asked me for a favour that would take up most of my lunch break
- A kid in the lunch queue accuses you of cutting in
- A student swears near you and then denies it
- You're asked to hold an assembly
- Some kids ignore you when you ask them to walk on the left
- You come across a fight in the playground
- A student makes a suggestive comment about you

And so on. It's not that you're literally speechless. It's just that there are so many ways to say things, it's hard to know how to get it right.

Example:
You take over a new class, and some of the boys make a comment about your appearance, or your clothing, or ask if you have a boyfriend. There are so many ways to respond to this.

- You could ignore it and hope it doesn't happen again. But that would normalise it, or suggest it doesn't matter, when clearly it does.
- You could shout at them and tell them it's disgusting. But what if they wanted you to lose your temper?

- You could smile and try to make out you're not bothered by that kind of thing. But that might encourage it.
- You could flirt. I hope I don't need to outline how awful this is as a response.[1]
- You could tell them off somehow. Draw a line and indicate they've crossed it. But how?

Or another common example:

A student walks into the lesson, dragging their leg behind them, applying makeup and listening to music on their headphones. Everyone stops and stares at the bravado, and the lesson stalls. What do you say? A rebuke? Send them out? Shout? Make a joke? Be sarcastic?

There are no hard answers here, only principles.

When I ran the *TES* online behaviour forum, I frequently encountered people who seemed to have the same problems, time and time again. I used to write them hand-crafted, artisan answers, which would take me a long time, and which frequently repeated themselves. After a while, I started to ask myself if it wouldn't be easier if I just wrote about 20 stock answers for the 20 most common behaviour situations that came along? That way, I could answer 20 questions in 20 minutes and knock off early. I didn't, because most people didn't just want a solution: they wanted reassurance, and that needed to be personal.

But it set me thinking. It seemed that there were a finite set of difficulties that teachers commonly found themselves in. At first it seemed endless, but after a while, most teachers recognise that some things happen time and time again. A student will be late. Someone will forget equipment. Someone isn't trying very hard. Someone is staring out of a window. Someone is having a fight. Someone is bunking, and so on.[2]

---

1. True story: I was once on a panel at a university discussing behaviour. I was the only teacher on it. A young woman stood up in the audience and asked, 'I have some year 11 boys who make suggestive comments. What should I do?' The esteemed academic next to me on the panel said, 'Have you tried flirting with them?' Jaws fell, and everyone looked at her as if she was quite mad. It demonstrates the gulf that often exists between the theoretical understanding of behaviour management and its practice.

2. Of course there are always exceptions, and I will never forget the lad I caught peeing in a waste paper bin, or the two sixth formers that a colleague caught making sweet music behind the school bins. Such matters are never covered in your *Hong Kong Book of Kung Fu*.

The flight simulator

With that in mind, the best way to be as ready as we can be is to practise what we will *do* and what we will *say* in such circumstances *before they happen*. In this way, we walk into these events as prepared as possible. In other words, we build routines for *ourselves*, not just the students.

Frequently when something goes wrong in a classroom, there is a very real tendency to fall into what psychologists call the 'WTF' moment.[3] We get so caught up in the crisis of the moment that we freeze like a deer caught in headlights, and our reasoning goes out of the window. We become helpless spectators of the moment rather than captains of it.

How do other fields cope with this? Unsurprisingly, rather better. Even when I trained to be a waiter, we had two weeks' classroom training. *Two weeks*. We sat and discussed fire safety, handling hazardous chemicals, the history of the company, the values of the company, the menu, the drinks menu, the provenance of ingredients, handling drunks, allergies, cleaning cycles, food preparation and hygiene…and that was to be a *waiter*. Once I'd graduated from that and was set free in the wild, I then had several weeks of shadowing an experienced waiter, gradually being allowed to take tables on quiet shifts, well below capacity, and always supervised by a mentor, right at my shoulder.

Only after *that* was I signed off to fly solo. And once I did so, I had to follow the processes and procedures of the job's expectations. Work was regularly appraised, beautification schedules were checked off by line management, and working closely in contact with other staff members provided constant challenge to your standards. In some ways it was a maddening environment, but from a training point of view, it set you up to succeed, not fail.[4]

Contrast that with running a room as a training teacher. The theory you learn in your institution is sometimes hard to map onto the classroom, and relevance can be hard to glean. If you're lucky, you'll be given a supportive mentor who can explain what you should be doing; but often you're not, and you just have to learn by yourself, alone in a room with your students. This can lead to some great insights, but it can also lead to some terrible training experiences.

---

3. Actually I don't think it's called that.

4. I can't stress enough how oddly militaristic it was, when the end result saw you doing conga lines and singing 'Happy Birthday' to hen parties. But it was incredibly disciplined and well trained. Our conga lines were immaculate.

Throwing someone in at the deep end is rarely a good way to train anyone in anything. We wouldn't train an airline pilot like this, because the cost of failure is so high.

One way to avoid this is by putting new members of staff through a kind of a flight simulator; something that would give you a feel for the job before diving into it. So what would that look like in teaching? Two things:

1. Exposing teachers to circumstances where they can experience what it might feel like to do the actual job, but in as controlled a condition as possible.
2. Providing them with suggested verbal and behavioural habits in advance of needing them. In other words: scripts.

A **script** is simply a prepared set of actions, and a suggested set of phrases to say, in order to cope with a situation as efficiently as possible. An actor's script enables them to be someone else. A teacher's script can enable them to say and do the right thing until they get a sense of what that might look and feel like for themselves.

The idea is that by preparing some small responses and cues in advance of difficult circumstances, the teacher will be able to react efficiently.

What a script is not

A script is *not* a ritual to be followed slavishly. It is a good, basic skeleton of how to respond. They are not the last word in perfect responses. The minute you think of something better to say, you use that instead. Actors make the script their own.

I've already provided you with a script of how I tend to speak to parents on an important call discussing pupil misbehaviour. The key thing is to think, as far ahead as possible, what you will say and do *before* you need to say it. Often when we speak to people, we get so caught up in social pleasantries that we forget the point of the conversation, or we try to avoid saying important but difficult things.

And when we get stressed, we often say the wrong thing, or focus on what feels right in the moment. But that might not be what *needs* to be said. A parent might *need* to hear the hard truth that their son is being lazy. A student might *need* to hear what will happen to them if they don't improve. Instinct is not always the most reliable guide to communication in a professional relationship.

What a script is

Graham was my trainer when I worked bars. He was funny, clever, able to cope with any circumstance or scenario. I learned a lot from him about people. There was no drunk he couldn't handle. No party he couldn't entertain, no lost child he couldn't placate. He knew every ingredient and nook and cranny of his role. And then one day he simply handed his notice in. It was unthinkable to us; he was as much a part of the place as the tip bell or the peanut rail. I asked him why he was leaving. He said, 'Because there are no more surprises left.'[5]

He had mastered his role because he had, in advance of any possible problems the job could throw at him, all the solutions. He was three steps ahead of everything because he had already worked out what to do. Without challenge, of course, that could lead to inertia and ennui. But it also led to mastery of one's circumstances.

There are finite problems you will face as a teacher. It makes sense to have the right thing to say before you have to say it, and the right thing to do before it needs to be done.

Having a script creates the *impression* you are calm, prepared, and focused. It minimises errors generated by having to think on one's feet. It means you don't fall into e.g. sarcasm when what you need is sincerity. It means that you say what needs to be said rather than what springs into your mind at the time.

Important:
- Scripts can – and should – be ad-libbed to suit the circumstances, as long as you stick to the main points.
- Scripts should not be a straitjacket or replace sincerity and professionalism. They should be a scaffold for these.
- Scripts do *not* entail speaking robotically. In fact, they are a great way to develop better speaking skills rather than a way to deskill oneself.

Look at a satnav. I use mine all the time to visit schools in unfamiliar areas. It saves me hours and hours of parking up and checking my route, making U-turns, correcting my course – and has added years to my life thanks to reduced blood pressure. But I have very little sense of where I am going and would struggle to remember the route I took the next time. In some ways, I

---

5. 'And when Alexander saw the breadth of his domain, he wept, for there were no more worlds to conquer' – Hans Gruber in *Die Hard* (1988). Not Plutarch, as Gruber claims.

remain blissfully ignorant of how to actually get around. I have outsourced that completely to the satnav. It could drive me off the cliffs of Dover and I would follow its directions, unconcerned.[6]

It is easy to see how such devices can deskill a driver. It used to be that when I wanted to go somewhere, I bought a map and worked out the route. You very quickly got a sense of where you needed to be and where the next turn was. If you lean entirely on the satnav, it takes a very long time to internalise the actual routes you need, because there is no pressure to do so.

Similarly, if you read scripts robotically then you could easily come across as insincere and inflexible. But if you use them as prompts and learn to weave them into your conversation, you learn to talk with greater purpose. PowerPoints can deskill teachers in a similar way. You can see this effect on those who simply follow them without detour, as opposed to those who use them as prompts to keep them in the right direction, ensuring that key details are drawn out.

When I started to do interviews on air, I was struck by the discipline needed to come across sensibly. If you turn up to Radio 4 to do the Today programme to talk about some new behaviour policy, you might have lots to say, but you find that no sooner has the interviewer asked you how you are than they're bidding you good day.

You quickly realise that what you need to do is write down the three points you simply must get across, and say them with as much urgency as you can muster. If you've done that, then you can prattle and riff as you please. If you don't, then your time has been wasted, because you didn't say what you thought was important.[7]

Chunk your behaviour phrases

Scripting means having key 'chunks' or phrases ready *before* you need them. That also means behaviour phrases, or mini sequences of behaviour you prep before you need to use them.

If someone walks into your lesson late, you can respond in many ways. But why waste the energy? Work out what you want to say in advance, then say it. I will

---

6. And one day, probably will, when Skynet finally becomes self-aware.

7. I can see now why politicians are often accused of answering the questions they want to answer rather than the ones they were actually asked.

suggest that the middle of a lesson is not a great time to be inventing witty bon mots and quips or trying to look clever. You have a lesson to teach, and that requires all your focus.

Repetition, repetition, repetition

Repetition creates emphasis. You don't need to think of new things to say all the time. This isn't a dinner party. Repeat yourself as much as you need to. If something is true, then it is always true in identical circumstances. Like a road sign. Road planners don't fret about 'How shall we tell them what the speed limit is *this* time?' They stick up another sign, same as the last one, to remind you. Repetition creates emphasis. Repetition creates emphasis. What does repetition create?[8]

Key into what they already know

A useful feature of repetition is that the phrases become familiar. The response becomes expected. The consequences become part of the culture. In other words, you are building up norms of expectation that become more embedded with each repetition. You cue them up to expect with greater certainty what will happen, rather than leave them to wonder if today you'll let things slide.

Prep your behaviour

Have you ever followed a 20-minute recipe at home for a delicious meal, but it takes you an hour and a half from fridge to fork? Then you may have wondered how restaurants can take your order and see it dropped in front of you in under 15 minutes. The answer is prep. Chefs come in at 7 a.m. and start chopping onions, making sauces, portioning up veg mix, and cooking off anything that can be done in advance. When you ask for your dinner, it is already half made.[9]

In a similar way, the teacher should prep their own language and routines before they need them. This saves time thinking about what to say, and makes it less likely they'll do the wrong thing.

---

8. **EMPHASIS!**

9. The only way fast food is fast is because it's almost entirely ready before you ask for it; the only way to have high-quality fast-ish food is by having brilliant chefs and very few customers.

Examples of classroom scripts

- Thank you, 4B, it's time to begin the lesson so I need: jackets off, bags on the floor, books out and attempt the starter.
- Thank you, Jasmine, Drake, Eddie, great start already.
- Thank you, Bronwyn…. thank you Roz.
- Just waiting for five people to start learning.
- Thank you, Martin. Just four now.
- Good, that's everyone. Next time let's get that done in half the time.

Here are some script examples for getting attention in order to transition from one activity to the next, reprinted with the kind permission of Dixons Music Primary (DMP). Notice how clear and sequential the steps are. Both behaviour and language are scripted for the teacher by the school in order to create as much consistency and clarity of culture as possible.

Dixons Music Primary scripts

- All instructions should be clipped and clear.
- Remember to avoid any humour/side comments/rhetorical questions/sarcasm – it just won't work (it might work for the few near you and their reaction will confuse the rest etc.).
- Always allow time for students to follow the instruction you gave before speaking again.

Transition Routine 1 Attracting attention before a transition
Teacher to raise hand. This is the DMP 'Signal for Silence'. **Children to stop, raise their hand and turn to track the teacher.**
Teacher to wait for silence, giving non-verbal praise e.g. 'thumbs up' for children doing the right thing. *Note:* *Avoid speaking when your hand is up; cut off any conversation whether with a student / another adult when hand goes up* *Only use DMP Signal for Silence to attract attention in all lessons across school.* *The rhyme '1,2,3 eyes on me' with students responding '1, 2 eyes on you' [stopping at this point] can be used in EYFS/KS1 only* *No rhymes or clapping rhythms to be used in KS2 e.g. hocus pocus*

Transition Routine 2
Sitting as a group to moving around classroom
(e.g. 'carpet to tables' during Maths Mastery lesson or 'sitting to group work' during a music/ PE lesson)

Teacher to clearly state that a transition is about to happen and ensure all children are tracking before beginning the transition routine. For EYFS/KS1 use something like 'It is time to transition to tables, track me.' For KS2, 'It is now time to transition to tables in our natural state. Track me.'

1	Teacher to **show** 'One' by holding 1 finger up. *Children to stand but continue to track the teacher.*
2	Teacher to **show** 'Two' by holding 2 fingers up. *Children to face in the correct direction but track the teacher.* *Note: Children may be facing in different directions depending on where they are going next*
3	Teacher to **show** 'Three' by holding 3 fingers up. *Children to move in a calm, silent manner, facing the direction of the table they are on.*
(4)	Teacher to clearly say 'Four' (hold up 4 fingers) *Children sit down, get out equipment, then track teacher for next instruction.* *Note: This additional step may be needed if equipment has been previously set out in the middle of tables. E.g science or maths equipment*

Transition Routine 3
Sitting at tables and moving to another place e.g back to carpet or lining up
(e.g 'back to carpet' during EYFS/KS1 lessons or 'leading out of the classroom')

Teacher to clearly state that a transition is about to happen and ensure all children are tracking before beginning the transition routine. For EYFS/KS1 use something like 'It is time to transition to the, track me.' For KS2, 'It is now time to transition to line up in our natural state. Track me.'
Note: Equipment should have been tided away before the transition is started.

1	Teacher to **show** 'One' by holding 1 finger up. *Children to stand after tucking chair in but continue to track the teacher.*
2	Teacher to **show** 'Two' by holding 2 fingers up. *Children to face in the correct direction but track the teacher.* *Note: Children may be facing in different directions depending on where they are going next*
3	Teacher to **show** 'Three' by holding 3 fingers up. *Children to move in a calm, silent manner.*
(4)	Teacher to clearly **show** 'Four' (hold up 4 fingers) *Children to track teacher for next instruction.* *Note: This additional step may be needed if children sit on the carpet for teacher input. E.g in EYFS/KS1*

Transition Routine 4
Corridors lunchtimes and breaktime

Teacher to complete Transition Routines 1-3.
Teacher to remind children of expectation of silence in the corridors and link to earning autonomy. EYFS/KS1: 'The rule is silence, in order to earn your next autonomy badge you must show that you can be trusted in the corridors.'

KS2: 'Remember that we are moving around school in our natural state.'

Teacher to adopt a 'transition position' situated between classroom and corridor. Teacher to praise good behaviour and address inappropriate behaviour as outlined in the DMP Behaviour Policy.

Note: It is the responsibility of all staff to model silence in the corridors and address behaviour during transition periods.

Transition Routine 5 Entering and exiting assembly	
1	Teacher to complete transition Routines 1-4. *Note: Teacher to remind children of the importance of being role models for younger children and the importance of tracking the front at all times, link to visions 'Being the best school in Bradford'. Reinforce 'natural state' at KS2.*
2	Class to enter assembly led by the class teacher. Teacher to lead children across the hall to create a row facing the front. Teacher to indicate when the next row will begin. **Children to remain standing in silence until the whole class have entered in rows.** *Note: Children should be strategically placed in rows to pre-empt any disruption that may be caused in assembly. Key children **must** be placed next to the adult.*
3	Teacher to stand in front of row to ensure all children are tracking. When all children are tracking, teacher to use a signal to indicate sitting down.
4	Teachers to complete feedback/intervention with pupils during assembly. Timetabled adults to stay in assembly to address behaviour. Note: *Adults should be facing their class, not facing the adult leading the assembly. During singing assembly, all staff must model singing alongside the children.*
5	Adults to listen for their class being dismissed. Once the name of the class has been called, teacher to stand at the front and ensure all children are tracking. When all children are tracking, adult to use a signal to indicate standing up. Adult to dismiss class row by row and ensure silent transition taking children into the hall.

The good script

A good script is:

- As short as possible (but no shorter).
- To the point.
- Clear, linear, concrete.
- Functional rather than emotional.
- Practised beforehand to ensure strong delivery.

Try it yourself, however awkward this might feel. Write down a script about what you might say:

- To begin a lesson.
- Issuing a detention.

- Phoning home for a negative reason.
- Phoning home for a positive reason.
- Dismissing a class.
- Instructing a class to change activity.
- Asking for quiet.
- Getting focus and holding it.

Write it out in full if you can. Read it to yourself. Film yourself saying it. Say it to a very good friend, with a glass of wine if needs be. Ask for tips. Think about how to refine it. Then turn it into a few bullet points that you must say or things you must convey. Then deliver it without notes. Do it not once, but several times. Do it until you are entirely bored of it, and you're hitting the key points every time, but you don't need to copy each sentence slavishly word for word. That's when you're ready to try it in the wild.

And don't try to script every possible response. Don't try to script a whole conversation, because life is not that simple. 'Everyone has a plan,' said Mike Tyson, 'until they get punched in the mouth.' Life will punch you in the mouth like you're a piñata. So instead of trying to script every possible branch of conversation, get your key points scripted, and drop them in with urgency.

Scripting behaviour

The same principles apply with your own behaviour sequences. Before you encounter a difficult circumstance, ask yourself: *What will I do? What will my response be?* Or before you encounter an everyday circumstance, ask the same question.

- *How will I welcome a class?*
- *How will I give an instruction?*
- *How will I announce the best reader prize?*
- *How will I teach them to transition between activities?*
- *What will I say so that they know what they should do?*

These questions can be examined with as much attention to detail as you can bear.

- *Where will I stand?*
- *Where will my resources be?*
- *What will my behavioural script be when someone is late? Not just what I will say, but what I will do.*
- *Will I ask them to wait outside?*

- *Will I let them sit down?*
- *Will I immediately set a sanction?*
- *What then?*
- *How will I 'behave' myself in a detention?*
- *Or a restorative conversation?*
- *Or a meeting with parents?*
- *What will I do at a parents evening?*
- *Will I have books ready?*
- *Will I start with behaviour or results?*
- *Will I start with small talk?*

If you want to look into this aspect of behaviour management, Lemov's *Teach Like a Champion* (see bibliography) is an excellent resource.

This doesn't mean over-plan everything – remember Professor Tyson's advice – but it does mean that you have a sketch of what you might do before the bullets start flying, rather than working out your strategic responses in the battlefield. Remembered, decisions made under stress and pressure are often sub-optimal; but those made in advance, in calm circumstances, are usually more thoughtful and useful and wise. So utilise wise 'you' and take their advice, rather than subjecting stressed 'you' to the captainship of the moment.

Scripts are there to help, not hinder. The more you use them, the less you need them. Once you assimilate them into your normal conversation, you know that the training wheels are coming off, and you have grown as an educator. But many people need them for a long time, and many of us still use them no matter how late in our careers we get.

PART 3
BEHAVIOUR FEEDBACK

The meeting of two personalities is like the contact of two chemical substances: if there is any reaction, both are transformed.

Carl Jung, 1933, *Modern Man in Search of a Soul*

CHAPTER 10
BEHAVIOUR FEEDBACK

This is the third leg of the tripod of teaching behaviour effectively.[1] So far we have looked at the huge importance of students receiving strong, clear, consistent signals about how they are expected to behave. Then they have that message reinforced by patient, constant reteaching in order to support the development of their skills, knowledge and understanding of this behaviour. Slowly, they learn better ways to behave, gradually building up the muscles and habits and reflexes they need to flourish. Most people can be relied on to be motivated variously by kindness, the desire to fit in, the desire to succeed, to belong to a group and so on. These are powerful forces, and they are supportive and nourishing ones.

But these strategies won't guarantee perfect behaviour from everyone. It does a lot of good with a lot of students. But they are not enough. Not for everyone, not all the time.

Take the rules of the road. *Most* people are happy to obey them for a variety of reasons: they like to drive safely, self-preservation, kindness, the desire to not frighten others, and so on. But they aren't enough either. Good road behaviour cannot be guaranteed by merely teaching it clearly and teaching it well.

Even if everyone in the world was taught to drive perfectly, and knew *The Highway Code*, there would still be many people who broke those rules. They would be angry, in a rush, showing off, careless, etc. There would be many people who would overestimate their competence or underestimate the road conditions. There would be those who enjoyed going fast, and those who enjoy being in front of everyone else. In short, there are many motives to drive badly that convince some people to ignore what they've been taught. And this assumes everyone is well taught and knows the rules completely. Five minutes in London traffic will remind you this is not the case.

---

1. The Tripod of Teaching Behaviour Effectively sounds like one of those ghastly diagrams from the 1990s that everyone in education seemed to adore: the 'bicycle of learning', the 'kebab of guided instruction' and so on.

So, we still face a challenge getting everyone to behave; simply knowing what to do is not enough. And even if only a few people are selfish drivers, that is all it takes for accidents to happen, and to many more than just themselves. Any teacher will tell you how misbehaviour from even just a few children can have a radical impact on the quality of the learning environment. Remember Hobbes's quote: 'If it be known that there is one thief in a city, all men have reason to shut their doors and lock their chests.'[2] And that's also true of classrooms, where a handful of students can make it impossible to teach. Even if we assume that only a small minority of people blatantly, wilfully break the laws, that is all it takes for us to have to take precautions.[3]

And that ignores the fact that society is not, of course, divided evenly into two neat categories: the good who uphold the laws, and those who are evil and wicked and do not. Most of us are capable of breaking rules in certain circumstances. The frequency and type of rule-breaking will vary from person to person, but good behaviour is a continuum.

Every great man and woman you can think of had vices. Mere mortals like you and me tell little white lies, creep over the speed limit, fail to declare copyright infringement, make illegal U-turns and so on. How deeply or often we do depends on a) our character and b) the circumstances in which we find ourselves. Some people are more resolute on these things than others; some people more dissolute. Some people are never tested and therefore never sin; some are tested constantly and do not.

As Paul the Apostle memorably said about the battle we all face to do the right thing despite our inclinations: 'For what I want to do I do not do, but what I hate I do. And if I do what I do not want to do, I agree that the law is good.'[4]

In the classroom, this means that there are no absolutely good or absolutely bad children; there are only children who are capable of behaving well and less well depending on the circumstances they find themselves in. Some children will arrive oven ready, impeccably mannered, trying hard and being kind. Some of the children in this group will behave well no matter what you do – and sometimes despite what you do. Then there are children who are so persistently defiant that they seem to have based their conduct on the opposite of what you have asked them.

---

2. Hobbes, T. 1588-1679 (1968) *Leviathan*. Hardmondsworth: Penguin Books.

3. Also known as the 'Why we can't have nice things' principle.

4. Romans 7:15-16, New International Version

Influences on student behaviour

Most children will behave, or not behave well, depending on influences from their personal circumstances and school circumstances.

Personal factors include:

- Upbringing
- Home culture
- Personality
- Values and expectations
- Peers
- Media

And so on. You can often do little about this.[5]

School factors are the environment you provide for them:

- Clear expectations
- Taught (not told) behaviours
- Habituation
- Routines and norms
- Modelling, examples, demonstrations
- Repetition of expectation
- Patient correction of errors

The room you build, in other words. As we have mentioned, this needs to be as immersive as possible, so that students receive as much information as possible about what good and bad behaviour looks and feels like. But even clearly explained messages only reach so far, so often. There are many reasons why students may know *what* to do but feel they don't have to do it.

In the real world, it is possible to swear or speak unkindly of others, mess about, be lazy, and nothing obvious happens. The world is often terribly unfair: the good suffer and the wicked prosper. It raineth on the just and the unjust alike. This might explain why so many religious traditions emphasise that justice is located in the universe *after* death (Heaven and Hell), or *between* lives (karma and reincarnation). The classroom needs to be better than that.

---

5. And sometimes you can. But don't expect to be able to unpick the stitches of the tapestries of their lives easily.

You cannot rely on one strategy alone to motivate all children to behave.

Of course we must react to misbehaviour. It is, as an approach, only dangerous when we see it as the solution to all misbehaviour. It is a tool, or a series of tools, which have tremendous utility in the right context and next to none in others. But you still want those tools in your toolkit. They are even more useful when we realise their limitations and strengths.

No classroom can be run by e.g. sanction alone. But no classroom can be run by restorative approaches alone, or social norms alone. Good – even great– teachers rely on a magazine of motivational devices to inspire and persuade as many students as possible (as much of the time as possible) to demonstrate good behaviour.

Consequences themselves can be very complex. It is often only the inexperience of using alternatives that makes so many teachers reach for the consequence codes/sanctions so often.[6]

What do consequences look like?
There are at least five types of consequence. After a behaviour we could:

1. Encourage (attach a reward to a desired behaviour, like a merit point, a star sticker, a smiley face, etc.)
2. Discourage (attach a sanction to the action in order to deter future misbehaviour)
3. Clarify/redirect (did they understand what they were supposed to do?)
4. Support (offer a targeted provision specific to their circumstances, such as counselling or a teaching assistant)
5. Teach (teach them something they need to know/be able to do – e.g. reading – in order to reduce further misbehaviour)

1/2 Encourage/discourage
These tactics, focusing on sanctions and rewards, are so ubiquitous, and yet so badly done, that I've devoted entire chapters to them. We'll come back to these.

---

6. Look at any school's behaviour policy. I'll bet you that, 9 times out of 10, it's almost entirely devoted to the consequence code, or some kind of sanction pyramid. That's not wrong to include, but a school behaviour policy should also be an embodiment of how to behave well, not merely how to set sanctions for misbehaviour.

3 Clarify/redirect

One simple response to misbehaviour is to check the student's understanding of what it is they need to do. Often, if a student is off task and amusing themselves with inappropriate behaviour, part of the cause might be that they don't understand what they have to do pedagogically (i.e. the work that has been set) *or* they are unsure how they should behave.

Neither of these excuses misbehaviour, but they can be factors in the choices a student makes. Effective classroom management means making it as easy as possible to behave, not simply expecting everyone to behave perfectly and routinely reading them the Riot Act when inevitably they do not.

Clarification is part of a process that sees some misbehaviour as a result of deeply ingrained habits to act in ways that aren't useful or appropriate for the classroom. If we accept that good behaviour can be taught, then good teaching practice demands that we check for understanding.

Examples:

'Do you know what it is you should be doing?'
'What's the rule on shouting out?'
'Can anyone tell me why this line-up isn't right?'
'What's the third thing we insist upon in this classroom?'

And so on. Using clarification acknowledges that some (not all) misbehaviour stems in part from unconsciously behaving poorly rather than choosing to behave poorly. If a student doesn't know what a good line-up looks like, or what the uniform expectations are, then punishing them for this is unfair and ineffective as a means to change their behaviour (although it will do wonders for their capacity to feel simmering resentment). We wouldn't direct a student to build a jet engine, then reprimand them half an hour later for not doing so. We would acknowledge that we have asked a very specialised and highly skilled task of them, and then teach or remind them what to do next.

This is why a simple reminder, warning, or redirection can be such a powerful tool.

Of course, this strategy, like all others, has limited utility. You can only clarify so much before you realise students are wilfully ignoring your expectations. If students think that they will *only* get endless clarifications from a teacher

CHAPTER 11
SANCTIONS

Good behaviour cannot be secured in all students by brilliant instruction alone. Many students will understand perfectly well what they should do and still ignore that for a variety of reasons. For boundaries to count at all, they must be patrolled, and they are patrolled with consequences. There is no escaping it. There has never been a human community that has survived without sanction, penalty and rebuke.

Sanctions and rewards are two of the most common tools of behaviour management you'll find in most classrooms or schools. This approach is as old as the stars. Historically, sanctions have often been associated with penalties: from brutal and abusive sanctions like the belt or the cane to the more benign detentions, lines, litter duty, lost break time, extra work, calls home and so on. This is such a common approach, it is a wonder that so few teachers are taught very much about its successful use. Often teachers are simply told they have to use it.

I'll explore sanctions and rewards in some detail for several reasons: because of their ubiquity, because if they are properly applied they can be very useful as a behaviour modifier, and because their implementation is rarely explained properly.

Consequences are associated with the behaviourist theory of human actions and decisions. In behaviourism,[1] the focus is on providing external stimuli to change behaviour. In the classroom, the teacher controls the environment, using sanctions and rewards to stimulate behaviour this way and that. This is called 'operant conditioning'. Rewards and sanctions are typically referred to as *reinforcements* and *punishments*:

> A **reinforcement** is any stimulus you use to *encourage* the behaviour in the future, more frequently.

> A **punishment** is using a stimulus to *discourage* behaviour.

---

1. Skinner, B. F. (1976) *About behaviorism*. New York, NY: Vintage Books.

We can differentiate further by adding one more factor: positive (adding something to) and negative (taking something away). This gives us four categories that are useful to understand:

- **Positive punishment** – adding a stimulus the student doesn't like to discourage behaviour, such as reprimanding a student, giving them more work as a punishment.
- **Negative punishment** – removing a stimulus to discourage behaviour, such as setting a detention, time out, losing golden time, taking away a game, etc.
- **Positive reinforcement**: giving a stimulus after the desired behaviour, to encourage more behaviour like that: food, presents, merits, praise, and such.
- **Negative reinforcement** – removing a stimulus to promote the behaviour: 'You can leave the table [the unwanted stimulus] if you finish the three questions.' I'll take away the thing you don't like, if you behave in the way I suggest. Or the student starts working to stop the teacher nagging. Negative reinforcements are not punishments.

Negative sanctions are likely to be most effective in high-trust environments, i.e. when students have a strong expectation that they will happen. But perhaps oddly, rewards are most effective when they are *unexpected*.

Aren't sanctions cruel?

Only cruel ones. Commentators like Kohn have often described sanctions and rewards as inappropriate, ineffective and immoral. We certainly need to be careful not to use sanctions inappropriately (see below). But the research simply does not support the conclusion that we should *not* use them. As Marzano says: 'Quite the contrary, the research … strongly support[s] a balanced approach that applies a variety of techniques.'[2]

One meta-analysis[3] found that disciplinary intervention resulted in lowered misbehaviour in 80% of subjects in the studies. It found that classroom

---

2. Marzano, R. J., Pickering, D., and Pollock, J. E. (2001) *Classroom instruction that works: Research-based strategies for increasing student achievement.* Alexandria, VA: Association for Supervision and Curriculum Development.

3. Stage, S. A. and Quiroz, D. R. (1997) 'A meta-analysis of interventions to decrease disruptive classroom behavior in public education settings', *School Psychology Review*, 26, 3, pp.333-368.

management systems with no reward/sanction system reported the least improvement in behaviour and that sanctions featured in the most effective systems. Not *any* sanctions, though, and the evidence stresses that mild sanctions are usually the most effective. And all the evidence we have suggests that the best way to maximise the effect of a sanction is to make sure that students are absolutely convinced it will happen. In other words: *The certainty of the sanction is far more important than the severity.* Brutal or excessive punishments are not only cruel, they are less effective.

Also remember: *no one strategy works universally. Use as many strategies as necessary to move the behaviour needle in your classroom.*

Is that all you've got? Subjectivity and consequences
Reinforcement and punishment are in the mind of the beholder. On Twitter, for example, many people are actually encouraged to act cruelly by people insulting them. It's possibly negative reinforcement; as one online correspondent said to me, 'You're distracting them from their day-to-day lives, which are likely punishing.'[4]

Or, as another said, 'I suspect many are abusive [online] because they are lonely, and half-consciously hope you'll respond to their insults by fighting with them, because that would be a validating acknowledgement of their existence. To the perpetually ignored, even a slap can feel like a caress.'[5]

This is similar to some children who wrestle with deep feelings of worthlessness, for whom any response – however punitive – is validating. Attention can be toxic or healthy, but at least it is attention.

When you describe behaviour management to some people, they automatically think you mean merciless punishments, incarceration, the belt, the cane and so on. But as I hope I have made clear, most of your classroom time should be spent on the *proactive* phase, i.e. teaching children the habits and norms of good behaviour. *Reacting* to misbehaviour with consequences simply reinforces and completes the circuit of that phase. Do both, in order to make both more effective.

---

4. Twitter exchange with @sentientist, Dec 2, 2019

5. Twitter exchange with @G_SBhogal, 11:47 PM, Nov 17, 2019

So, what is the purpose of sanctions?

Sanctions have one primary useful effect, when they have any effect at all: they deter. They do not cure, or transfigure. They are not magic. No one ever sat in a detention and thought 'My God, what have I been doing with my life?' Students are not Jean Valjean in *Les Misérables*, paralysed with guilt and shame, then transformed by the healing power of forgiveness and grace. No, the aim of sanctions is to deter; to make the recipient think, as they stew in the juice of their discomfort, 'I might not do this again.'

What are sanctions?

First, what are they not? They are not retribution. They are not a means to get one's own back on a child after some slight or injury or insult. They are not a way to restore balance to the universe, or a way to pay a debt to the community. They are not revenge. Everything in your behaviour management toolkit must serve a purpose and that purpose must be moral as well as practical. Revenge is neither.

Who are sanctions for?

The deterrent effect of a sanction works on two levels: the personal and the communal. For the person receiving the sanction, there is a behavioural nudge: if I do this (X) again this penalty (Y) might happen again, so I might not do it again. This is operant conditioning in its simplest form. So, in theory, we might hope to see the student discouraged from repeating the action in future. At the communal level, we might see the incident frequency decrease across the class or year group, because everyone else sees the sanction carried out and understands that it would apply to them too in the same circumstances.

It's not just a response to the present misbehaviour, but an attempt to direct future behaviour.

Do sanctions work?

The simplest answer is 'sometimes', and also 'to different degrees'. One of the things people against *all* sanctions frequently say is, 'Some children aren't deterred by sanctions, so what's the point?' Or more specifically, 'This student repeatedly gets sanctions but they're still misbehaving, so they clearly don't work, so they are pointless.' But they are simultaneously right and wrong. They're right: sanctions don't have much impact on some students. But they're wrong when they say that means we shouldn't use them, because they have *some* effect on lots of us.

248

Picture this. You're driving along a motorway. You know the speed limit. You know how to drive. But the road ahead is clear, and you have somewhere to be. The temptation to break the speed limit, even a little, is high. You have the motive, means and opportunity. It's a crime scene waiting to happen.

What's to stop you? Potentially, lots of things. Some people obey the speed limit because they want to be a good person; some because they want to be a good driver; some because they don't want to harm others; some because they don't want to endanger themselves; some might have had a relative involved in an accident; some don't like going too fast.

These are all social reasons, motivations, inspired to different extents by one's identity, personal beliefs, appetites and habits.

That's enough to keep most people within the legal limit, but it's not enough to guarantee that everyone obeys it. If your safe-roads policy relies on good people acting morally, then your optimism will be dashed against the jagged rocks of life, and by 'life' I mean 'other people'. Even people who believe themselves to be good people will break rules from time to time. Crucially, they will rationalise doing so retrospectively: 'I was in a hurry, so *this* time it was OK.' Or 'I'm a really good driver so it's safe to speed.' Or, 'I'm really angry and I deserve this.' Or 'I have a plane to catch,' and so on.

Then there are people who know the limits but see everyone else going ten miles per hour over and do the same, encouraged by the social norm they see. Or some who wouldn't consciously speed but are careless enough to let their speed creep up. Add to this scenario that there are plenty of people who don't care about speed limits, who think they're a good driver, who love driving fast, who want to show off, who are inexperienced and so on. Clearly, you can't rely on the honour system to keep motorways safe.

Proactive socialisation can only go so far, with so many people. There will always be rule-breakers. In fact, there is even an argument to be made that, if everyone around you is obeying the rules, then there is an obvious advantage in you *not* doing so: jumping the lights, going the wrong way up a one-way street, using the wrong side of the road to obtain some temporary advantage. This is called the free rider problem in social ethics. The criminal takes advantage of a law-obeying community by exploiting the agreements, promises, boundaries everyone else keeps, and breaks them for personal gain. From this perspective, rule-breaking can even be seen as rational.

Consequences affect everyone, even when you aren't the direct recipient of them

What then? Well, we know what then: *consequences*. Financial ones (speeding tickets, etc.) behavioural ones (licence points leading up to the loss of the licence), instructional ones (attending a driving course), or even incarceration in extreme cases.

Do these deter? As an answer, I offer a thought experiment to you: were we to remove all penalties and consequence for bad driving, do you think there would be more or less of it? The point isn't that deterrents successfully prevent all misbehaviour – clearly they don't, because people still break the rules; the point is that they act as a brake on the frequency of the misbehaviour.

Another thought experiment to try to persuade you: imagine a road with speed cameras every 500 metres, and they were all definitely switched on, and you knew it. Then imagine the same stretch of road, with one speed camera every ten miles and you thought it might not be working anyway. Which of these scenarios, if any, would deter your behaviour more successfully? If you said anything other than the first, then nothing will convince you. Will people still speed? Yes, absolutely. Maniacs and teen racers and getaway drivers, and married couples having an argument, and angry people late for meetings, the careless, the feeble minded, the man on the edge of a breakdown and so on. But not as many as before, and that is the whole point. Only outliers will fail to conform.

Consequences in the classroom

Transfer this to the classroom. As I mentioned, sanctions work on two levels. The first level is individual: a student who experiences a sanction might think twice about repeating the misbehaviour. *Some* students will be deterred, and some will not – but did I mention that some will? That's better than before. The justification for sanctions is not that they are panaceas, but that they aid good behaviour because they reduce rule-breaking. They aren't universally effective, but as I repeatedly mention, no one strategy is. No medicine or surgery heals all ills. No joke amuses everyone; no tool fixes everything. The idea that one behavioural strategy can be the answer to every behavioural complaint is the root of a great many absurd conversations about behaviour.

The second level of a sanction's effect is social: the community sees that behaviour has boundaries and that these boundaries are patrolled with consequences – which include sanctions. And by doing so, the community can experience the deterrent effects vicariously, without having to incur them personally. We see what happens to others, and we imagine it happening to ourselves. We realise that if we also behave in way (X) then we too will incur sanction (Y), and if (Y) is more trouble than we care to incur then (X) is less likely to happen.

The theory is reasonably straightforward. In practice, it's a little more complicated.

When and with whom do they work?

Sanctions have a deterrent effect, but that effect is not experienced evenly throughout a population of students, or even consistently by one person. There are multiple factors that make sanctions more or less effective, and it is vital that teachers are aware of this in order to get the most out of the system and, crucially, not to use sanctions in a way that fails to have any impact or, worse, encourages worse behaviour.

Three main factors are important to understand in terms of a sanction's effectiveness:

- Certainty rather than severity
- Consistency is key
- Sanctions affect different people differently

Certainty rather than severity

As the speed camera scenario above illustrates, it is the certainty of the penalty that matters most. Knowing that you *will definitely* be caught by the speed camera massively increases the effect it has on your driving behaviour. Thinking you might get away with it has the opposite effect. Some people might still be deterred, but the effect falls off a cliff with some people. In other words, the best way to ensure that your sanctions have an impact is to make sure that they are highly consistently applied, and that you are as vigilant as possible when you apply them.

Consistency is key

Shouldn't we make exceptions? Yes we should. But sanctions must be applied as consistently as possible. Every rule has exceptions, and any rule that tries to be absolute is a cruel and unfair one, because it is unable to cope with the complexity of circumstances that life throws at us. In society, even killing somebody – which is generally frowned upon – is allowed or tolerated for a variety of reasons in exceptional circumstances: self-defence, acts of war, in response to prolonged mental cruelty, insanity etc. Allowing these exceptions doesn't obliterate the fact that there is a strong prohibition against it, and steep penalties for those found guilty of it. It simply means that the rule is not artificially simple: there are caveats and exceptions to it.

So too in the classroom. We can make exceptions as long as they are

- Exceptional
- Logical
- Internally consistent

Here's an easy example. A student with Tourette's syndrome might find themselves unable to restrain their swearing, or their audible tics, no matter how hard they sincerely try. When you teach such a student, it would be absurd to reprimand them for the outbursts, because we cannot be held responsible for actions over which we have no control. I cannot be held responsible for something that I didn't do, or that I did without being aware of it: the sleepwalker who breaks a vase; the baby who ruins the rug with a beetroot smoothie. Responsibility requires agency.

OTHER EXCEPTIONS

What about less visible difficulties that students may face – difficulties that suggest an exception must be made? What if a student is going through some testing personal circumstance that suggests they need support other than a penalty? Where is the room for exceptions in this circumstance? Tourette's is a clear and obvious circumstance where it would be unfair to set a sanction, and it is also something that other students can understand with a little explanation and context setting. Students understand that their comrade can't help the outbursts and realise with a little help that this doesn't mean that there is no rule against e.g. swearing, or that they are allowed to do so by implication.

They realise the norm still exists, and they understand that the norm is a little more complex than just an absolute ban on the behaviour. In fact circumstances like these can be a useful opportunity to teach other children about students who face different challenges, and to learn about tolerance and respect.

We should also make exceptions for less visible difficulties, or for student circumstances that are private or protected by the covenant of disclosure. If a teacher needs to make an exception for a student, for example by not applying a sanction that would normally apply, then it is important the class still understands that:

- The behaviour wasn't ignored by the teacher.
- It still mattered.
- Action is being taken.
- There is an exception happening.
- The exception has a reason.
- We can't always discuss these because sometimes privacy and dignity are more important.

The teacher needs to reinforce these points in a simple conversation with the class, but not necessarily in front of the pupil. And the beauty is that if primed in this way, most students shrug their shoulders and say, 'OK.' As long as they understand that there's some reason for it, they're often far more forgiving than we think they might be.

Also, many of them will already know if their classmates are going through difficulties, because of their existing social alliances.

Even better is if the class can be primed to understand that exceptions will happen exceptionally from the very beginning, long before such exceptions need to happen. That way, students are ready for the event where you may need to act differently with one pupil. This ensures that the teacher's rules, while highly consistent, do not become a straitjacket.

Zero tolerance is a very useful *attitude* to have, rather than a method. But remember that it is largely a slogan (see: 'Zero tolerance – a slogan, not a strategy?', p. 141). Never permitting any exception might be cruel and could be stretched to absurdity. Imagine you have a rule that states, clearly, that students must ask permission to leave the room, and that anyone not doing so will provoke a sanction of some kind. Now imagine the room catches fire. Would you still expect the same adherence as before? I hope not – you would expect self-preservation to overtake compliance, and excuse anyone for doing the obvious and sensible thing.

In which case, true 'zero' tolerance has not been observed, rightly. I have been to more 'zero tolerance' schools than most. I ask them if they would expect a child to submit homework if they were hit by a bus. They say, 'No, of course not.' So, what they have in reality is 'a very low tolerance for misbehaviour'. And what we are left with is a more sensible discussion about where the boundaries should be, and what our tolerance levels are.

STOICISM AND UTOPIA

> It matters not how strait the gate,
> How charged the punishments the scroll,
> I am the master of my fate,
> I am the captain of my soul.

'Invictus', William Ernest Henley

The reasons why – exceptions apart – we must still have very low tolerance for poor behaviour is explored in the philosophy of Stoicism, a term which broadly means being prepared to cope with the pressures and trials that life will inevitably provide. Attempting to prevent children from addressing this by keeping them away from any distress has the opposite effect than the one we intended: it makes them more incapable of dealing with difficulty. We actually need to expose children to consequences in a relatively safe environment, and we need to teach them that they matter, and that their actions matter because they have consequences. To do otherwise is to pretend we can keep them safe from all cares, when we obviously cannot. Such thinking is utopian, and as Christopher Hitchens loved to point out, the word utopia translates as 'no place'. As a blogger called Anonymous Educator once wrote:[6]

> A perfect world doesn't exist, either as a golden age to return to or a promise in the future. We need to teach our students that life is a series of choices and show them the consequences of bad choices while still in the relatively safe environments of our schools because when they leave our buildings, the consequences are more severe. This means having a set system of behavioral expectations which is rewarded or punished consistently, one which escalates all the way to expulsion/exclusion. We can't change the circumstances of students' lives, but we can teach them (and remember, teaching is our job) that their actions have consequences. Most of the time, good actions yield good consequences, and bad actions yield bad consequences.

---

6. Anonymous Educator (2020) 'On the value of discipline', www.bit.ly/2PjtUPT [retrieved 25/04/2020]

EXCEPTIONS MUST REALLY BE EXCEPTIONAL

Despite that caveat, teachers must endeavour, must truly strain with every muscle they have, to communicate very, very, very low levels of tolerance for routine-breaking. In order for a consequence to be seen as a norm, it must be highly consistent.[7] A norm is that which is experienced, because then it becomes expected in the students' imaginations. There are very few exceptions made for those who drive over the speed limit: they are normally only for professionals engaged in police or ambulance work or coping with some other emergency such as evading an accident.

SANCTIONS AFFECT DIFFERENT PEOPLE DIFFERENTLY

Many teachers have noted that sanctions have different effects on different students, and that the greatest impact seemed to be on students who identified with the school culture and were normally well behaved. Some research even suggests that there is 'a wealth of evidence that a focus on punishment *alone* [my emphasis] will not impact many of the most severe types of offenses or re-educate the highest rate offender'.[8]

But, as we shall see, this does not mean we should stop using sanctions. They still have an impact on many students, even if that impact is varied. Their inability to deter some of the most committed and challenging students is no more reason to advocate against their use in general than the fact that some people are allergic to penicillin means we shouldn't utilise it in most treatments requiring antibiotics.

As David Didau says, they 'signal to those members of the student body who are able to weigh up risk and reward that there are sanctions in place, that poor behaviour will be met with predictable, proportional and fair consequences'.[9]

Sanctions affect not only the individual but also the community. Not using sanctions on any one student because 'they never turn up' or 'they never seem

---

7. Perhaps I mentioned this?

8. Atkins, M. S., McKay, M. M., Frazier, S. L., Jakobsons, L .J., Arvanitis, P., Cunningham, T., Brown, C. and Lambrecht, L. (2002) 'Suspensions and detentions in an urban, low-income school: Punishment or reward?' *Journal of abnormal child psychology*, 30(4), pp.361-371.

9. Didau, D, (2019) 'Do detentions work?' The Learning Spy blog, April 29 2019, www.bit.ly/3fswbmm [retrieved 30/01/20]

to have an effect' also has an impact on the community, who now see sanctions as optional, inconsistent or unfairly issued.

PROSPECT THEORY

The idea that incentives (rewards) and disincentives (sanctions) affect different people differently is a tenet of prospect theory, one of the foundational theories of behavioural economics. Developed by Daniel Kahneman and Amos Tvesrsky in 1979, it describes how differently individuals respond to the prospect of gains and losses.[10] For example, although we might predict that losing £1000 would be exactly the same magnitude of disincentive as gaining £1000 would be an incentive, we find that this is not the case. People are often not perfectly rational agents.

Prospect theory describes how people make decisions based on the loss or gain depending on their relative positions (the *reference point*). The incentive/ disincentive is relative to who we are and our context. A rich man wouldn't think much of a £10 fine for speeding, but they may consider being publicly named and shamed as unbearable, and give thousands to cover it up. Conversely, a homeless man might think exactly the opposite in terms of the impact it would have on their behaviour: having their name published might mean little, but financial loss, however small, might be disastrous.

Prospect theory explains that people faced with risky choices that could lead to gains are far more risk averse than people facing a risky choice that leads to possible losses. All things being even, we will do more to avoid a discomfort than to seek some gain.

Sanctions do not deter everyone equally. If the main effect of a sanction is to deter, then we must take into account the fact that people are not brute matter and do not all respond in identical ways to identical stimuli. We should expect this. People are complex, and what appeals to me might not appeal to you. What horrifies me may delight you. We can look at the same painting or piece of music and be moved in entirely different ways. So too with any kind of reward/ sanction stimulus.

So, deterrents work differently on different people. Who do they work most on? Sadly (for our purposes) everything we know about this area suggests that

---

10. Kahneman, D. and Tversky, A. (1979) 'Prospect theory: an analysis of decision under risk', *Econometrica*, 47 (2), pp.263–291.

the people who are most deterred by the threat of a sanction are the most law-abiding and socially compliant people. In other words, exactly the group who least need to have their behaviour modified.

This shouldn't surprise us. These people have already bought into the rules and norms of the community most earnestly, so we should expect them to be most determined to avoid a social penalty, the scorn of the community, or the disapproval of people from whom they might seek approval.

And of course, the mirror image to this is that there is a small subset of people who are utterly unmoved and undeterred by sanctions. There are many reasons for this:

- They may lack the imagination to realise what will happen to them if they are caught.
- They may be unusually impulsive and fail to appreciate anything beyond the moment.
- They might struggle to grasp probability and think it unlikely they will be caught.
- They may be natural gamblers and believe the risk is worth it.
- They may be so goal-focused that they ignore the risks of their misbehaviour.
- They may simply not care.
- They may have such challenging home circumstances that mild school sanctions seem irrelevant.

There is probably a subcategory here worth remembering: people for whom sanctions are a perverse form of incentive; they might see it as a badge of honour to be in detention, for example. Or there may be something in the penalty that they seek, invisible to those of us who seek other things.

For example, if you're homeless, the sanction of incarceration may seem like a benefit on a cold night. Some students with profound behavioural problems provoke physical confrontation with others in order to be restrained – because this is the only time that they experience any form of human contact or comfort. Such distressing considerations are a sad reminder that what might be a privation for some people might be a luxury for others. There are also children who will deliberately activate a sanction in order to achieve some other end, e.g. to be removed from a lesson they dislike, or in order to harvest adult attention, even if the behaviour is toxic and the attention negative.

Through this lens, it is easy to see why some people might claim sanctions are useless. And if they only deterred the conspicuously virtuous and had no effect on anyone else, then that might be true. But behaviour does not work like that and people are not like that.

Personality types are a continuum. So are people's responses to the threat of sanction. Some people are very deterred, some not at all, and most people are somewhere in between, on a bell curve of impact. The important takeaway is that most people are deterred to some extent, and some more or less than others.

Any strategy that deters most students to varying degrees from misbehaviour is a useful one to use. Sanctions work like any tool: sometimes.

Severity
Sanctions must *not* be severe. They must not be disproportionate. They must not be excessive. They must not be used as revenge or retribution. But they are not and should not be. Sanctions must be proportionate to the misbehaviour they seek to redress and deter.

More principles of effective sanctions

- Have an escalating tariff. Small misbehaviours incur small sanctions. Bigger ones, bigger sanctions. If a behaviour is not amended by a small sanction, then the first port of call for a teacher running a room should usually be to escalate the sanction.
- Repeated misbehaviour should prompt escalated sanctions. If a behaviour occurs frequently, then it is vital that the student realises that multiple misdemeanours add up. It's little use to attempt to deter a student from perpetually talking in classes with the same short sanction.
  The famous definition of madness is 'doing the same thing and expecting different results'. If a student repeats the same misbehaviour frequently (such as talking over others in several classes) then this needs to activate a steeper sanction. In some cases, this is all that is required to convince the student that matters are becoming more serious. Teach them that their actions *do* have consequences.
- But repeated misbehaviour should also sound alarm bells. Not only should sanctions escalate, but the prudent teacher must ask if something else is going on in the student's circumstances that, if addressed, could improve their behaviour. The first stop here is

a pastoral conversation with the student to discern if anything is upsetting them, if they understand how their behaviour is harming their education or that of others, if everything is OK at home, and so on.

It is also a useful point to assess if the student needs some other, more tailored form of support to amend their behaviour, such as small group work on their social skills, remedial work on the curriculum, some form of counselling, or other therapeutic intervention, specific to their personal circumstances. This is often one way in which students in need of help start to access greater levels of school support – *if* the school and teachers are alert to the possibility that the student might need some form of tailored provision.

The potential pitfalls of using sanctions

I hope I've made it clear that sanctions are only one tool we can use, are not universally useful, and affect people differently. Keeping these things in mind will help us to avoid using sanctions unfairly. It is a sad and demonstrable fact that some people find it very easy to treat others differently depending on their perception of them or their relationship to them.

This can be seen in prison sentencing, where there is evidence that middle-class people are often treated more leniently than working-class people, for the same crime. The former made a 'foolish error' whereas the latter is a 'hardened criminal'. The same effect is seen with more or less good-looking people.[11]

It is vital that teachers try to be as scrupulously fair as possible when issuing sanctions (and rewards). Remember that these are used as mechanisms to influence future behaviour, and should be allocated where necessary, *not* because you 'felt like it' or through some desire to 'get your own back'. Never sanction when angry unless you are certain you are in control of yourself and that it is what you would have done in more calm conditions.

Attribution bias

Attribution bias[12] is when we unfairly or incorrectly imagine reasons for other people's actions rather than our own. For example, we are far more indulgent with our friends than people we dislike. We might see our best friend act rudely

---

11. Hollier, R. 'Physical attractiveness bias in the legal system', The Law Project, www.bit.ly/31ih89L [retrieved 01/07/20]

12. Heider, F. (1958) *The psychology of interpersonal relations*. New York, NY: Wiley.

and think, 'Oh she's having a hard day today, I wonder what's up,' but we might see someone in a political party we don't like doing the same thing and think, 'What a dreadful person.' We attribute internal causes (character, free choices) more when people we like do good things, or when people we dislike do bad things; and we attribute external factors (they were forced to do it by others, etc.) more when a person we like does bad things, and vice versa. Basically, we filter what people do through a lens of what we think about them already.

So if you already think of a student as rude or aggressive, you are more likely to attribute their misbehaviour to their bad character. But when dealing with a student you perceive to be kind and virtuous, you will likely explain any misbehaviour as being caused by external factors: maybe they're just having a bad day?

Obviously this is a very dangerous mistake for teachers to make. So be extremely careful not to build up layers of prejudice through which you judge some students more harshly than others, or privilege some over others. One of the most frequent cries you will hear from students is that 'You're so unfair!' or 'You're picking on me!' A lot of the time, this is simply tactics, the desire to get away with something, or a sincere belief that they have done no wrong. But be careful to make sure that they aren't right.

Sanctioning unfairly can be minimised or avoided by:

- Focusing on the behaviour rather than the student. Is what they did prohibited by the class norms, routines or rules? Then apply the consequence code scrupulously and consistently. At first, students will rebel against what they perceive as your inflexibility (although see exceptions under 'Consistency is key', p. 251), but if you hold the line on this, they will see you as fair and strong-willed. Best of all, the deterrence of sanctions will be magnified, and you will end up using penalties less.
- Having a clear understanding of your own tariffs and the school policy on consequences – you know the standard.
- Clearly communicated and understood sanction norms with the class – they know you know *they* know the standard, and everyone's shared understanding supports everyone's adherence to it.
- Scripted language and behaviour. Know what to say in advance of having to say it (see 'Scripts', p. 221).
- Data – make sure you periodically check who you sanction, when, and why. Are there any patterns? Scrutinise this data, and satisfy yourself that you haven't developed favourites or scapegoats.

Other dangers to be avoided:

- Using sanctions as your exclusive strategy to modify behaviour
- Antagonising students into worse behaviour – avoid this by using scripts, by preparing all students to know when and why sanctions occur, and above all, practise speaking to students assertively rather than aggressively. It is too easy to let off a little steam, and it even feels good sometimes. That's why it's dangerous. When you feel yourself getting upset or emotional, get a grip of yourself by remembering, 'I am angry and this is a dangerous state for me to make decisions.' Also, have a removal procedure in place so that if you have to use it, you can do so with ease, rather than anxiety (see 'Removing students', later).

What makes a sanction effective?

Fletcher-Wood summarises the research on this in an excellent article from 2019.[13] He argues that sanctions aren't as effective when:

- They aren't immediate. We prefer immediate rewards and delayed costs. As he says, 'being funny among peers now may outweigh the cost of a detention next week'.
- They are uncertain. Delayed sanctions are uncertain because a lot can happen between now and then. Perhaps they can duck out of it somehow? And if the teacher is notorious for not turning up, then students are far more likely to test the boundaries.
- They are 'rote punishment', i.e. simply sitting still. Some students are perfectly fine with a little sitting quietly. There is less sanction effect from that for some. Consider getting them to do something.
- They create *unnecessary* conflict. While sanctions by necessity entail *some* conflict, they should be issued fairly and consistently. They should be seen as natural consequences, not spiteful or malicious acts. Make sure they are issued in a professional tone that conveys necessity and procedure, not an emotional backlash.

Therefore teachers need to:

- Set them as soon after the misbehaviour as possible.
- Use them consistently. The more you do this, the less you have to use

---

13. Fletcher-Wood, H. (2020) 'When do detentions work?' Improving Teaching, www.bit. ly/3ftfPdo [retrieved 16/02/2020]

them. When the threat of the sanction becomes as real as the sanction itself, you drastically reduce the number of sanctions you issue.

- Make them productive. They shouldn't be fun, but they should be instructive.
- Make sure students know why they are there, and what to do next.[14]

Repetition

If a sanction doesn't produce the desired effect, and you have no immediate cause to suspect some deeper issue, then the first port of call should be to repeat the sanction, but also to escalate it. That means the same sanction is applied again, but potentially at a more serious level. Most schools have a consequence code that includes an escalating series of sanctions. Use it. If the penalty for their first offence is a 20-minute sanction, then repetition of the same offence the next day might be 40 minutes. If it reoccurs, there should be something more serious, to reflect the fact that the behaviour is becoming a pattern, rather than a one-off.

Frequently, low-level mainstream misbehaviour can be amended if the students can be persuaded that you will never give up – that what is wrong on Monday is wrong on Friday and the next week and the next. In many ways, they want to see if they can wear you down. So you have to be made of more enduring stuff. You need to be the one who outlasts them.

Escalation

If a sanction is not carried out properly (e.g. a student fails to attend, or attends but misbehaves in the sanction) or if the sanction is not completed before the student repeats the behaviour, sanctions should be escalated. Twenty minutes becomes an hour, for example, or a detention with a classroom teacher becomes a detention with a head of department and so on. Again, refer to the school consequence system in this matter. It is important that you uphold the school behaviour policy, in order to reinforce the school behaviour culture. Students can easily tell when a teacher is working outside of the school system, and they will play that to the maximum advantage they can.

And if a student is incurring repeated sanctions then the teacher must involve other members of staff – line managers, pastoral staff, etc. If it is really persistent, and repetition and escalation aren't working, then more serious and complex interventions may be required.

---

14. Fletcher-Wood, H. (2020) Ibid

Sanctions have a social function as well as an individual one

Sanctions have varying degrees of impact on students if applied in the ways suggested above. But they do not only affect *that* student. Students operate in group contexts. As I mentioned, classrooms are like Rubik's Cubes: move one square and you affect all the other squares. Sanctions demonstrate to the rest of the class that there are boundaries and specific expectations. Some research suggests that removing sanctions has a disproportionate influence on the rest of the class seeing this. In one experiment, students were shown a classmate deliberately cheating, and their behaviour was recorded. In the absence of a sanction, cheating doubled among the rest of the students.[15] In other words, if others don't see sanctions issued for clear misbehaviour, they feel incentivised to copy the behaviour, knowing that no consequences will follow.

Even normally honest people can be tempted to be dishonest if they feel like they might get away with it. There are very few angels or devils in humanity. Most of us are a mix of virtues and vices, and most of us are capable of breaking the rules under different circumstances. Teachers, as ever, should strive to make good behaviour as easy as possible and remove or reduce obstacles – such as temptation – whenever they can.

For this and many other reasons, teachers should remember to keep sanctions as part of their repertoire and ignore the often well-meant but ultimately harmful advice found in some behaviour training to dispense with them entirely in return for the fool's gold of entirely relationship-based approaches.

What is a good detention?

Detentions are such a common strategy used in schools (especially, but not exclusively, secondary/high school), it's worth putting them under the microscope.

What is the aim of detentions?

As with all sanctions, the aim is to deter. In order to deter, a detention must come with a consequence that the student does not want to experience or repeat. But it goes without saying that the severity must not be so great that it becomes disproportionate. Certainty not severity, remember?

- It must involve a mildly tiresome experience for the student.
- The student needs to understand what behaviour of theirs has caused it.

---

15. Ariely, D. (2013) *The honest truth about dishonesty: how we lie to everyone–especially ourselves.* London: Harper Perennial.

- It must feel like it has an end, and when it is finished, the slate can be more or less wiped clean.
- It should end with a threshold conversation (see below).
- It mustn't be interpreted by the student as a reward, or something they would enjoy doing anyway, e.g. letting them read their book, or play on their phones, or have a nice chat with the teacher about their favourite type of ant.

Threshold conversations

A threshold conversation is one that indicates to the student that they have gone from one state to another. It is designed to acknowledge the past and look to the future. The student stands at a threshold, or in a door frame, about to step into a new world. Threshold conversations are used to create a narrative about what just happened, and what needs to happen next. Without this framing, students will write their own narratives, often toxic ones, where they are the hero and the world is *so unfair*. Challenge that and give them another way to look at things. Make sure this conversation includes:

- What they did wrong in order to be there
- How they behaved in detention
- What they should have done instead
- How they can do better in the future
- A gentle but firm reminder of what will happen if the behaviour repeats
- Establishing whether they need to talk to you about any unusual circumstances affecting their behaviour
- An indication that the slate is now clean
- The expectation that they will do better
- A clear message that you want them to do better and you believe they can
- Telling them that they matter. Their behaviour matters. You want them back in the class and doing well.

If you want to have a pleasant pastoral conversation with students, then that can also be useful, but don't pretend that this has been a sanction. If you confuse and conflate the two then you risk losing any deterrent effect, and students won't feel its impact. In fact, you may even encourage the misbehaviour, because students may see your detentions as a way to access your attention and company, instead of being able to obtain it in more positive ways.

Example:

A teacher sets a detention for a student who rarely tries in lessons, and that day spent the whole morning throwing pens at his peers. The teacher wants to get to the bottom of things, so decides to use the time in detention to chat to the student about what's going on at home. But there is another student in detention at the same time, and in the course of the conversation, he also gets involved in the discussion. The students are calm and cooperative, and the teacher spends ten minutes chatting to them about television. Things are going so pleasantly that the teacher says, 'Look lads, do you want to get off early? Let's not see any silliness again.' The next day, the behaviour is repeated. The teacher, now cross, shouts at the student, 'What did we talk about?' And the student replies, 'Television!'

Example:

Same student and reason. This time the teacher insists that the detention is sat in silence, as the student writes out a few paragraphs describing what went wrong that day. At the end of the detention, the teacher sits next to the student and asks, 'OK, what went wrong today?' The conversation is shorter, and both parties leave having agreed what to do next.

In fact, some say this is a good sign – they want to connect with you – but do not reward misbehaviour by simply having a friendly chat with them. Instead, let them know that your time and focus are available to those who try to do their best, or those in need. You can still have civil conversations with all students – I would recommend it – but don't make that conditional on misbehaviour.

When students are in trouble, they need to feel like they have done something wrong. They need to be given a sense of how to improve and be forgiven, but they first need that sense of gravity. Otherwise, why not misbehave, if they just jump straight from misbehaviour to forgiveness?

The detention should *feel* serious. It should, for example, be completely quiet, or especially quiet. Much clearer guidelines of what they can and cannot do in detention should be conveyed. Clarity of expectation is important.

One of the hardest things for the teacher is to maintain their standards in these environments. It is so easy to loosen up and pal around in detention time,

Example:

'I can see you had a tough day meeting the standards today. Tell me in your own words what happened, and what didn't go as well as it should.'

'OK, thank you for putting that so maturely. When you speak like this I know we can get past this. I want you in that lesson doing as well as I know you can. I think you're right. I think that [student summary] did happen. Did you see how that affected [classmate]? It made it harder for him to finish. Did you mean that? No. Do you think you did as much as you could have? No, you're right. Tell me, do you find this work easy or hard? Some of it easy, some of it hard. OK, what bits are hard? What do you think we could do to fix that?'

'Do you see why I can't have you doing that in our lesson? Do you understand the systems I have to follow? I need everyone to be safe and learning. I can't do that if people do [X]. So what do we need to do next time…?' etc.

CHAPTER 12
REWARDS

Along with sanctions, rewards remain one of the most popular default strategies for behaviour management you'll find in education.

Rewards can be a very useful motivator, and they should be a part of every teacher's everyday toolkit. As with sanctions, the problem doesn't lie in using them per se, but in *how* to use them and *when* and *why*. Used properly, rewards can help to encourage better habits. It is possible to use rewards badly, use them well, and even indifferently, with no impact. We'll now consider some of the factors that make them more or less useful in the classroom.

It's easy to see why people like to use them. Rewards are one of the most convivial parts of managing the behaviour of a class. Sanctions often go against our instincts, unless we are one of those unhappy souls who takes pleasure in another's distress. But rewarding students? That feels entirely pain free. It feels nice to be nice. It feels like students are getting what they deserve, and that life, for once, is fair, or kind. It is also, to be honest, delightful to see the response, or their parents' response.

But sadly, we cannot reward students endlessly into good behaviour, in exactly the same way we cannot punish a child into being good.

The many forms of reward
A reward is a benefit given to a student in return for some action they have carried out. It's similar to (but not quite the same as) a payment. We give a reward for four main reasons:

- To change a student's behaviour
- To motivate other students to change their behaviour
- As a teaching strategy
- Because they deserve recognition

Rewards always have a social context in the classroom. They never occur in a vacuum. When you reward a student for something, you do so in a community. What is rewarded gets *noticed*. In the simple behaviourist model, you are seeking to reinforce the behaviour by attaching a positive or desirable consequence to the action. Parents and teachers alike are familiar with the ancient tactic of bribing children to behave. If a child is dragging their feet getting ready for a car journey, promising them a favourite snack once on board can work wonders for little minds. But there are pitfalls as well as advantages to this strategy.

The reward transaction

The behavioural calculus is pretty simple: *If I do X (which I'm not keen on) then I will achieve Y (which I am very keen on). Therefore, to achieve Y I will perform X.*

This form of transactional strategy of behaviour can work for teachers, but only up to a point. Much like sanctions, the following factors need to be taken into account:

- Students are more motivated by rewards as incentives when they are capable of understanding that the reward is connected to the behaviour. This means that students tend to be more motivated by rewards when they are calm, rational agents who possess the imagination to conceive of a possible future where the reward occurs.
- Students also need to be capable of self-regulation, at least enough to control their immediate desires in order to achieve some greater goal. This means that they can't be too impulsive, or impulse driven.
- Rewards, like sanctions, affect some people more than others. They act as an incentive to more behaviourally able, ambitious children with the imagination to connect present actions with future gain. In other words, often the already fairly well-behaved child. This shouldn't be surprising, because these children have already bought into the behaviour system. But it is important (and frustrating) to realise that if we are not careful, rewards frequently target children who, by most accounts, need the least incentivising. Still, we are where we are.
- Children with the least ability to connect present and future actions or to self-regulate (often the least well behaved) are the least likely to be motivated by rewards that require them to do so. Many children look at our carefully designed, year-long incentive schemes and just think, 'Nope. I'll never manage that.' Which means that they won't be influenced much by them.
- Well-behaved children are frequently not motivated so much by extrinsic rewards (e.g. a prize) as by intrinsic ones (e.g. they enjoy the subject, they like being well behaved etc.). So even with these children,

we might find that simple token-based rewards don't have as much impact as we would like.

But this doesn't mean we should abandon rewards, even long-term ones. Already well-behaved children deserve recognition too, and rewarding them acknowledges their effort and character, while holding it up as a role model to others. Also, rewards do have some effect on other children, just not as much. They still have an impact.

All children deserve recognition of their achievements. This is true no matter what their circumstances, but for some children (especially those from less advantaged circumstances), it is even more important. Excellence should be rewarded because it deserves to be rewarded and celebrated. Plus, the community sees what behaviour is celebrated, and therefore desired. This helps to normalise the expectations, exemplify them in concrete, and draw a picture for other children to aspire to. Plus, they deserve it.

Problems with rewards

Traditionally a reward is used to incentivise behaviour. But this can lead to several problems.

1. We condition children to expect a reward for doing what should be normal

If we give out rewards in order to modify behaviour, then (if we are consistent) we end up rewarding the same behaviour repeatedly. This is fine…until we reach the stage where the student starts to expect the reward every time they behave – and why shouldn't they? If we have clearly explained our reward system, they will understandably believe us. But this can lead to children behaving *only* for the reward, and not because they believe it is the right thing to do, or that they should just do it for its own sake. Worse, it can lead to behavioural slip-back if the rewards are removed, and the student then feels disincentivised to repeat the action. 'Hey, where's my lollipop?'

One way we can resolve this is by making sure we don't constantly reinforce every behaviour with a reward (*continuous reinforcement*). Students can become desensitised to the effect of a reward – it just becomes normal for them. Like a child with too many birthday presents, they stop valuing the gifts because there are so many. They become desensitised to the stimulus.

We can avoid this to some extent by making use of *intermittent reinforcement,*[1] i.e. rewarding less frequently and more inconsistently. For example, rather than constantly giving children a merit for performing some simple act of kindness, you could reward them for kindness one week, then good spelling the next, then punctuality the next. Research suggests that intermittent rewards are far more effective as a reinforcement than continuous reinforcements. Keep them on their toes, and students will often try harder.

2. Some children are disproportionately rewarded

Whose behaviour do we seek to modify the most? Poorly behaved children's. So, who often ends up receiving the most rewards/merit points? The poorly behaved child. Which leads us to the odd situation in some schools where the best-behaved children have no reward points, and the worst-behaved children are sitting on a tower of them.

I've seen schools where coaches have been hired for students as a reward trip to some theme park, and every seat is occupied by a little rascal/pirate, and all the well-behaved children left behind are gazing at them through the window and thinking, 'Who do I have to punch to get on that?'

Beware of what you incentivise. Beware of the behaviour you normalise without meaning to. It's important to note children's sense of fairness. People prefer fair inequality over unfair equality – inequality should be meritocratic. This means that children are fairly happy to see someone get a reward (but not them) if they think the person deserved it, e.g. for being the fastest in a race. But they are less happy when 'everyone wins a prize for turning up' because it doesn't seem fair. We are happy to share windfalls equally (like someone bringing in an enormous birthday cake to the classroom), but resent equal sharing of anything that requires effort.[2]

3. Reward value is contextual

Rewards are worth different things to different people. Just as a £100 fine provides a very different deterrent to a billionaire as opposed to a poor man, a £100 reward also generates different levels of incentive for different people. The promise of £100 probably wouldn't tempt Bill Gates to your table, but many millions of people around the world do much more for much less. Naomi Campbell allegedly said, 'I don't get out of bed for less than ten grand,' and who are we to argue? I knew a man

1. Miltenberger, R. G. (2008) *Behavioural Modification: Principles and Procedures.* Belmont, CA: Thompson Wadsworth.

2. www.go.nature.com/2Dw6kNa

who was mugged and flung into a skip for the £20 in his pocket. That great reward you think everyone will work hard for – say, a book token – will disproportionately incentivise bookworms or students looking for birthday presents for their family, more than a student who cannot read, or has no interest in doing so.

Success reinforces motivation

Success is addictive. Doing well at a subject in school can be extremely rewarding, and that sensation of reward can be highly motivating. For many teachers it is the Holy Grail of motivation: to see students trying hard and behaving well and achieving because they appreciate the value of that achievement. In fact, if a student is highly capable at something, then there is evidence to suggest that an extrinsic reward might actually be *demotivating* for them. This might be because they are already motivated by the intrinsic pleasure and fulfilment of mastery and competence, and anything external to that could detract from that pleasure. But:

> On the other hand, we're not intrinsically motivated to do everything. … Learning a musical instrument is a classic example, particularly when you're just starting out. You're just playing scales and it can seem extraordinarily dull … and lots of people give up. … And here, perhaps, extrinsic motivation can play a part. … That bump in the road, that effort gradient beyond which you actually start seeing the benefits of your labour, feeling a sense of success and becoming intrinsically motivated is where a bit of extrinsic motivation can help.[3]

You may need to use extrinsic motivation (treats, sanctions) in order to build up intrinsic motivation (I do this because I want to). One can help build the other.

Also, people often talk about the 'carrot and stick' approach to motivation. But if you are dangling a carrot for students, remember that the rabbits will try harder to get it than the polar bears.[4]

How often should I reward students?

Skinner's research into rewards suggested that when students receive the same reward for the same action, the incentive drops off very quickly. If you give the same prize every time for a correct answer, it soon stops having a motivational

---

3. Nick Rose quoted in Hendrick, C. and Macpherson, R. (2017) *What does this look like in the classroom?* Woodbridge: John Catt Educational.

4. Also: keep a bucket of raw meat.

effect on the student. They get used to it. It loses its value to them. It can even disincentivise them against repeating the action! But Skinner discovered something else that was more surprising: students are more motivated by rewards when they are more inconsistent. When you don't know exactly when the reward will be, you try harder. This is akin to the slot machine/one-armed-bandit effect; the gambler persists even more in the game, because success could come at any moment. The uncertainty increases the anticipation.

A similar effect can be found in channel surfing or scrolling through the internet. Intermittent reward creates a greater incentive to repeat the behaviour – as anyone who has stayed up on Facebook or Twitter long after they stopped enjoying it can testify. You never know when someone will say something nice about you, and you never know when you'll come across something you love.

What are the most common ways of rewarding students?

Privileges: Allowing students to do things that others cannot. These could be: jumping to the front of a queue at lunch; being given first choice of reading book; being allowed to present a report to the class; entry to a common room reserved for the scrupulously behaved.

Material goods: Prizes, lunch with the headteacher,[5] book tokens.

Status symbols: Smiley faces on the board, phone calls home, public praise, student of the week, head of the table, class monitor, school prefect, name on the board etc.

These things can have some use as short-term modifiers of behaviour, and if used judiciously they can have an effect on some students some of the time. But research suggests that offering tangible rewards (e.g. money or marshmallows) dependent on task behaviour has a negative effect on previously high motivation, especially for younger students. In other words, if a student was already motivated to behave the right way, then offering them a physical reward can actually damage their motivation to repeat the behaviour. They have become used to the treat. So beware of using this option frequently.

But the best extrinsic reward is…

---

5. A dream for some, a nightmare for others.

Praise

Praising the student is one of the most common and best ways to reward a student. For it to be as effective as possible it must be:

- Sincere. Students can spot BS[6] and insincerity from space. Students need to believe you, and in the absence of terrific acting skills, it's useful if you believe it too. Which means it's best if it's honest and deserved.
- Proportionate. Gushing praise is cheap. If you flood a market with a commodity, the value of that commodity drops, and so too in the classroom. Praise too easily dispensed, or dispensed in unrealistic levels, loses value quickly. If everything a student does is 'amazing' and 'fantastic' and 'out of this world' then where does that leave genuine exceptionality? Praise is not an arms race. Not everything is perfect. 'Good' is fine.
- Targeted. 'Good' is fine, but 'Good because X…' is better. Praising a student for some specific action or outcome that is clearly defined has much more impact on their future behaviour, and is taken on board far more easily. Don't say 'This painting is amazing!' Say, 'This painting is really good because you remembered to use perspective this time, and the dark tones help the background recede.'

These three principles help praise to be as effective as possible and to avoid the most common errors. Praise is free, and praise gets right to the heart of what most people want: to be recognised, to be valued, to be noticed, to feel that we matter to others. These kinds of 'goods' matter most to most of us.

Example:

A student always turns up to your lessons with a creased shirt, a dirty collar, no equipment, smelling of cigarettes. For whatever reason, one day they turn up in a clean shirt and pens in their pockets.

A good example of praise might be to walk up to that student (in a moment when no one else can hear), and say, 'Your uniform looks great today, I appreciate that.' It may not have been their efforts, but maybe – maybe – that student will feel three inches taller because they were noticed; they mattered. Someone saw who they were and it mattered.

---

6. ButterScotch

But that praise might seem low value to the student who turns up every day in a clean uniform, equipment ready. So tailor the praise to the student and their circumstances.

Once every six months, say, ask **that** student (and a few of their peers) to remain behind at break. Tell them that their uniform is always great, their punctuality is perfect, and their effort in class is exemplary. As a result, you'll be sending a praise postcard home to their parents/guardians to say so; thank you. They mattered too.

Praise like this is very powerful – especially for children who do not receive much praise. It is very easy to over-praise the extremely capable for being continuously excellent, and equally there is a danger that we only focus on the very poorly behaved or least able. There is a large bubble of children in the middle who also need sincere, targeted, proportionate praise, so make a conscious effort to find the best in them.

'Catch them being good' is a common aphorism in education, and it is sensible in many ways. But catching them being good also requires judgement. Crucially, to make this kind of praise as effective as possible, it requires that one knows the students – their capacities, their circumstances, their journey – and the more you know the better the praise can be.

How frequently should I praise?

There are no easy answers to this, but there are good principles to guide us:

- When someone has acted in a way you want them to repeat
- When someone has done something you want normalised
- When someone has acted in an exemplary way that you want others to aspire to
- When someone who normally struggles does something exceptionally good *for* them
- When someone who normally behaves well does something extraordinary (like a great act of kindness)
- When someone looks like they need a pick-up, or seems daunted or anxious

None of these principles are the law. Praise can be dangerous too: it can normalise mediocrity if you keep praising actions that are easy to perform. It can, like any currency, be devalued by giving too much of it away. It can also be devalued by using praise of excessive heights.

Deliver your parcel in one piece

In this context, the parcel is the message you actually want to communicate. You can deliver it in one piece, achieving the aim you want, or you can drop the parcel and break what's inside. Praise can be undercut by tone, by body language, by sarcasm. A good way to get better at using praise is to remember that we rarely hear praise in our daily lives, and children are normally quite insecure about their performance, so issue it confidently. The beauty of it is that you don't need to pretend to be someone you aren't. You can praise in many different ways or styles. If you are smiley and warm, praise in that manner. If you are curt and serious, praise in a curt and serious way. The key thing is to be you, or at least a professional version of you. You on a good day, perhaps.

Example:

> I cannot forget old Mr Monaghan who taught me history. He was as serious as a stick and smiled as infrequently as an eclipse. But when he passed your book back to you, paused and said, 'That was a good answer you wrote about the Rosetta Stone,' he couldn't have spoken with more impact had golden confetti rained down and ticker tape billowed from the windows as he said it. Thirty years later, I still remember this.

Which consequence do I use?

We have now looked at several categories of sanction, and several of reward. We have considered other options such as clarification, teaching, or support. Teachers often tie themselves in knots wondering how to respond to misbehaviour. But there are a few principles that can make it a lot easier.

- Be as *consistent* as humanly possible. If there is a whole-school behaviour policy (and there should be), then stick to that like glue. Use the ladders and advice and consequences it dictates. Remember that norms and habits and routines are built on consistency. The more the better. If your school recommends using warnings, moving seats, setting sanctions etc., then do so. Teach the students that your rules are sincere and will actually happen.
- Have *exceptions* when you need to, but make sure they are *exceptional*, logical and transparent.

- Use a *combination* of any responses when you need to. You are not bound to only one. This fact is liberating, and much overlooked. Teachers should not try to respond to all behaviour with the same tools, as if all behaviour had some kind of easy fix. Don't use only sanctions, or only rewards, or only norms or only restorative conversations.

Imagine this scenario: a student is staring out of a window when they should be writing up an experiment. The teacher asks them to get started, but the student tells them to, 'Get stuffed.'[7] Unbeknownst to the teacher, the student didn't understand the objective, or what to do. How should the teacher respond?

Example 1:

The response could be a combination of sanction (to demonstrate boundaries) and an attempt to discover what the student doesn't know yet about the science in order to re-enter the curriculum. The latter is more time consuming, but in reality, if this is not done, the student is unlikely to go home and bring themselves up to speed.

If this is to be dealt with properly, a more complex response is required. Note: the sanction is still an essential part of the response; it is not a minor part of it. Do not mistake complexity for over-tolerance of unacceptable behaviour.

- The sanction: to reinforce boundaries, to express disapproval, to attempt to discourage repetition of the behaviour
- The investigation: to reduce the desire to misbehave in the future by building alternatives for them

Example 2:

Or the response should simply be a sanction, because (after all) the student should have been paying attention to the instructions in the first place, and no amount of confusion justifies being rude to someone. After the sanction, there should still be a conversation to unpick what they did wrong, what they should do next, and how they can choose the right behaviour next time.

---

7. Or words to that effect.

CONSISTENCY IS THE FOUNDATION OF ALL HABITS

Practice makes perfect. Perfect practice is better. Habits only last as long they are performed. As soon as we stop practising, we start to lose that habit.

CHAPTER 13
PARENTS

Parents are, for most children, the biggest influence on their upbringing. Most students still spend the majority of their non-school time in the parental home, under their roof, under their rules and norms. In other words, parents are potentially one of your biggest allies. Of course, when things do not go well, parents can also present enormous obstacles to the student's education. Especially if the parent has a toxic view of education.

Often, with the most challenging students, we find challenging circumstances in their backgrounds and home circumstances. Children do not create themselves. They are the products of their contexts. Some children are fortunate to have loving parents who carefully and patiently equip them with powerful, positive habits and social skills, learning skills, social and cultural capital. Some are less fortunate, and some experience both sides of the coin.

The vast majority of parents know and love their children far more than we ever will. This is self-evident, given the difference in scale between the time we spend with them and the positions we occupy. Most parents are motivated by the intrinsic love and desire to see their children safe and happy and thriving. I take that as axiomatic, and understanding that is key to working successfully with parents. It is shockingly easy to see parents as obstacles to 'what we want to do with the student'. They deserve as much support and respect as we can manage.[1]

But there is a percentage of parents who love and want to support their children and do so in a toxic or dysfunctional way: the parent who refuses to support the school against their child because they see it as a way to show familial loyalty; the parent who thinks the teachers are pushing their child too hard by asking them to redraft work; the parent who doesn't want their child to learn about

---

1. A relationship that goes both ways, of course. Teachers should set dignified boundaries and parameters of common expectations with parents, preferably from the start of the relationship.

'other cultures';[2] the parent who refuses to let their child go on a school trip; the parent who doesn't agree with *some* school rules so tells the student not to bother with them.

There is a long list of ways in which parents can love their children, but still hurt them by helping them to make bad choices. Some parents have had bad experiences of school themselves. They may have a deep mistrust of institutional authority. They may even have a good reason for this. Some parents have a deep-seated disdain for education in principle: perhaps they had a bad experience as a student; perhaps they come from a family culture where employment focused on careers that don't require schooling, for example casual unskilled labour, the service industry and so on.[3]

There is also a smaller cohort of parents who struggle with mental health issues that generate irrational or unreasonable demands towards school, which map unhappily onto their children's experiences throughout education.

And finally there is the smallest cohort of parents: those who are toxic on other levels; those who commit emotional or physical abuse on the ones they should hold the dearest, perpetrators of neglect and abandonment and other tragedies.

But most parents, the majority, care far more deeply about their child then you ever will. All of our communication must be framed respecting that relationship between children and their parents. Anyone reading this who has children will intuitively grasp how dear their offspring are to them, and most people who do not can appreciate this too. The teacher must not, at any cost, convey to the parent that they have any personal dislike of the student. That is one reason why smalltalk or saying something positive to begin with can help so much.

Build bridges before you need to cross the river

One of the biggest mistakes we can make is to treat the parent as a problem. It may be that they turn out to be challenging, but it's unreasonable to begin from that assumption. Too many teachers only speak to parents when they need to report misbehaviour, which can lead to a narrative that parents are only people

---

2. I heard that a lot. Of course, I ignored it, given that my job was to teach an objective understanding of comparative religions and philosophies. I wonder if maths teachers ever got, 'I don't want my kid learning those weird Arabic squiggles,' as much.

3. Or robbing. I taught enough kids where the craft seemed to be passed down the generations, like a fob watch or other heirloom.

you speak to when things go wrong. On the other side of this equation, many parents with challenging children feel that the only reason schools want to call them is to nag them about their terrible children. That isn't healthy. How long do you think it takes before even a reasonable and helpful parent starts to first dread, then despise a call from school? We can only endure criticism for so long before we start to blame other people for our ills.

The best thing any teacher can do is to call home *before* you need to. Where possible, proactively call (or email) parents to introduce yourself and simply tell them:

- How much you're looking forward to teaching their child
- What it is you'll be teaching them
- Ask if they have any questions
- Ask if there's anything you need to know

NB I say 'where possible'. If you teach primary, or small classes in other settings, it might be possible to make a quick introduction to every parent. But if you have multiple large classes, this is impossible. In which case, make the phone calls you *need* to: target the parents of children that you know you might need to talk to at some point.

Use these conversations as a teaching vehicle to help the parents understand what is expected of them too. Many parents, perfectly well intentioned, will support their child against the school in every circumstance. It is important that parents appreciate the kind of message this sends to children about how to behave at school.

This is important because it builds relationships. You're going to need it with some families more than others. And what better way than a neutral, friendly introduction, a handshake to set the tone of how things will proceed. It's a great chance to quickly outline some of the class norms, equipment rules, etc., and offer support if they need it. Many parents will have questions they didn't want to bother anyone with. Some will be mistrustful – 'Why are you calling me?' but most will be pleasantly surprised.

The alternative is speaking to a parent for the first time when the child has gotten in trouble, and it's easy in that circumstance for the parent to feel defensive. Who wouldn't? They love their child. Now a stranger phones them out of the blue to tell them their child is trouble. For some, the implication is unavoidable: 'What are you going to do about it? This is your fault. You're a terrible parent.' No wonder so many parents get defensive, especially if they are already under stress, working two jobs, staring at rent demands etc.

And when you do speak to parents, try not to go cold straight into a behaviour conversation. Use small talk of any kind to begin with, or have a brief conversation about progress, then segue into behaviour. Frame the conversation neutrally, because any behaviour conversation has the capacity to get heated quickly.

Ask for their help

Another big mistake many teachers make when speaking to parents is to make them feel that *they* are in fact in trouble, not the child. This is a great way to make an adult with unhappy memories of school feel like garbage all over again. Remember these people are potentially your greatest allies, so cultivate their alliance. It's no good just assuming all parents will be supportive. Most may be, but their idea of support may be very different to yours.

Scripting a phone call home

Given that a phone call home for misbehaviour can be such a minefield, it's worth thinking about how best to make one. I've seen some dreadful calls that go a bit like this:

> 'Hi, is that Mrs Ryan? This is Mr Bennett. Your son was disgusting in lessons today, and I want to know what you're going to do about it.'

You can almost hear the embarrassment and anger coming over the phone from afar. This is how you antagonise and alienate people – people you will need. Far better to try a script a bit more like this:

> 'Hi, is that Mrs Ryan? It's Mr Bennett from school. Ryan's fine. I just wondered if this is an OK time to chat about how he was today? Thanks.'

A polite introduction. And an acknowledgement that her time is valuable. Plus an essential reassurance that the child hasn't been hit by a bus or something. If you're a parent and a school calls home, it's easy to think the worst. Then carry on...

Value mapping – build an emotional bank account with parents

> 'Ryan's done some great work in my lessons. Did you see the homework he made last week on [fill in the blank]? He can behave really well when he wants to.'

This is preamble, but it plugs into a simple truth – the parent sees the best side of their child. They love their child. You need to acknowledge that the child is valuable to them. You've value-mapped with the parent – shown that you share values – which is a useful technique if you want to try to gain agreement from someone. It's a way of saying to someone, 'I'm like you. I'm on your team.'

We don't just think rationally; we think emotionally too. We filter and interpret and decide subconsciously what and who we're going to listen to, and who we're going to trust. Showing someone you care about the same things is a great way to get on the same page and encourage agreement. Then you carry on:

'I'm afraid Ryan's let himself down a bit today.'

'Let himself down.' It implies this incident is not normal, which implies that normally he behaves well. Expressing regret at this point echoes the regret the parent is probably feeling. You're not angry; you're just disappointed. You're on the same page as the parent. Which is a great time to use…

The Benjamin Franklin effect

'And I need your help getting him back on track. Have you got five minutes to talk about that?'

And that's where you want to land. *I need your help.* People are far more likely to support you if you ask them to help you. This is sometimes called the Benjamin Franklin effect.[4] People are far more likely to help you if they have done you a favour, or think they are. It's thought to be an example of how we deal with *cognitive dissonance.* If we think we dislike someone, but we've done them a favour, it feels weird: why would we do a favour for someone we don't like? So we reconcile this conflict by changing how we feel about that person. Maybe we *do* like them a bit.

---

4. So named due to Franklin's observation in his autobiography where he said, 'He that has once done you a kindness will be more ready to do you another, than he whom you yourself have obliged.' Franklin famously made an alliance of a rival legislator by asking to borrow one of his books and thanking him profusely for doing so. 'We became friends, and our friendship continued to his death.' Franklin, B. (1928) *The Autobiography of Benjamin Franklin*, p48. Boston: Houghton Mifflin Company. This also has a darker side. There is a phenomenon where some soldiers develop a hatred of those they are ordered to kill. The cognitive dissonance this provokes is resolved in a less happy way: they dehumanise their opponents, to rationalise that their deaths were justified.

It's a subtle way of getting people on board with your directions. People are far more likely to offer help if asked for it. It's harder to resist (although not impossible, of course) when someone reaches out so obviously. It's like when someone puts a hand out to shake yours, and the cue is irresistible. Or when someone starts to clap next to you. The unconscious instinct kicks in, and the norm takes over.

You need their help with Ryan. That alone is a powerful cue. Then in the same sentence, another power move: *I want to get him back on track.* What parent doesn't want this? Some maybe, but most do. And finally, *have you got five minutes?* Their time matters, which means they matter. And what parent would say 'No I have no time to talk to you about helping my son'? Of course, some *will* say exactly this. But most won't.

In that simple exchange, you've gone a hundred miles further with this approach than the blistering, blunt, reprimand delivered in the first. I have never heard a parent reject the second approach. This is the script I used to use. You will use your own, but try to include the following beats:

- You matter.
- Your child matters.
- Their learning matters.
- Their behaviour matters.
- I care about all of these.
- I need your help to help them.
- Let's make things better together.

Calling home is no time to get your own back, take out your anger, or tear a strip off someone for being a bad parent. You might feel entitled to all of that, but that's not what this conversation is for.

And if you've started with a pre-emptive phone call *before* you needed to call in the first place, then you have credit in the Bank of Relationships with the parent, and you can draw from it. If you go in cold to a conversation like that, you have to be nimble. But if you've already created a narrative where you are a supportive and professional adult interested in the student's well-being, then you are light years ahead, and success is far more likely.

Of course, when you ask parents for help, some will confess that they need your help. My advice is to give what you can. Some parents are desperate for some kind of counsel. Many have very little by way of a support network to fall back on. You can make an ally of one another in this process. I once had a conversation with a single parent who was struggling, and I suggested that she should take away her son's Xbox for a while so that he had an added incentive to work: to get back his console. 'Oh I can't do that, he'd be lost,' she said. I assured her that she could, and she did. Sometimes people just need a nudge.

One final point: voicemail. It seems to me that a disproportionate number of parents of challenging children have phones that go straight to voicemail. Few things are as excruciating as the clumsily phrased voicemail about misbehaviour. Some teachers leave five-minute epics. No one likes to listen to long voicemails. Have a short script ready of what you will say if you have to leave a message. And make sure that the core message is simply the need to get in touch with the parent and could they call back/you will call them at a set time.

Communicating effectively with parents

Develop a script that is positive and professional. Practise it with your mentor or coach or sympathetic partner. Parents have lots of expectations of teachers and these expectations vary enormously. Some parents view teachers as their soul mates and natural allies, and culturally segue into easy alliances. This is ideal – parents and teachers should have one huge thing in common – the interest and well-being of students.

For some it is not – on both sides – and we can only regret that. Some parents see teachers as obstacles to their children's happiness. Some parents see them as their intellectual or moral inferiors. Some see them as tradespeople, hired to do a job and provide a service. Some are suspicious of them. Some are threatened by them. Some are openly hostile to them. You represent the state, institutional authority, a threat to their children, a past in which they failed or flourished. You are not just *you*. By assuming the mantle of teacher, you assume the cultural baggage and ornamentation that those robes confer. The privilege is also a burden, as all privileges should be.

So your ongoing communication with parents should aim to continually disarm their anxieties and build rapport. Be friendly and personable, but be professional, cautious, courteous, careful in what you say (and especially what you promise). Let them know that you:

- Care about their child's safety
- Care about their child's education

- Love your role and subject
- Believe their child can succeed
- Expect their child to do well
- Are prepared to work hard to make that happen
- Need them to understand that their child will flourish if they follow the norms and routines
- Are there for their queries if they have any

Volunteer information before it is asked. Be proactive with home communication. This is where emails can become very useful. Don't make them chase you for it.[5] If you supply them with what they need to know before they need to know it, they're far less likely to be anxious.

Avoid sarcasm unless you have a solid, deep relationship with the parent. See the good in their child and let them know. Ask for their help. Don't treat them like the problem. Most aren't.

Many parents are anxious that they don't know what to do to help their child do well. So tell them. Parents can add rocket fuel to a student's understanding if they themselves understand the work, or at least where the child should be aiming. But understandably, this can cause a great deal of anxiety for non-experts. The medicine for this anxiety is information. Give them syllabuses and take time to talk through what they are expected to achieve week by week. Parents who don't know this kind of information find it easier to give up trying, throw their hands up and admit that they have no clue if their child is doing well or not until you send a report home.

Managing parent behaviour

In many ways, you need to do what you can to manage the routines that the parents have with you, with the school, and with the education of their children. So be clear what you expect from them. Be clear what they can expect from you. Tell them how to get in touch with you. Tell them how they may *not* get in touch with you. Boundaries are as important with parents as they are with anyone else. If you don't set boundaries, they may assume that there are none.

---

5. I am reminded of Chris Rock's sarcastic, satirical advice about the wisdom of running from the police: 'If the police have to come and get you, they're bringing an ass-kicking with them.' Rock, C. (2000) 'How not to get your ass kicked by the police', The Chris Rock Show.

Never say, 'Call me anytime.' They will. Never give your personal mobile or similar, unless there is a pressing or urgent reason to do so (e.g. a school trip where the school mobile has been dropped down a drain). Manage the accessibility of your social media portals. Children and parents *will* search for you online, so be in control of what they find.

And finally, try not to bring your emotions to any conversation. Strong feelings easily become your master, tricking you into thinking the wrong words are the right ones to say. Good sentences are written with words, not feelings.[6] You need to know what you want to say to them before you have to say it. Things said in anger are frequently hasty, righteous and aggressive. So too are things said in desperation or frustration. Take time between feeling a spike in your emotions and speaking to parents. Script what you have to say. Give yourself time to breathe. The quality of your communication will rise as your blood cools.

---

6. The poet Mallarmé listened to the painter Degas complaining about his inability to write poems even though 'he was full of ideas'. 'My dear Degas,' Mallarmé responded, 'poems are not made out of ideas. They're made out of words.' God knows how Degas ever painted anything with that attitude.

CHAPTER 14
INTERPERSONAL SKILLS

We are all familiar with people who are persuasive, or great leaders; people for whom we would go an extra mile, every time; people who can convince us to do things we're reluctant to do. If a teacher has any of these skills in their repertoire, they can be great at running rooms. They might only rarely have to touch the formal school system. We all know teachers who just seem to have 'it'. You wish you ran classes like them. You wish you had relationships with your class like them. These are the people who make some people say 'behaviour management is all about relationships'.

Is behaviour management all about relationships?
No. And yes.

Firstly, in excellent classroom cultures, we usually see excellent relationships between students and staff. But that doesn't mean we aim *straight* for building a great relationship. We need to understand how these relationships are achieved. When you focus on trying to build them, but you don't have a clear idea how to do it, you can make a lot of mistakes.

Secondly, even though this is true, in large communities, even classes, we cannot rely on behaviour to be entirely based on individual relationships between a single member of staff and each and every student. Otherwise what happens when students take a dislike to a teacher (as frequently happens, even to blameless members of staff)? If a supply teacher comes to school, are students excused from trying hard or allowed to be rude because there is 'no relationship'? No. Behaviour management is about relationships *and* adherence to systems. To put it another way, the student must be taught to have a relationship with not only their teacher but also the whole school community and the institution itself.

One way I can tell a school has taught students to comply with and value the school culture is by watching a cover lesson. If I can't tell from behaviour alone if it's a cover lesson, then I know the students behave because they know that is how they should behave in school, and the school has made its culture clear. If the behaviour is weak, then I know it's because they only behave for *this* teacher or *that one*.

Good relationships with your students help with behaviour immensely. But you must also teach children that they need to behave no matter what. Teach them to be responsible for their own behaviour instead of outsourcing it to others. Or to put it another way, students need to learn to have a relationship with the school community, not just with you.

The first thing to be aware of is that relationships are built on trust. People need to trust you – to trust that you are consistent, that you are who you say you are, that you mean what you say, that you will be there for them, that you are a reliable adult.

The second thing to be aware of is that trust is built on structure, predictability, reliability, dependability. In other words, it is built on routines and consistency.

This leads us to a conclusion that surprises many:

> *Good relationships are built on norms, routines, and predictable consequences. Routines make relationships possible.*

We'll explore this later, but for now understand that everything this book has explored so far has been done with the aim of building up relationships. But not in a woolly or confused way; with a clear purpose and understanding that relationships are not magic or based on 'like at first sight' or 'getting' the kids. They are based on being the kind of person with whom it is possible to have a relationship.

Be wary of trying to simply observe competent teachers and copying exactly what they do without understanding this. Some schools will ask new teachers to do this. Worse, they might encourage them to rely solely on interpersonal techniques and relationships to manage classrooms because 'Look at Ms Smith – she doesn't need to use sanctions.' Worst of all is when a school punishes a teacher for using the behaviour system!

Two problems

First of all, successful teachers you observe probably had to build up these relationships over a long period by *using the formal systems*: by using norms and routines, and teaching them patiently, and setting sanctions, and calling home and having a thousand pastoral conversations. You cannot judge a person's technique simply by watching them in the moment, if they have taught the class for some time. Much of what they have done to build these great relationships has been done in the past. All you are seeing is the fruit of their labour. So don't judge yourself against this, or simply try to copy it.

In 1877, the painter James McNeill Whistler exhibited some paintings at the Grosvenor Gallery in London, including *Nocturne in Black and Gold*. However, the art critic John Ruskin derided it as slapdash, and undeserving of the high price it asked: 'I have seen and heard much of cockney impudence before now, but never expected to hear a coxcomb ask two hundred guineas for flinging a pot of paint in the public's face.'

Whistler was incensed, considered this libellous, and took Ruskin to court. Giving evidence, he rejected the claim that it wasn't worth the asking price because it took so little time to paint (two days). He said: 'I am not asking this high price for a brief amount of work. I ask it for the knowledge gained during the efforts of a lifetime.'[1]

In other words, what you saw on the canvas – a few ounces of oil, a few hours of work – wasn't the source of the value; it was the artistic sensibility and skill developed over a lifetime that was demonstrated by the object. Whistler won his case.[2]

A high-functioning teacher running the room efficiently is like an iceberg, or Whistler's *Nocturne*; what you see happening in front of you is a fraction of what it appears to be.

The second problem is that many schools expect teachers to be able to manage behaviour using *only* interpersonal skills. But that way, madness lies, because this often results in schools expecting teachers to be able to do it *without having been trained to do so and without formal systems to fall back on*. It's almost as if they've said, 'Climb this mountain but don't use your feet. Or hands.' Then they come back five minutes later and say, 'Why didn't you do it?'

---

1. The Annual Register: A Review of Public Events at Home and Abroad for the Year 1878, Part II, Remarkable Trials: Whistler v. Ruskin, p215-217. London: Rivingtons.

2. A somewhat Pyrrhic victory though. The court only awarded him one farthing in damages, and he wasn't allowed to recover his costs. Still, he had a 200-guinea handkerchief to dry his tears.

Interpersonal skills are subtle, and not everyone develops them easily. Some aspects can be taught. If you're careful, you can observe them in others, but the catch-22 is that you often have to know what it is you are observing in order to discern it. Otherwise you spot some trivial, eye-catching trick or technique and think, 'That's great, I'll do that too.'

Example:

> A new teacher from secondary school, struggling with behaviour, is sent on a terrible training course. There they are shown endless videos of preschool teachers greeting their classes with fist bumps, masonic handshakes, and elaborately choreographed high fives. 'Oh boy,' they think, 'that looks easy – and fun!' They try to transplant the technique into the entry routine of their challenging year 11s. Unfortunately it goes down like a sandbag dropped from the rigging of a ship. The class refuse to do it and openly mock the teacher, who wonders where it all went wrong.

Example:

> When I was a new teacher, I struggled with behaviour. Because of this, I asked my mentor what I should do with a ferociously horrible year 10 class. 'Have you tried putting the worst behaver in charge of the lesson?' they said. 'It might teach her empathy.' I had not thought of this, mainly because it sounded a terrible idea. But I was desperate enough to give it a go. It was, of course, a disaster. She spent the next 40 minutes doing an impression of me and pretending to be a teacher. A boy at the back of the room said, 'Sir, what are you doing?' 'I have no idea,' I replied. When I spoke to my mentor later, he asked me how it went. I replied, 'Not well, to be honest. Did it work when you did it?' 'Oh I've never tried it,' he said. 'I just thought it might help.'

Two schools

Very frequently, you will walk into the classroom of an experienced teacher who has taught a class for some time. The behaviour is excellent, you are told. 'Go and see what she does.' So you go to the lesson, waiting to see the tricks and tips that separate the bad from the good teacher...only to see nothing special at all. The teacher directs students to do things, and they do them. No one objects or fusses much. You leave the lesson thinking, 'Perhaps she's hypnotised them' or 'Kids just behave when she tells them what to do.' Neither is true.

What has happened is that the culture of the classroom has been professionally and thoroughly instilled in the class for years, until they have become habituated into working the way they need to in order to flourish. From the outside, this good behaviour seems easy or inevitable. You can scarcely imagine these children tossing their desks over in a tantrum or telling the teacher to fuck off. The problem is, you cannot see what the teacher has done to build this, because it has been done in the past. You can only witness the present. What you are seeing is *now*, and the hard work has been done *then*.

I call this *two schools syndrome*. Every school has at least two schools within it. The first school is the one that experienced, high-status teachers inhabit. They may have light timetables, lots of formal authority, or easier classes. To them, behaviour seems great, and they go home with a happy whistle. The second school is the one occupied by low-status, full-timetable teachers with the hardest classes and the least authority. To them, the school is a trial. Teachers in the latter category aren't always capable of learning much from teachers in the first.

What teachers should you watch, and when?
Still, watch other teachers closely. Watch teachers who are excellent at their jobs and know how to handle classes, but watch them when they take over a *new* class. This is more interesting; this is when you are more likely to see the nuts and bolts of their formal and interpersonal skills laid bare. September is fertile ground for observing good teachers take over tough classes, and really see what it is they are doing to move the behaviour needle.

The visible and invisible ladders of consequences
One of the most useful techniques I have witnessed in teaching is what I call the *invisible ladder of consequence*. Good teachers use it all the time without even knowing it. It is almost never taught formally, and if every teacher consciously understood its basic structure, we would see the need to set formal sanctions shrink.

What is it? It is the sum total of every little cue – verbal or otherwise – that we give to students to encourage them to behave, short of issuing formal sanctions and rewards. The way we speak to them; when we speak to them; every hand signal, eye contact, and non-verbal communication. It is tone, volume, pitch and pace; it is word choice and connotation and every other subtle syllable and sentence of how we communicate with others.

295

The *visible* (or formal) ladder of consequence is easier to understand: it is usually the beginning and end of some schools' systems: consequences codes, formal warnings, incremental sanctions, reward systems, report cards, points taken on and off the system, smiley faces and sendings-out and exclusions and report cards and parental meetings and everything the school writes down in its behaviour policy.

The invisible ladder of consequence is different. It could also be called the social ladder of consequence. It is a series of nudges and reminders and cues that attempt to herd children into better patterns of behaviour than they currently exhibit, without having to issue anything formally. It could also be called interpersonal skills, or social skills, or influencing skills.

Imagine a teacher confronted with an initially noisy or uncooperative class. So there they stand, like some character in a first-person shooter, looking at their armoury and wondering which weapon to select.[3] Until an action is taken, there are a million things one could choose to do: shout at them, stare at them, beg them, wait for them, start and pretend they're listening. They could even threaten sanctions. But there are options here, without going down that path. Consider two scenarios in order to understand what is possible. In the first, the teacher will lean into warnings, sanctions, and consequences. In the second, they will explore the invisible ladder of consequence.

Scenario one

A teacher walks into a noisy classroom for the first time. The students don't acknowledge his entrance and are engrossed in whooping, capering, bag-flinging and every shade of loafing. Apart from being seated, they're as far from being ready to learn as nature allows.

The teacher looks at the chaos and sighs. He sits at his desk and decides to use the school's formal consequences system to get good behaviour. 'Stop talking!' he shouts, just loud enough to be heard over the cacophony. No one seems to respond. So, in line with the school policy, he does what the handbook tells him. 'Everyone – that's your first warning! Settle down now or I'll see you after school!' He waits a second, but no one responds, so he shouts, 'Second warning! Get to work or you'll get a detention.' A heartbeat passes. 'OK, everyone in this room has a detention with me after school! I warned you!' The class springs to

---

3. The BFG, normally, and the 10K if you can find one.

its feet in a Mexican wave of defence lawyers shouting, 'I object!' They'll see him in court.

Good luck with the rest of that lesson.

Scenario two

Same teacher, same room, same entrance, same initial behaviour. The teacher stands in front of the class and, volume raised just an ounce above the noise, shouts, 'Let's get started please!'

He raises a hand as he does so and purposefully makes eye contact with as many people as possible, holding their gaze for just a second to indicate he's not afraid to do so, but moving on before it becomes a stare.

Now he scrutinises the room a little more closely than before. There was an impact, but it might only be a few kids, easy to miss unless you're looking for it. A few of them will have responded – the three most compliant kids, perhaps, the ones tuned into doing as they're asked, or just the ones who think learning is important. The volume dips, perhaps just a little as he has that group's attention. What happens next is vital. He needs to keep this faint momentum going. They won't focus on him for long.

He praises the compliant loudly and clearly. He name-checks them. 'Thank you, Rebecca; thank you, Reuben. Books open, work's on the board, great start.' So those two are getting attention and praise. The slight decrease in volume allows the teacher to be heard slightly better.

The next most compliant kids hear and see this and figure they may as well join in. There may even have been a few kids who were just so lost in their conversations they barely noticed the teacher. So you get them next. They also get spotted, and praised. 'Thank you, Tanisha, Dami; thank you, Olu. Great start: books are out and open, starting the task from the board, well done.' This adds a few behaviour cues. The teacher doesn't just say, 'Get started.' He says what that means, however obvious it may seem to him. Nothing is too obvious to say when directing behaviour.

a third of the class to get started and get ready.' This indicates that most students are on the right path, and it's now the minority who need to attend to that norm.

He adds a little geographical specificity: 'I'm just waiting for a couple of rows at this side of the class to switch on. Great stuff, Tabitha; thank you, Natasha, Mason, Iqbal.' Then he ramps this up a fraction: 'Just waiting for a few tables in **this** row.' He ramps it up more.

Then he uses geographical proximity to add some urgency, by moving closer to some of the still-noisy hotspots. He taps the table of those who need to get with it, but still makes it sound like he could be talking to anyone. He lets them change their behaviour without losing face.

Next he uses more eye contact, repeats the instructions, repeats the praise.

If you have a very good relationship with some of the students you need to get through to (and I stress a very, very good relationship) and they are simply very distractible, tap their shoulder lightly to give them a symbolic nudge.

He refers to the work on the board, and asks a few rhetorical questions about it. 'I wonder who'll be able to tell me most about what we did last lesson in a few minutes when we're all ready?' He keeps praising the compliant, and drops hints about the lesson content. 'We're going to be looking at some fascinating people from history today; I hope we can get as much time as possible to do so. You're going to love this.'

More invasive: 'I'm just waiting for a few people at these tables. I'm just waiting for a few people at this table.' With eye contact.

Then, after he's used all of his patience-voodoo on the class, the intervention gets sharper and sharper, more and more targeted. Finally, names are mentioned: 'Ryan, Chelsea, I really need you to get started, with books open. Everyone else is doing great, and you can too please.' Full eye contact. Delivered not in a hurried, hectoring way, but in a matter-of-fact way, as pleasant as he feels like. At this point, he's encouraging them to do the right thing. The threat of consequences is in the background, which is where it should be.

Now, if by this point they still aren't going along with what he wants – if he can stand right in front of them, look them in the eye, name them and ask for their cooperation but still receive none – and it's deliberate and conscious, **then** he can move on to the formal ladder of consequences.

> 'Ryan, that's a warning. Please get your book out now and start the work on the board. I don't want to have to speak to you at the end of the day. I want you to work as brilliantly as you did last week.' Notice how direct that is, much more prescriptive, clear and unambiguous: 'Do this.' Note also how it is encouraging, and aspirational: 'I want you to succeed.'

> And if Ryan is still talking or not complying, the teacher then gets on with the formal ladder of consequences: 'Ryan, you've had a warning, and now I need to see you after the lesson. Turn it around now.'

This sounds a little laborious, but the beauty of this approach is that everything I just described could take about 30 seconds, even with a little take-up time for each step. When you watch a teacher do this who is fluent in the language, it's fluid and almost invisible; but the cajoling, the encouraging, the nudging, the threatening, the steel and the love are all there woven throughout the interaction. They need to know you mean business. They need to know you care about them. They need to know that this is a lesson.

This is one of the hardest things to learn to get right. It is a deeply experiential thing to learn. The best thing to do is to watch people who are very good at it, and film them if you can. Also, have yourself filmed, and watch what *you* do very closely. How do you sound? How much time do you give them to comply before you jump on the consequences? It can make you very conscious (in a good way) of things you need to improve.

These are some of the soft skills of behaviour management that teachers are expected to learn, mysteriously, by osmosis. If you hear a line manager saying, 'We need to get your detentions down' or something, you have every right to say, 'Yes I also would like that. I should point out that the school behaviour policy requires me to set them. Can you arrange for me to be trained in de-escalation techniques please?' We can but hope.

But they can be learned. Some people are naturally (or have learned to be) better than others at these types of processes. Some people really struggle. No school should expect all of its teachers to be naturally fantastic at these things and to rely on them solely. That is why we also need good school systems – to provide a scaffold for everyone's classroom culture.

The invisible ladder of consequences summary

1. Most schools have a formal consequence system. Use it.

2. Teachers should be trained to also use the invisible ladder of consequences

- Take up time
- Face saving
- Task correction
- Reinforcing norms
- Tactically ignoring
- Positive language
- Questions and choices
- Tactical pauses
- Reminders

Visible ladder
Warning...second warning...name on board...move seat...lose golden time... call home...parked...sent to headteacher etc.

Invisible/tacit ladder
Redirect class, no names...praise the compliant by name...redirect with a no name reprimand...redirect with no names but more warning...name non-compliant...

Other tactics: move closer, 'the stare'.

CHAPTER 15
DEALING WITH CRISES

One of the biggest worries teachers have is 'How will I deal with a fight or an argument, or something equally rough?' And who could blame them? Unless you are used to conflict, or have professional experience dealing with physical and verbal confrontation, these circumstances are shocking and intimidating, not only because the risk to one's own safety is great but also because they are so rare.

Few of us are trained to deal with our own conflicts, let alone someone else's. What makes it even harder is that teachers are expected not to walk away from such events, as most of us will sensibly do, but to walk towards them – to resolve them, even. Teachers are like firefighters[1] in this respect: they often have to walk towards the fires everyone else walks away from.

Unless teachers are given training on handling these situations, they risk making poor choices because decisions made under stress are often poorer. Cognitive biases, which are shortcuts in the way we reason, become more pronounced when someone is under stress.[2] For example, we become far more likely to:

- Selectively search for evidence (*confirmation bias*). You unconsciously expect a student to annoy you, so you look for signs that they are doing so.
- Stop looking for new evidence (*premature termination*).
- Be unwilling to change our views when new evidence comes to light (cognitive inertia). You blame a student for talking even when some honest students tell you they weren't.
- Want to see things in a positive light (*wishful thinking*). You give too much leeway to a student because you hope they will behave, even though they haven't shown you they can.

---

1. But this time in a good way.

2. Maqsood, T., Finegan, A. and Walker, D. (2004) 'Biases and heuristics in judgment and decision making: The dark side of tacit knowledge', *Issues in Informing Science and Information Technology*.

- Distort our memories to support what we have chosen (*choice supportive bias*).
- Be more willing to believe what we have been told frequently (*repetition bias*). 'This is the worst class. They're all little monsters.'
- Conform to group decisions (*groupthink*).
- Underestimate the uncertainty of events.
- Stick to a decision based on the effort that has already gone into it (*sunk cost fallacy/framing bias*).

And so on. These and many other effects do not bode well for high-quality decision-making. And when you're faced with a fight or an argument, you have to think fast.[3]

And that risks making things worse or handling things badly. In many mainstream settings, violence is uncommon, even rare. In some schools you may never see a fight. But in many, you will, at least occasionally. And in some, they will be as regular as a heartbeat. Being prepared for these situations will go a long way to helping teachers feel like they can handle them.

Conflict comes in many forms. In this context, I'm referring to any of the more extreme forms of dispute: fights, shoving, verbal aggression, anything that threatens the safety of others, chairs thrown, etc. Sadly, many teachers only start to think what they should do when they encounter them, and by then it is too late for strategic thinking.

One of the most important skills that a teacher can have in their repertoire is knowing how to de-escalate conflict. How to take a situation that is getting out of control and get it under control.

Remember the Serenity Prayer:

> *Grant me the serenity to accept the things I cannot change,*
> *courage to change the things I can,*
> *and wisdom to know the difference.*

This neatly describes how we should deal with crises in classroom behaviour. Sometimes, like a firefighter, we must simply accept that the fire is happening, and consider what we need to do to best cope with it. Sometimes we need to

---

3. Needless to say, the same effects apply to children under stress.

think about how we prevent fires. Sometimes we think about putting them out, and sometimes we think about what to do next once it starts to die down.

Example:

> In nightclubs, I often saw bouncers/security deal with aggressive customers. Sometimes they did so by responding with brute force. Sometimes that was necessary and right, and unavoidable, but sometimes it was not, and it created more harm and disruption than walking away would have done. Sometimes they persuaded people to calm down. Sometimes they enlisted the help of the customers' companions.

So, how can teachers deal with crises?

Prevention is better than cure

Prevention runs through this book like the veins in a blue cheese. Little fires are easier to put out than big fires. But easier still is making it hard for fires to catch in the first place. Better a fence at the top of a cliff than an ambulance at the bottom of it, remember?

The most effective room-runners create an environment where misbehaviour is less likely – and good behaviour more likely – by:

- Proactive approaches – norms and routines, clearly, patiently taught, retaught, enforced and supportively reinforced.
- Reactive approaches – consequences, rewards, sanctions, mentoring, coaching feedback, pastoral conversations, support arising from that.

Strong culture makes escalation less likely

Consistent classroom cultures create strong norms that discourage the escalation of minor misbehaviours into major ones, prevent minor misbehaviour becoming entrenched norms, and offer a supportive scaffold for students who need a little assistance reaching the norms that will help everyone to flourish. This is the best way to deal with the problem of major conflicts, crises, fights and so on. In environments like this, escalation is less likely: fights and other problems are less frequent because even minor misbehaviour is either unthinkable or extraordinary to contemplate. Sweat the small stuff more so you end up with less of the big stuff.

There is some evidence that this can be more broadly applied to reducing crime in public areas. The famous 'broken windows' strategy of New York in the '90s provides an interesting example. In 1982, Kelling and Wilson wrote about an experiment to test the long-held theory of some police officers that 'if a window in a building is broken and left unrepaired, all the rest of the windows will soon be broken'.[4] Zimbardo[5] had tested this by placing two cars with the bonnet up in a poor borough of the Bronx, and one in wealthy Palo Alto, California. In the Bronx, the car was stripped bare in under 24 hours; in Palo Alto, it was left alone. So Zimbardo smashed the car a little with a hammer in Palo Alto, and within hours, it had been similarly decimated.

The results *seemed* clear: sweating the small stuff mattered. If residents saw that social norms had already been broken, they were more likely to break other norms. The theory behind this was that once people see tacit permission to misbehave, they think about other ways in which they can misbehave. Possibly they sense that rules are not as closely observed in the vicinity of the distressed norm.

After the article, Kelling was brought in to advise then mayor Rudy Giuliani on bringing crime down, and the broken windows strategy was implemented. Crime plummeted, but it would be too easy to attribute it to the policy alone, as multiple other factors also converged on that outcome. But more recent studies[6] have homed in on and supported one specific claim: that evidence of public disorder (e.g. graffiti next to a no-graffiti sign) encourages other disorder (such as littering or stealing). This maps onto classrooms too: when you sweat the small stuff, and provide an environment that constantly deters even small misbehaviours and immerses students with normative nudges, then not only is low-level disruption kept at bay, but so too are more serious misbehaviours.

The UK's strictest school

I once spent a day at the Michaela Community School in North West London, one of the UK's most successful (and famously, strictest) comprehensive state schools. It serves an extremely poor demographic, is non-selective, and infuriates many people by achieving some of the best grades in the UK, beating almost every top private school.

---

4. Kelling, G. L. and Wilson J. Q (1982) 'Broken Windows', *Atlantic*, March 1982.

5. Zimbardo, P. G. (1969) 'The human choice: Individuation, reason, and order versus deindividuation, impulse, and chaos', *Nebraska Symposium on Motivation*, 17, pp.237–307.

6. Keizer, K., Lindenberg, S. and Steg, L. (2008) 'The spreading of disorder', *Science*, 322(5908), pp.1681-1685. https://doi.org/10.1126/science.1161405

My guide, an articulate, keen year 9 student, asked if I wanted to know anything. 'What would the teacher do if a student swore at them?' I asked. I wanted to get a sense of how high-tariff misbehaviour was handled. Her reaction was memorable: she acted as if I had suggested we were on the moon. 'That would never happen!' she said, 'But if it did…actually, I don't know. They would be in really big trouble.' She couldn't even countenance it. Not because she didn't understand what it was, but because even minor misbehaviour was so uncommon.

This also wasn't because these were the charming offspring of diplomats; they came from one of the poorest and underprivileged inner-city cohorts in London. In conversation, they told me how they had all seen terrible behaviour in their primary school experiences. They just didn't see it here. The culture was so clear and unambiguously ambitious.

Years ago, when I was a teenager, I used to go to a karate club in Glasgow. Every six months, Sensei Enoeda from Japan would come over and grade us for our efforts, and attempt to conceal his disdain at our comedic attempts to master the Shotokan discipline. One student asked him via a translator what the best way to win a fight was, and he memorably replied, 'To not be there in the first place.' Which at the time seemed a cute answer, but was in retrospect profound. The best way to de-escalate behaviour is to prevent behaviour getting to the point where you need to de-escalate.

The best strategy to deal with serious misbehaviour is to create a classroom climate where even minor misbehaviour is unusual, and always – always, challenged in some way when it does occur. The best way to deal with big fires is to make it harder for little ones to get bigger, and for little ones to even catch in the first place.

Whole-class culture-building techniques are a rising tide that lifts all ships. They provide a healthy and reassuring framework for all students; they provide a nudge and a guide to students who need only a little assistance; and they provide a vital framework of how to behave for the students who struggle most with the classroom expectations.

In addition to this approach, the most successful room-runners offer the most challenging students as much targeted support as they can. They 'walk towards' the issues rather than hoping everything will work itself out by itself. Many complex interventions are beyond the classroom teacher's ability to provide –

lack of time and training make sure of that – but the teacher can often make some headway by targeting the neediest, helping them deal with negative habits and emotional states etc. This should be done in conjunction with the school and its various mechanisms that are there to support you.

This is the proactive approach to behaviour – targeting the most challenging students before their patterns of behaviour can disrupt the lives of others. It is supportive, moral and effective. It is not magic; not every student's misbehaviour finds its remedy in this method. But it helps. Sometimes it helps a lot, sometimes a little and sometimes not at all. But it helps a lot more than *not* doing it.

To back this process up, many schools have some form of inclusion unit, where students who are struggling to cope with mainstream classrooms can be taught. Work is set that is rooted in the curriculum, but it can also be therapeutic work to learn new behaviour, attitudes, and skills that help them cope and thrive rather than merely survive.

Taken together, these approaches will do a great deal to deter or redirect a lot of higher-end misbehaviour. But these approaches are of little comfort to the teacher who has to deal with it when it happens. Reducing its occurrence doesn't mean eliminating it, and because human nature is what it is, even in an immaculately run classroom or school sometimes behaviour will go to red alert. In some classes, it will be almost common, and in some circumstances (e.g. schools for challenging students) it may even be relatively constant. How should teachers handle this?

Much of the best practice in this arena comes, perhaps unsurprisingly, from sectors where the most dramatic and explosive behaviours are seen most often: PRUs, alternative provision, as well as early years, kindergarten etc. I owe a great debt to colleagues in these sectors, and I believe mainstream teaching has a lot to learn from these pioneers and pilgrims.[7]

How to de-escalate

First, we need to understand the different stages of behaviour intervention and identify the one at which we are attempting to intervene. This will dictate two things:

---

7. As an aside, because behaviour management is much misunderstood and frequently poorly trained at scale, we should look to these environments of clinical expertise as templates of what we may do in more mainstream contexts.

1. The aim of the intervention
2. The strategy

Stage of intervention:	
1. Before event occurs	Aim: prevention
2. As event begins	Aim: defusal
3. As event occurs	Aim: containment
4. As event ends	Aim: de-escalation
5. After event	Aim: resolution

The earlier the intervention, the more effective it is. The later, the more energy needs to be expended to achieve the aim.

Stage 1: Prevention – the power of proactivity

Even with powerful, well-taught norms, behaviour goes wrong. Once the misbehaviour begins, it may well seem like norms weren't enough. And that may be true. This does not mean that these strategies were the wrong ones. It does mean that no strategy, by itself, is capable of creating perfect behaviour.

We're looking for *best bets, most likelys* and *highly probables*. We look for as many approaches as possible, and hope that using a range of strategies means we capture as many students as possible with them. Most of this book has been dedicated to proactive strategies, and rightly. As I have noted, the structure and reassurance they provide often has the most impact on those who need the most structure. Proactivity means you will often be unaware of the misbehaviour you have prevented.

Stage 2: Defusal

Once a misbehaviour begins, intervention must be as early as possible to prevent it snowballing into a more serious misbehaviour. Fires do not put themselves out. If a teacher hears two students needling one another at the back of the classroom, or a small object has been thrown at someone, haste must be had in the effort to stop a train sliding away becoming a runaway one. Catch the pebbles before they become a landslide.

NUDGE THEM BACK

A nudge is a concept popularised by Thaler and Sunstein in their 2008 book of that name.[8] They defined a nudge as:

> Any aspect of the choice architecture that alters people's behaviour in a predictable way without forbidding any options or significantly changing their economic incentives. To count as a mere nudge, the intervention must be easy and cheap to avoid. Nudges are not mandates. Putting fruit at eye level counts as a nudge. Banning junk food does not.

A nudge is anything we can do to change the environment to make a given choice more likely than another alternative. A famous example is the painting or sticking of flies onto men's urinals, encouraging a better aim by providing a target. The world of public spaces is full of nudges, from footprints stuck on the floor of corridors, tempting us to follow their example, to putting fruit snacks nearer to checkout tills in order to encourage healthier eating.

Critics have claimed that even successful nudges tend to have short-term influence over behavioural choices. Even if that is true, nudges that are cheap and easy to administer must surely be useful additions to a teacher's repertoire of influence.

Left to their own devices, a student who is misbehaving may well stop themselves and get back on task. But often they will not, especially if they are involved in a situation that is emotional, upsetting, confrontational or connected to their status. At this point, it is useful if the teacher can provide a gentle nudge to encourage them to course-correct. This must occur as early in the misbehaviour as possible. The teacher clearly addresses the student(s), redirects them towards the preferred behaviour, and away from the misbehaviour. This can be done in two ways:

1. Focusing away from the misbehaviour and towards the right behaviour

What should you be doing now? What question are you on? What is the answer to X? What is the rule for X? What do we need to do when someone annoys us?

---

8. Thaler, R. H. and Sunstein, C. R (2008) *Nudge: Improving decisions about health, wealth, and happiness.* New Haven: Yale University Press.

This has the advantage of being framed in such a way that the student is encouraged to think about the behaviour they should be following, not the one they are not. It provides clarity and an example of what to do next, making it easier to do it. It also provides an opportunity for the student to change course without too much loss of face, as it can be phrased to sound like a question rather than a reprimand.

2. Focusing on the misbehaviour or its consequences

'Stop doing [X]; if you do [X] then I will have to [Y].' This is much more clearly designed to address the misbehaviour rather than tease out and encourage better behaviour. But it is certainly the best option in some circumstances. If a student is about to hit another with a lead pipe, shouting 'Sit down and revise for your test!' seems an odd choice of language compared to the more serious and imperial 'Stop doing that at once!'

It is an act of professional judgement that dictates which angle is used, and when, or to decide what tone, register and message needs communicating.

The message must be prompt, it must be clear, and it must be confidently issued. The student has been given the chance to pause, to reflect on what they are doing, to grab a lifeline that will prevent them from greater misbehaviour. For some students, this is all it will take.

- The teacher should be on high alert at this stage and remain hyper vigilant to see how the scene develops over the next few seconds.
- Hold eye contact or remain performatively observant of what is occurring.
- Move closer to the pupils and remain there. Ask one of them to come closer to you in the seating arrangements.
- Do whatever it takes to show the students that things need to start getting better.
- Let them know they have to change course before things get serious.

The student is reminded of the norms and routines that have already been taught, and this gives them a chance to refocus on their behaviour. Policing behaviour like this requires high focus, concentration and mental effort. It cannot be maintained throughout the entire lesson, but it must be employed judiciously when required.

The overall benefit of this approach is that it gives students the chance to course-correct with minimal loss of status and suggests ways to change their behaviour at the point at which it is easiest to do so. This approach works best when students are aware what the norms are but need help to stop doing what they're doing.

THE LADY, OR THE TIGER?

In 1882, Frank Stockton wrote 'The Lady, or the Tiger?' a story about a king in a faraway land who used a bizarre trial by ordeal to decide an accused person's fate. They had to pick one of two doors; behind one was a lady that they would then have to marry, but behind the other, a ravenous tiger.[9] Setting aside the odd value anachronisms represented by this choice, we can see a large, carnivorous nudge at work. You still get to make the choice, but you won't like where one door leads.[10]

The language of choice is a well-worn example of this technique in behaviour management. The idea is to cue the behaviour they should be doing, and simultaneously suggest what else they might choose to do...along with the penalty for this choice.

> 'You need to get started on the task or I'll have to record on your report that you weren't trying.'

Or, more positively:

> 'If you stick with these questions, you'll be finished before the bell, and you can have all of your break with your friends.'

The language of choice gives notional control of the situation to the student; they can pick an option. In reality, the teacher is framing the reality of the situation, and suggesting to the student how they should view their present moment. Remember that many students (and people) can be impulsive and find

---

9. Stockton, F. R. (n.d) *The lady or the tiger, and other stories*. Toronto: Musson Book Company.

10. It's unclear what happened to women prisoners, unless the kingdom was more progressively liberal than the story suggests. In *The Simpsons*, Lenny and Carl are told that behind one of the doors is a tiger, and behind the other, Homer Simpson. When it turns out that both doors lead to tigers, it is revealed that one of the tigers is called Homer Simpson.

themselves easily caught up in the moment. For such people in such moments, a reminder that there are other things at stake that they have temporarily neglected can be edifying.

Like any other technique, this is a useful rather than a miraculous strategy. The student is still free at this point to think, 'Well, I don't care for either outcome actually,' and carry on their business.

Try not to wade in too quickly. Look for danger cues, e.g. fists clenched, tears, voice starting to raise etc. If you can keep calm yourself, you can spot these clues that emotions are starting to boil over a lot more easily. If you try to intervene in an argument that's just about to become a punch-up, sometimes treating it with a reprimand or light-hearted banter can make it worse. Notice if it's becoming more than just messing about.

Stage 3: Containment

In the children's movie *Playing With Fire*, Dr Amy Hicks explains to smokejumper Jake Carson, 'Kids are like fire. You can't control them. You've just got to contain them until they burn themselves out.' Rarely has a metaphor been more apposite[11] than when students are going through a meltdown or are in the middle of an outburst. When emotions are running high, reason is thrown out of the window, and many children find it hard to make calm, rational decisions.

If a student has reached the point where they are being violent, or lashing out, or attacking property or people, or violently and verbally abusing others, the teacher then has to recalculate what success would actually look like in this scenario.

It might well be preventing the maximum damage to people and property. And as the quote above demonstrates, fire burns out; so too do high emotional states. No matter how anxious, angry or abusive a student is, one thing must always be remembered: that state will not last forever. It will pass. Emotional states regress to a mean, which means that both elation and misery will pass, in time. This is the reasoning behind the Samaritans policy of 'keep them talking': even the most desperate of souls starts to feel slightly better after being in the pit of despair for a while.

---

11. Or harder won. That's 96 minutes of my life I will never get back.

FIREFIGHTING

Let's assume at this point the behaviour is in full flow: the fight is in progress, the argument is raging. You are beyond prevention or defusing. When behaviour is highly challenging, quickly assess the context.

What do I need to know here? A moment's thought and pause might be all it takes to realise who the aggressor is in a fight, and who the defender. That could save you making a big mistake about where to focus your energy.

Am I the right person? The answer is usually 'If you're there, then yes you are.' Never walk past or away from a meltdown, even if you can. But you might need assistance. I once tried to calm down an inconsolably angry boy, but when that failed, we got his brother out of another lesson to help us, which was exactly what he needed at that point.

What is my objective here? It might seem obvious ('end the fight') but sometimes there are alternatives. Another day, we had a young man storming throughout the school in a violent temper, punching walls and cabinets. Eventually he ended up on a flight of stairs in the fire escape, boiling with rage. One colleague was shouting at him to get a grip of himself and come back into lessons, he'd never seen such disgusting behaviour etc. The young man was having none of it.

I sat down half a flight below and faced away from him. I told him that I would just sit quietly here because I was worried about him, and I'd wait for him to feel a bit better, at which point we could talk if he wanted. It took half an hour, and eventually he did. The objective at that point wasn't, 'Make a disruptive student obey me, and take a good telling off for good measure.' It was, 'Contain the fire until it goes out.' Once that had happened, we could work on other strategies and aims. There's time later for reprimands and phone calls and pastoral conversations. Of course, I had time to do all this. This is a lot easier in a functioning whole-school system. If you're alone, this is incredibly hard.

AVOID INFLAMING THE SITUATION

There's a lot you can do to throw fuel on the flames when students are angry or upset. But conversely, there's a lot you can do to help them calm down. None of this works all the time. A lot of it helps a lot of the time.

- Approach calmly, with a low consistent voice.

They need to see someone calm, not someone that makes them feel more threatened or defensive.

- Acknowledge any distress if necessary.

'I can see you're upset.' This can surprise them. They were probably expecting an attack, or a criticism.

- Ask what is happening.

If they're talking about what's happened, that's a lot better than simply reacting emotionally to what's happening. Legend has it that Churchill said about diplomacy, 'Jaw-jaw is better than war-war.'[12] Talking is not fighting. It's a good start.

- Be clear about what you need to do.
- Reassure them that you are there to help.
- Demonstrate empathy.
- Control your own emotions.
- Be aware of your body language.

Are you standing too close to them? Are you saying calm things but look like you're ready for a fight? Stand at ease, arms down by your side, unclenched fists. Relax the muscles in your face and make gentle but assertive eye contact without staring.

SAFETY FIRST

A word about safety. Intervening when a student is upset, angry or otherwise emotionally agitated always carries with it certain risks. When a student is in a state like this, they are less likely to be thinking rationally, far more likely to react impulsively, and more likely to perceive the world through a very tight lens. Comments are far more likely to be interpreted as threatening or insulting, and everything that happens to them seen as a potential threat. They are more likely to lash out, verbally or physically, even if in normal circumstances they would not do so. It makes sense in that charged moment.

---

12. He didn't, but Harold Macmillan did, misquoting him four years later in 1958.
    Churchill had actually said, 'Meeting jaw to jaw is better than war.'

When dealing with agitated adults in bars, I always had to remember that a tense situation could become a tragic one in an instant. People are too used to a diet of action films and adventure fiction to properly appreciate the perils of violence, where simply falling over can be fatal if you land on the wrong part of your head or throat, concussion often means brain injury, and no weapon is harmless. Even the toughest of tough guys in door security would take a step back the moment any drunk pulled a weapon.

The decision to intervene is a complex one, but often one that has to be made on the spot. As with all such decisions (see 'Scripts', p. 221), the best way to prevent a bad decision on the spot is to try to make it in advance, rather than decide in a stressful situation.

YOUR OWN SAFETY

Can you handle this alone? Even if you think you can, you shouldn't. Summon assistance whenever possible. If you cannot leave the scene, send someone you can count on to be sensible and act with urgency. Better still for there to be a prearranged, taught behaviour involving a nominated person who goes for help when certain clear trigger points have been reached.

Only physically intervene solo when circumstances absolutely demand it. Two people will use less force than one person. Two people are more capable of administering restraint (if required) than one.

Should you intervene physically? Another key question. What is the aim of the intervention? It might seem the natural thing, to pile into a problem, and some people are certainly primed to do something rather than nothing. But sometimes, doing nothing is better than doing the wrong thing, at least in the short term. Are they a danger to themselves, or others? Are they likely to calm down without being restrained, held or made contact with? The most capable security guards I ever worked with got physical as rarely as possible, because they recognised the dangers of doing so without a clear objective, and because they used other tactics – such as interpersonal skills – before, instead of, or even during restraint.

Are you trained to restrain? This is key. Unless you have had specific training in safe methods of restraint, only ever do so as a last resort (for example if they or another student are in imminent danger) because physical confrontation is, for the untrained, a dangerous business. Noses are easily broken, and this can happen just as easily by accident as on purpose.

What are the risks to yourself? No staff member should feel they are duty-bound to place themselves in danger. Circumstances vary from role to role, sector to sector, and country to country, but there is balance between a duty of care towards your students and an employer's duty of care to employees. Jobs that expect physical contact must state so clearly in their contracts, and crucially, train staff to deal with it.

On the other hand, we must consider the moral duty we have as adults to do what we can to prevent the harm of others, and many parents would be disappointed if a professional in charge of their child's care didn't step in when they were in danger.

THE AUDIENCE

Audiences change the behaviour of actors. Students behave very differently with an audience than without. Because a lot of their actions are influenced by how they think they will appear to others, just knowing that others are there will have an impact. Status is very important to most people. Many students, especially ones literally fighting for their prestige, will do almost anything rather than back down in front of a gang of peers.

In bars, I saw this often. Most fights in bars are about nothing, or trivia – a spilled drink, a dirty look, whatever. But bucks and bulls would batter each other into the ground over such things. I also observed something very interesting: many of them would give up at the slightest excuse to do so, as if they never wanted to fight in the first place. All it would take would be a simple restraining arm from a friend and a shout, 'He's not worth it!' and their violence would melt away, usually growling that the other guy had *better watch it* next time. If the other assailant has his own lieutenants doing the same, the fight is over, and honour has been served.

What is fascinating about this is that they seemed desperate for a way out, and being given permission and opportunity to take one had a huge impact on their behaviour. And the reverse is true. *Not* being allowed a get-out, or an escape hatch, means that their choices diminish to one option: the tiger.[13] Without the audience winding them up, so much aggression withers.

In the classroom, you can use this effect if you can get the angry students away from others, into a calm, quiet place with no external stimuli to encourage them

---

13. Or both doors lead to a tiger. Or the lady has knuckledusters.

to react badly. If the incident is taking place in a public area like a playground, ideally you would be able to dismiss the audience by simply asking them to disperse – and *sometimes* this is possible. But often, other students find it impossible to resist standing and staring, because action is mesmerising.

Many people love a bit of drama, especially when it's not happening to them. You'll be crawling along a motorway wondering what's happened, until finally you see a car crash on the other side of the road, completely unaffecting your own lanes physically. But everyone else has slowed down to rubberneck at the free theatre…after which the road instantly clears. Drama is addictive, which is why people buy more books about murder and sex than fractal geometry and crop rotation.

Dispersing crowds is hard. One strategy that can help is to pre-teach students how they are expected to behave when a fight breaks out. Teach them that they should disperse, go about their business and leave the scene immediately. Teach them that their presence makes it worse, and makes it harder to stop the fight. Drop in some warnings that anyone who doesn't do this might be spoken to afterwards etc. This will *help*. It won't make every child do it, but remember, that's not the outcome we hope for from any intervention. We're looking to make things better, not perfect. Never let the perfect be the enemy of the good.[14]

Pre-teaching children to not be passive participants in the problem is helpful. You can specifically prohibit some behaviours, so they know what they shouldn't do as much as what they should. It has been suggested that, because people are often motivated by the impression they make on others, it is possible to build accountability cues – preloaded messages that teach children what 'good behaviour' means when a fight happens. Therefore, when a student sees a fight and tries to stop it, they already know that *others know* they are doing the right thing, and not just interfering.[15]

Where I taught in East London, children would shout 'Beef! Beef! Beef!' merrily when a fight broke out (a 'beef' was a dispute) and it was treated like the circus had suddenly rolled up in the playground, rather than the violent opera

---

14. Voltaire quoted an unnamed Italian poet in his *Dictionnaire Philosophique* in 1770: 'Il meglio è l'inimico del bene.' It later appeared in his poem 'La Béguele' as 'Le mieux est l'ennemi du bien.'

15. Bommel, M.V. et al. (2012) 'Be aware to care: public self-awareness leads to a reversal of the bystander effect'. *Journal of Experimental Social Psychology*. 48 (4), pp.926–930.

of tragedy teachers saw. That's the kind of behaviour you could specifically prohibit, as long as you publicly follow up with students who do this. Research suggests that *altruism* (helping another with no obvious reward) is increased when people see one another as being part of the same social group. Because perception of group membership is highly subjective, it might be useful to reinforce a group identity for your students. If they allow others to get clobbered, they are letting down their 'team'.[16] Group membership and group cohesiveness matters.

Another technique that can help is to name students and ask them to leave, preferably specifying the destination. It is much harder to ignore a specific instruction than one that is addressed to a whole group. This is a version of the 'bystander effect'. This is a theory in social psychology that suggests individuals are less likely to offer help to a victim when there are other people present. The greater the number of bystanders, the less likely it is that one of them will help. When people are in crowds, they feel less responsible than when they are faced with a decision alone.

Some research suggests that in ambiguous situations, bystanders may look to one another for guidance, and misinterpret others' lack of initial response as a lack of concern. This causes each bystander to decide that the situation is not serious, making them less likely to do nothing to help, and more likely to passively observe.[17]

You can ask for assistance by giving named students a task to do. This reduces the abdication or diffusion of responsibility that can occur when you give a blanket command aimed at everyone (and therefore no one).

Remember, students in a fight – or emotionally distressed – are far less tuned in to reasonable arguments. Instead, keep your instructions:

- Clear – not ambiguous
- Direct – addressed to a defined individual, with a command
- Specific – 'Do this exact thing'

---

16. Levine, M., Prosser, A; Evans, D. and Reicher, S. (1968) 'Identity and emergency intervention: how social group membership and inclusiveness of group boundaries shape helping behaviours', *Personality and Social Psychology Bulletin*, 31 (4), pp. 443–445.

17. Meyers, D. G. (2010) *Social Psychology (10th Ed)*. New York, NY: McGraw–Hill.

Example: 'Jim, put the chair down and walk towards me,' not, 'Hey, what's all this going on here then?'

These factors help achieve cut-through in any scenario. In a challenging situation, it is even more necessary.

THE STUDENTS' SAFETY

Restraint or any form of physical hold should only be a last resort, use the minimum force necessary, and only be done to prevent greater harm to others or the student themselves. The main aim is to remove them, so if you can persuade them to lay down their arms voluntarily then that is always better. Remember that all fires burn out, and no child remains angry forever. This is why it is so useful to remove them (or get them to remove themselves) to a space where they can calm down to autoextinguish their emotional bonfire.

When adrenaline hits the system, the body starts to sweat, the heart rate increases, breathing becomes rapid and shallow, pain sensitivity is reduced, physical strength is augmented, and the gut slows down digestion. The body is ready to run or take a swing, but if the situation doesn't permit this, even greater stress occurs. Adrenaline is released under any circumstances that are stressful, exciting, dangerous or threatening. That means that even in the absence of an actual threat, the same fight-or-flight mechanism is unleashed, because your adrenal gland can't distinguish between a sabre-toothed tiger and an annoying boy flicking your ear repeatedly.

Because of this physical component to the behaviour, being upset or angry is not a thing that most people can switch on and off. When a child's system is awash with adrenaline, it takes around 40 minutes to an hour or so for it to break down. Which is why, when we isolate a student after a fight, we give them plenty of time to calm down.

CALMING DOWN

A word on 'getting people to calm down'. You cannot 'make' someone calm down. Remember these wise words: 'Never in the history of calming down has anyone calmed down by being told to calm down.'[18]

---

18. Anonymous, quoted from Sgt John Farrell, North Eastern Police Department, www. bit.ly/2Dt7xp1

Calming down is not something you can do to someone (unless you have tranquiliser darts). Calming down is something that happens when someone is in an environment that enables calm to occur: a quiet spot, away from everyone, where the student knows they are safe from harm and distress. Plonking them on a chair outside the headteacher's office in a busy corridor, exposing them to mockery and scrutiny, is not conducive to calm. Leaving them alone (but supervised) for a short while, so long as they are safe and no danger to others, is. And never tell someone to calm down. It is more likely to antagonise an already agitated student by reminding them that they are not displaying calm and making them feel controlled and patronised.

Stage 4: De-escalation

Assuming you are not physically restraining an agitated student, there are several things that can be done to assist a diplomatic de-escalation:

- Remember 'jaw-jaw' is better than 'war-war', and if they're talking, they're not setting fire to the gym cupboard. Talking with someone helps them to focus away from the circumstance that is provoking their distress, and towards something – anything – else. So, get them talking.
- Show active listening. This means not cutting them off, not simply waiting for a gap to tell them what to do. Make them feel that you are treating them as a human being. I used to deal with a lot of angry restaurant customers, and what they were upset about wasn't so much cold fries or long wait times (although they were the triggers) but the fact that they felt they weren't being treated with dignity.
  The solution was – almost without exception – to *listen*. Listen without a sound, apart from listening noises. And then, once they had finished, listen some more. That often threw them. Agitated people are expecting to be interrupted, are expecting pushback. Don't give them it, if you can bear it. Just listen. Here, doing nothing is doing something.
  They will then start up again, and you just keep on listening, until they stop. Do this a few times and they exhaust themselves, because they're not fighting against anything anymore. They end up drained of ire. At most, ask for clarification, or repeat back one of their points to show that you heard them. For some people, being heard is a very new experience.
- Look at the person. Natural conversations require that we look away at times, and sometimes staring can make people feel more agitated. But eye contact is a powerful connector.

- Nod. It's a light cue of agreement, or perhaps approval. Let the listener interpret it as they will. But it's a basic human gesture that what they are saying matters, that they matter.
- Paraphrase back. This shows you've been listening and processing what they have to say.
- Use open questions. This keeps them talking and keeps them explaining and unpacking. It makes them think.
- Stand at a non-threatening distance. Or sit, if you can. Little non-verbal cues that suggest you're ready for a scrap, however implicitly, aren't helpful.
- Treat them with dignity, even if they are in the wrong. This is hard. They may clearly be in the wrong but remember what the goal is: to get everyone calm and safe with the minimum of damage to anyone or anything. Well-trained police know this. A good officer will show empathy and understanding, coaxing upset antagonists into calm spaces rather than battering them into them, if they can avoid it. People fighting for dignity and face will fight very hard indeed. Give them some for free and you are miles closer to a solution. It costs nothing but forethought, and the need to be right all the time.

ASSERTIVE, NOT AGGRESSIVE, BEHAVIOUR

Be assertive, not aggressive or submissive. Assertiveness is 'the ability to stand up for one's rights in ways that make it less likely that others will ignore them'.[19] This should be the default model of communication for a teacher at all times, but it is even more important when dealing with students in challenging circumstances. Marzano describes this as involving:

1. **Use of assertive body language**
   - Making and keeping eye contact
   - Maintaining an erect posture, facing the student, but keeping enough distance so as not to appear threatening
   - Matching one's facial expression with the content of the message

2. **Use of appropriate tone of voice**
   - Speaking clearly and deliberately
   - Using pitch that is not greatly elevated from normal speech
   - Avoiding any indication of emotion in one's voice

---

19. Evertson, C. M., Emmer, E. T. and Worsham, M. E. (2003) *Classroom management for elementary teachers (6th ed.)*. Boston: Allyn and Bacon.

3. Persisting until the appropriate behaviour is displayed
- Not ignoring an inappropriate behaviour
- Not being diverted by a student arguing or blaming, but listening to legitimate explanations[20]

Being submissive is also the wrong model. Aggression suggests that the student doesn't matter; submissiveness suggests that the teacher doesn't matter. Assertiveness suggests they both matter, and so does the content of what is being said. Rhetorically, when something is said confidently, it suggests that it is of value, and deserves to be heard. I once heard it described in this way: speak as if you were ordering a box of spanners over the phone. There's no need to be angry or pleading. It's just a matter of fact. 'I need a box of spanners and you sell them.'

CLEAR SEQUENTIAL INSTRUCTIONS
The most effective behavioural instructions are clear, in *sequence*, and direct.

'Put that down and come here,' followed by 'I want to help you,' is a good example.

'What did we say three weeks ago at the restorative integration meeting with your mother?' is not. It doesn't even have an implied imperative; it's a puzzle, not an instruction. Don't make them work hard to understand, or you've given them another reason not to do so. When students are agitated or upset, nuance is not going to be appreciated. Rational thinking is not their priority. Our decisions, at the best of times, are a blend of reason and emotion.

LOWER THE STAKES
When tempers are high, and blood is hot, students need a reason to get calm. Avoid accusing them of anything; try to focus on immediate steps to make things better. Tell them that you're there to help them, and that in order for you to do that, they need to 'X'. Remove the audience if possible. Remove them somewhere calm and quiet and away from what is triggering their outburst.

---

20. Marzano, R. J., Pickering, D., and Pollock, J. E. (2001) *Classroom instruction that works: Research-based strategies for increasing student achievement*. Alexandria, VA: Association for Supervision and Curriculum Development.

Stage 5: Resolution – as the gale subsides

At the end, students will start to calm down. Don't take your foot off the gas. There are still things you can do to help the process.

- It takes effort to stay angry – eventually all anger will end. Never forget this. Continuously heightened emotional states are unnatural to all but the most pathologically damaged personalities. Angry people become calm. Sad people's sorrows lift. Remembering this as a mid-/long-term goal will mean you avoid the mistake of insisting that everyone calm down instantly, with the collateral damage that this entails.

  But remember this applies to you, the teacher, too. If you are agitated or upset, try to manage your time so that you have space to catch your breath, calm down and find your balance.

- Be honest about what needs to happen next. No one likes to be lied to, and if you promise an outcome for a student that can't be achieved, they will never trust you again – deservedly. For the most agitated and damaged students, this trust is essential in order to work with them on improving their behaviour and attitudes. If a student is in trouble, say so, but also tell them what they can do to improve matters, and how the school can support them to do better.

  Repeatedly remind the student that they *can* do better, that you *want* them to do better, and that you want them to be part of the classroom/school community. They need to feel valued, even when they have let themselves down.

- Use clear, sequential directions. This format is always best, but particularly in situations where ambiguity and confusion could lead to renewed agitation.

- Positive reinforcement. Let the participants know you see them as a person of some merit, with potential, who can and has made positive contributions. This needn't be woolly platitudes. Reminding a student that they can do better, can be better and so on is not a lie, if you look hard enough.

- Use a calm voice. This may require some effort on your part. But do not bring more heat to the fire. It already has heat. It needs to cool.

- Fewer participants. Just like removing the audience changes the signals the student receives, when entering a cooling-down phase, don't swamp them with people, or make them feel they're being over-scrutinised. One-to-one chats are best for safe, calm landings.

- Remove to a safe space and let them calm down by themselves. Do not underestimate the power of students to cool down solo. If they feel under pressure to respond, and they're not ready, then give them time to return to a more balanced place. Remember: what is your aim here? If they've been removed from the rest of the student body then your ultimate aim is reintegration, but you can work towards that at an unhurried pace. Don't seek instant resolutions, because often these things can't be forced.

RESTORATIVE APPROACHES

In an effort to avoid using sanctions, some schools use restorative processes as an alternative. These strategies emerged from restorative justice programmes which emerged from the field of criminology. This was an attempt to avoid simply using arrest and incarceration as the way in which society dealt with criminals. Within the penal system, restorative approaches have also been used as a way to try to avoid simply adding prison time to already incarcerated offenders.

There are a number of programmes that operate under the banner of restorative justice, which is why I use the term 'approaches'. Broadly, restorative approaches take a community approach to the traditional crime/punishment issue. All of those with a stake in the offence are brought together in order to discuss the impact of the offence and how it can be resolved. There is frequently an attempt to 'restore' relationships that have been damaged by the behaviour, hence the name. In schools, this is also called restorative practice.

In practice, this often means that the teacher and the student discuss the impact of the student's behaviour, the student is encouraged to take responsibility for it, and both discuss how it can be resolved. Restorative approaches also have their roots in positive psychology, one of whose architects was Abraham Maslow. Restorative approaches are sometimes seen at odds with behaviourist approaches that emphasise consequences.

There isn't a good deal of data to help us understand if restorative approaches are useful or not. Case studies abound, but little at scale or of high quality. Most schools use restorative approaches in conjunction with consequentialist and other approaches, so it is very hard to pick the data apart in this regard.

Restorative approaches *can* be very useful. In fact, used in conjunction with whole-school processes that emphasise consequences, they can be a useful tool. Helping students discuss their behaviour, think more about the impact of their actions, and consider alternative choices they can make can be very important.

Helping students realise that others matter can help them to develop empathy and other important life skills.

The danger with using restorative approaches is that, when they are oversimplified, teachers can use them *instead* of consequence systems. As we have seen, teachers must not rely on one simple model of behaviour management, such as only using sanctions and rewards to achieve better behaviour. As this book strains to show, proactive systems that are sensitive to the motivations and psychology of children and groups, teaching them positive habits and norms, are by far the most effective way to move the behaviour needle of the classroom. And that also entails consequences. Without consequences, the deterrent effect is greatly reduced. And this is very costly for any whole-school culture.

When we focus on only one part of our behaviour strategies, there is a danger we ignore the usefulness of other strategies. Some children respond very well to restorative conversations. But some need to know they'll get in trouble if they misbehave. Some are moved by praise. Some need to be taught, and taught, and taught again how to demonstrate the right routines. By using a combination of all of these, we achieve the greatest reach and impact with the greatest number of students.

Although restorative approaches are often seen by some as a replacement for these other systems, there is an irony that some children in schools that rely primarily on these systems find themselves in restorative conversation after restorative conversation. To the student, this feels very much like a detention. If it walks like a duck and quacks like a duck, it may actually be a duck.

There is also an issue that many students see restorative processes as 'getting away with it', if all they have to do is learn what they are expected to say to progress through the conversation as quickly as possible. And if that perception is shared by the class community, it can have a very damaging effect on how they perceive the school and its expectations. Undoubtedly, many students think that if there are no consequences to their actions, then they can do as they please.

There is another danger, which is that students who have been the victims of misbehaviour frequently do not want to be participants in a restorative process. If you have been bullied, for example, you may not wish to spend any more time with your abuser, nor talk it through or develop some kind of relationship with them. With many issues, there is no relationship to restore. So restorative approaches must be avoided in these circumstances. Far better to use it as a response to two friends who have fallen out and come to blows. That is a perfect example of seeking to restore a relationship that has been damaged.

Restorative processes can sometimes be useful as a way to help build relationships with students, to generate the powerful narrative that what they did was wrong, and to make sure the student understands how to do better next time. It should also emphasise that the student is wanted and valued, but that their behaviour needs to improve. As we can see in the discussion about threshold conversations (p. 264), this can be a powerful way to help create a culture.

As a replacement for other approaches, it often falls short. Frequently, misbehaviour is not a misunderstanding or something 'wrong' with the student. Very often, misbehaviour is deliberate, intentional, lucid. And that means no amount of talking things through will work for some. It seems a kinder, gentler approach to replace consequential systems, but it is often a poor substitute for teaching children that their actions matter in more conventional ways.

EVERYONE WANTS TO MATTER

The need to matter, to be valued, to form sincere relationships with others, is at the heart of being human. Students need to know they can find these in their education, or they will seek them elsewhere.

CHAPTER 16
REMOVING STUDENTS

Ultimately, when a student is making it impossible to deliver a lesson to the class, or a student is in a state of agitation that is making it impossible for them to learn, teachers need to make a utilitarian decision based on the overall needs of the entire class. What decision can I make that will result in the greatest good for the greatest number of students?

This is inevitable and essential, because teachers are not private tutors, meeting the needs of an individual student. They are teachers of the whole class. In many ways, their position is similar to that of anyone in charge of a village, town, or community. How can I balance the needs of everyone, while meeting as many of them as I can, ethically?

If a student's behaviour is extreme enough that it doesn't respond to the gentle reminders and persuasions offered through mild sanctions, rebukes, reminders, normative messaging and the like, then teachers need to consider: do I need to remove this student from the lesson? Many teachers instinctively shrink from this strategy, believing – correctly – that their job is to provide an education to all, not just some of the students, and that simply removing challenging students from lessons is often not the best option for that particular student, as they lose access to mainstream education. And they have a very good point.

But there are other good points to remember.

If a student is misbehaving repeatedly, it often upsets the dynamic of the class to the point where everyone's learning is being seriously impeded. That matters. Everyone in the room matters. Their loss is not insignificant and is just as important as the potential loss of the individual student's access to learning; the difference is that these others have not created the conditions that make learning difficult. It is unfair they should be held hostage to the misbehaviour of a few. As Andrew Wiley, associate professor of special education at Kent State University, Ohio, says, 'The idea that the educational needs of all children can and must be met 100% of the time in the general education classroom is delusional.'

This policy, often associated with what was called the full inclusion movement, became popular in the late 20th century and had, as most things do in education, the best of intentions. 'Full inclusion means that all students, regardless of handicapping condition or severity, will be in a regular classroom/program full time. All services must be taken to the child in that setting.'[1]

But there is no practical justification for such an extremist view, other than a purely ideological or political sentiment. It is as absurd and misguided as attempting to deliver all medical services – psychiatric, oncology, paediatrics, geriatrics, counselling – in the same physical ward or GP's surgery, in an effort to promote some egalitarian utopia. Students need more than posturing. If they need help, they need help. If that help means small group nurture work for behaviour or a time-out as a sanction, or if the rest of the class need a respite from violence or verbal threat, then that needs to happen – not just for the good of the many, but the good of all.

The duty of care to all

Misbehaviour threatens not only learning but also, frequently, safety. Misbehaviour that risks the physical well-being of students or staff must not be tolerated in the classroom. The duty of care extends to all students, and when a student threatens that, serious action must be taken. It cannot be ignored, or it becomes normalised, and the students are exposed to harm on a daily basis.

The needs of the many

Not only physical harm, but emotional and mental harm, and the stress of being required to remain in proximity with aggressive students. In these circumstances, the student must be removed from the mainstream lesson. It is unconscionable to ask students and staff to endure harassment, intimidation or threats. It is bad enough for teachers; always also consider how it feels to be a peer of a student in a room where disruption is permitted. Kids *hate* it. They frequently ask, 'Why aren't the adults doing something about this?' *And they are absolutely right*. We must not forget our first duty to children – to keep them safe. It may be well meant to keep some students in the class 'to see if they improve', but the rights of the many must be taken into account here, not just the rights of the one.

---

1. Wisconsin Education Association Council website (WEAC.org) on March 1, 2014

The needs of the few – and the one

And what of the one? We often overlook the fact that if a student is misbehaving in lessons, then they are not learning. Removal can – and should – be a way for them to access the kind of provision that they may not be able to get in a mainstream lesson. They may need a pastoral conversation. Something may be going wrong in their lives, they may need therapy, they may need some kind of targeted focus that had previously been missing. They may need the boundaries to be patiently re-explained, they may need some form of sanction. All of these can often be carried out better outside of the classroom.

Teachers need to be robust in their understanding and acceptance of the need to remove students from the classroom at times. They may not like it, but this is not a question of what we like.

- Sometimes it is to protect the well-being or education of the rest of the class.
- Sometimes it is to demonstrate boundaries and uphold civil norms.
- Sometimes it is to help challenging students obtain the attention they need in an appropriate environment for their restoration or assistance or improvement.
- Sometimes it is purely to set a sanction.

But it is not even a 'necessary evil'. If it is necessary, it is not evil. If it is necessary, it is the right thing to do.

Have a removal strategy before you need it

Crucially, removal should not be done on an ad hoc basis. Removing a student from a classroom is (or should be) an unusual event, because student behaviour usually does not warrant removal from the mainstream classroom. But sometimes it does. And if the student needs to be removed, then they need to be removed. And they need to be removed safely and efficiently. There is a lot of potential in this situation to create even more chaos and distress, or even more disruption to everyone in earshot. It is a process that needs to be considered carefully. Which means deciding in *advance* how it will happen.

> Cue the students to know what to expect. Long before any students need to be removed, the students should a) be aware that removal is one possible outcome of persistent disruption; b) be aware that there is a process in place for how it will happen; and also c) understand the consequences of having to be removed. This foreshadowing should be

done as early in the relationship as possible, so the students are braced to expect it. This expectation will itself offer a mild deterrent to those whose behaviour gets too much for the mainstream room, and it also provides a reassurance to the students who may be wondering what will happen if their lessons are disrupted and their liberty or dignity is under assault. It is reassuring for students to know that in the event of extreme disruption, the teacher will respond appropriately to safeguard their well-being and education.

- By teaching the process by which removal will occur, the students know what to expect and are more likely to comply with the process. They will perceive less wriggle room, less room to manoeuvre or dispute what is happening. If a student can see the consequences bearing down on them, and still do nothing to escape them, then they may still dispute it, but they will know they have less of an argument.
- Removals must be done for very clear reasons. I usually told my students they would be removed from lessons for:
  - Persistent misbehaviour that ruins the learning of those around them
  - Rude, aggressive or dangerous behaviour that threatens the safety or dignity of their peers or the teacher. That way you can include one-off, high-tariff behaviours like telling a teacher to fuck off or throwing a book at someone. If you only define it as 'persistent disruption', then students can claim their behaviour was singular. I have also seen school systems where removals are not permitted, on the grounds that the student loses out on an education. I think it is important to make the case clearly and early with the students that their presence in the classroom is as much a privilege as a right, and that privilege can be temporarily rescinded for the greater good of all, and that sanctions are available in order to protect everyone, including the perpetrator.

I see far too many classroom teachers endure far too much misbehaviour on the grounds that they see sending a student out as a failure on their part, or in some way as an admission of weakness or lack of classroom skill. Some schools send an odd message to staff that says, 'It's your fault if you can't keep all your children in all your lessons.' While it may certainly be the case that some teachers remove too easily, it is still the right thing to do in many cases. It sets boundaries, indicates that some behaviours cannot be tolerated, and protects and safeguards the community of learners – and yourself.

Destinations

Of course, for this to be optimal, there should be a positive and supportive destination for the student who is removed. They should experience an in-school response that aims to teach them how to behave properly in the future. But even if they are required to sit quietly for a short period and work on sheets, this is not the primary concern of the classroom teacher, whose primary concern should temporarily be the needs of the community, and *their* rights in this matter. If we cannot keep them safe from harm and threat, then we are letting everyone down simultaneously.

Every school should have a removal system that places students deliberately in a calm, supervised space, preferably where they have meaningful work to do. Students should never simply be cast out of the lesson.

How to remove students

Again, preparation is key. Schools vary enormously in their processes, so it will be easier to include principles that should govern this rather than detail a precise system that must be followed.

- There should be fair warning that removal is about to happen or is in danger of happening. Of course, this may not be possible if the behaviour is spontaneous and serious. But in many scenarios, it will be possible to indicate where things are going. This may deter, or it may not. But at least it has been given a chance.
- Use *scripted language* to indicate a removal is necessary, to avoid emotional slip-ups, and deliver the message as coolly as one would when ordering a pizza. Students will often look for reasons to dispute your judgement, and if they suspect there is a personal agenda or an emotional dislike, they will often engineer this (in their heads) to indicate prejudice or a vendetta against them.
- Know where the removal destination is. Also, the student must know. And there must be someone waiting for them, ready for such an arrival. Schools often have such an area, where students can be temporarily monitored in the event of extreme misbehaviour. If the school doesn't, then it should have a subsystem in place where students can be removed to, for example, a designated classroom where the student will be taken and looked after. If the school doesn't have *that*, then it should do, because removal is a process that, while hopefully rare, is common enough to need systematising. It might be a pastoral leader's office, or a line manager's desk, but the key thing

is to know in advance of needing it. If your school doesn't have this process, then arrange one of your own. And press the school to rectify this error.

- Once removed, they should be provided with the opportunity to work in a useful way – this *might* be provided by the classroom teacher (or not; the teacher has a class to teach and should not have to conjure up lesson resources on the spot), but preferably the designated receiver will have a bank of prepared materials for such an eventuality. The point is that whatever the system is, there should be a system.

  What we want to avoid at this stage is an on-the-spot decision, hastily made, about where to send them and who will look after them and for how long. There needs to be a long thread of certainty and calm running through this process, which will already be prone to anxiety and disagreement. The calmer and more certain the process, the easier it will be to secure the student's buy-in. If it feels chaotic and impromptu, the student will discern (correctly) that they have more scope to mould the situation to what they want, rather than what is needed.

- The removal process may be facilitated by the teacher, or the student may be expected to take themselves to their destination. Or they may be taken by a classroom assistant. Or they may be removed by a designated member of staff who is summoned to the room. Or a trusted student may be sent to obtain that assistance. Or it may be dialled in via a school comms system. The point is that there should be a system, clearly understood by all parties. It should be calm, it should be prepared, and it should be predictable.

Removal rooms

Once a student has been removed from a class, what then? Typically, they will be taken to a place that can be called by many different names. But the simplest term for them is 'removal rooms'.[2] This is a broad category and doesn't tell us anything more than their function as somewhere to remove students to.

---

2. I have a list of about 40 names for such places. The Hub. The Green Zone. The Egg. Room 38. The Cooler. The Big House. Time-Out. And on, and on, and on. For some reason, removal rooms or support spaces seem to bring out the film noir poets and beatnik performance artists in us all.

Reasons for using a removal room include the following:

- First and foremost, because the student's behaviour and the goal of keeping them in the classroom are incompatible. This is usually because the behaviour is too challenging or disruptive.
- To give the rest of the class and the teacher the opportunity to learn in a safe and calm environment
- To remind the student that their behaviour has become, for whatever reason, intolerable. The reverse is disastrous for the health of the class: to tolerate intolerable behaviour is to normalise it; to encourage it; to expose children to continued abuse and teachers to continued distress.
- As a mild sanction
- To have conversations about the behaviour without disrupting the class
- To help students obtain further targeted support, sometimes in a separate area, an inclusion unit etc.

Obviously, removal rooms can serve many purposes simultaneously. They are an immensely practical part of a behaviour modification strategy and a strategy to reinforce the whole-school culture. They are not a substitute for doing anything else to amend the problem. They do not replace trying to deter students from misbehaving in the first place. They do not replace sensible norms and routines, designed to teach students how to behave in the first place. They do not replace the need to try to find out why a student is behaving in that way, and if there is something the school can do to accommodate or remedy that circumstance.

But removal rooms are not meant to be a replacement for any of these things. A student is unlikely to be helped, 'fixed' or substantially changed by being removed and then returned without any other work being done with them. By itself it is not restorative. What it is is a respite for everyone else, and a way to define boundaries of acceptable and unacceptable behaviour. More than that, it is a safety mechanism to keep students (and staff) safe, and to protect their dignity. It can be a place where students calm down, reflect on their behaviour, and plan better responses. It can be a place where students have important pastoral conversations with other members of staff that lead to greater efforts to change and grow.

To return to an earlier point: no one behaviour tool is enough; they are used in collaboration with a hundred other techniques and instruments. But none of this is to deny their utility as part of a greater mechanism.

When removing

Avoid engaging with detail if possible. If you have decided that a student needs to be removed, then the time for nuance has passed. You have determined that their behaviour has reached a point where removal is necessary; therefore, removal must happen. The discussion must come subsequent to that moment. You have a lesson to teach, and responsibility for around two dozen other souls at that point. Vitally, if you have decided and stated that it must happen, then you must not back down in the moment, persuaded perhaps by some special and exceptional level of pleading. Doing so normalises to the students that you are inconstant, and capable of being swayed by performative compliance. The time for good choices has passed; now actions must be seen to have consequences.

What do we remove for?

In some circumstances, the removal will be obvious – swearing purposefully at a teacher; using racist or misogynistic language; threatening the safety of another; pushing a desk over. I say obvious, but it may not seem obvious to some, and it is possible to think of exceptional circumstances where perhaps such things may be provoked by exceptional circumstances. But the teacher must ask, 'How can I guarantee as many students as possible can learn and thrive in a safe, calm, dignified space?' They cannot do this if the teacher permits students to swear at them, to threaten them, or even to ruin their education by persistent attention-seeking or grandstanding. Communities can be tolerant of many things, but the teacher who permits such things in order to be perceived as compassionate and tolerant must consider how the students actually experience such things. In many cases, students see it as a dereliction of duty, and a failure to protect them.

The most vulnerable child benchmark

Tolerance levels of what constitutes a sending-out will vary from school to school. Be guided in this by at least two things: the school policy, clearly spelled out, and your own moral compass where it is not clear. What would you tolerate for your own hypothetical children? What level of torment would you expect them to suffer? That should be the threshold that you use to moderate all of your responses. What would the *most vulnerable* child be expected to put up with? The anxious child? The abused or bullied child? The child going through mental health issues? Let these children's tolerance levels be a guide for what can be permitted in the classroom. That is why a common denominator of 'very civil, very safe behaviour' is the best guide for how safe a classroom should be. You may be OK with a little knockabout, a little banter, a little rough play, but is everyone?

To reiterate:

- If disruption is persistent, and making it impossible to run an effective lesson, *have the student safely removed to a safe place.*
- If students' well-being, health, physical safety or dignity is being threatened by someone, *remove that student from the class.*

Sending a student out shouldn't be seen as a first response – or a last resort. It is a tool to be used when *appropriate*. It sets the ultimate standard for what is acceptable in the classroom. Used judiciously, consistently and effectively, it acts as a brake for further misbehaviour. Used less than it should be, it acts as a temporary respite from time to time more than a deterrent, as students do not expect it. In many ways it should *not* be seen as a punishment, but a natural and logical response to a certain type of behaviour. It should be guided by a cool logic: we need to achieve X, but behaviour Y is preventing that, therefore response Z must occur to neutralise Y, restoring X.

No stand-up rows

Here is wisdom: if you're having an argument with a student, then you've already lost. Class time is too precious to waste on arguments with one student. It is entirely inappropriate to have an argument in front of a room full of students. The other students will perceive you as having lost control. The arguing student may well be arguing because they are getting attention, and possibly kudos from doing so. *They* may be unable to avoid doing so, so pre-programmed are they to respond immaturely or aggressively. But this is not what we expect from a teacher. The teacher must keep their cool at all times – or as much as humanly possible – and the children need to see a role model who can demonstrate what it means to act with certainty, dignity, and assertiveness, without malice or venom.

Scripting your removal language can be very useful here. If you're prepared in what you say, then your responses will be far cooler, far more rational and laconic than if you are responding emotionally, in the moment. Remember that decisions made in haste, under pressure, fuelled with emotion, are more likely to be unwise. Give yourself more of a chance to say the right thing by:

1. Saying as little as possible
2. Being direct, clear, and unambiguous
3. Avoiding sarcasm, gallows humour, or exasperation. Keep as much emotion out of it as possible, to convey that this is not an

emotional one, but a rational, reasonable one driven by process and necessity.

Sending out into corridors

This is an age-old technique often misused. Teachers may, in the heat of the moment, banish students outside the classroom, but often for very different reasons. As a result, its impact can vary enormously.

To cut through this confusion, we must ask the simple question: what is sending a student into the corridor seeking to achieve? What do we think happens in the corridor? Often they simply stand there, bored, until the teacher goes out, summons them, and they return, none the wiser.

Being sent into the corridor is often used as if it were a sanction, but it is a weak and vague sanction at best, and, as with any sanction, many students consider it as substantial as smoke. Teachers often use it as a way to make the student disappear for five minutes.[3] But they do not disappear. They seethe. They grumble. They meditate on how unfair the world is. They bunk and wander like goats. If the teacher is particularly forgetful or spiteful, they may leave them out there for long periods. This serves no purpose other than to build up a wall of resentment a mile high, and to drain any chance the student had of an education. Nothing magical happens in the corridor. I've even seen students synchronise their sendings-out, so they could meet in the same corridor at the same time. They may not be Moriartys, but they are not completely insensible.

The reason you send a student into the corridor must be either:

a.   Because you need to have a private word with them, in which case it must be done quickly.

b.   Because they're upset and need a little privacy or no audience in order to calm down. This should also be a short period of time. Any longer than five minutes or so and the teacher should formally have the student removed from lessons and taken to a supervised, pre-arranged space and environment (see above).

The takeaway here is that corridors are not places of sanction. Students are unsupervised and therefore not safe. They are not learning. They are not learning to behave well. They are not wondering how to be good people.

---

3. *Expellite discipulus!*

Sending a student into the corridor is an ejector seat for lazy teachers when issued carelessly. No teacher should use them as an easy way to achieve a micro-exclusion. If the student needs to go then do it by the book, or don't do it at all.

MY ROOM, MY RULES

The teacher is the authority in the classroom. This authority is rooted in necessity, compassion, and efficiency. Children need an adult. The teacher's power entails great responsibility.

FINAL THOUGHTS

There is much more that could be said, but if teaching is a performance then it is wise to know when to leave the stage. When I started to teach, it took me a few years to realise that I knew next to nothing about running rooms, and a few years after that to even realise that there were things you could usefully learn about it. The situation is still the same for too many teachers. It's high time we changed that. I have attempted to make this book accessible, evidenced where possible, but most of all practical. There are very few certainties in the theatre of the classroom, but many best bets and highly probables, which is where I have centred the techniques described. Nothing I have said is irrefutable or beyond challenge. But I have tried to be honest, to be serious, and to ensure that everything I have recommended is rooted in real classrooms with real students, not perfect mannequins that exist only in the laboratories of theory.

As a result, most of the strategies I have described are rising tides – ones that lift all ships. Structure, routines, positive norms, taught behaviour, high expectations, consistent consequences with boutique exceptions…these are the building blocks of every effective classroom and school I have visited, whether they cater for the youngest or the oldest, the most advantaged or the most in distress. The golden mean of these ingredients varies from circumstance to circumstance, but every teacher in every context would do well to attend to these factors and make their study the centre of their practice. For practitioners dealing with more specialist circumstances, and children with the highest level of difficulties in their lives, these methods are still the foundation of their best succour, although they will also have to seek specialist training to meet the challenge of their students.

Far too frequently I bang on about how much teaching saved me, gave me direction, purpose and meaning to my previously aimless and somewhat banal existence. But it is a testing profession, and its demands can break you, especially if you care about doing it well. It is a job based on repetition, the metronomes of the timetable, the curriculum and the tidal rhythm of the school year breathing in and out; but also one that surprises you every day. It offers you a front-row seat to the wonders of human imagination, while exposing you to every act of petty malice you can imagine. It is both the Lord's work and paperwork at the same time. It is a thankless task and a cornucopia of eternal reward.

And if you can get them to behave for you – for themselves – then it can be the best job in the world. I hope this has helped in some way.

Good luck.

BIBLIOGRAPHY

Ashman, G. (2018) *The truth about teaching: an evidence-informed guide for new teachers*. London: Sage Publications Ltd.

Aurelius, M. (2004) *Meditations*. London: Penguin.

Birbalsingh, K. (Ed) (2020) *Michaela: The power of culture*. Woodbridge: John Catt Educational Ltd.

Birbalsingh, K. (Ed) (2016) *Battle hymn of the tiger teachers*. Woodbridge: John Catt Educational Ltd.

Boethius (1969) *The consolations of philosophy*. London: Penguin.

Boland, E. (2016) *The battle for room 314: My year of hope and despair in a New York City high school*. New York City: Grand Central Publishing.

Boxer, A. (Ed) (2019) *The researchED guide to explicit and direct instruction*. Woodbridge: John Catt Educational Ltd.

Brower, F. (2019) *100 Ideas for Primary Teachers: Supporting pupils with autism*. London: Bloomsbury.

Carr, A. (1995) *The only way to stop smoking permanently*. Penguin books. London: Penguin.

Carrithers, M. (1992) *Why humans have cultures: Explaining anthropology and social diversity*. Oxford: Oxford University Press.

Caviglioli, O. (2019) *Dual coding with teachers*. Woodbridge: John Catt Educational Ltd.

Chalk, F. (2006) *It's your time you're wasting*. Cheltenham: Monday Books.

Chenoweth, K. (2017) *Schools that succeed: how educators marshal the powers of systems for improvement*. Cambridge, MA: Harvard Education Press.

Christodoulou, D. (2014) *Seven Myths About Education*. Abingdon: Routledge.

Cialdini, R. B. (2007) *Influence: the psychology of persuasion*. New York: Harper Business.

Cordasco, F. (1963) *A brief history of education*. Paterson, NJ: Littlefield, Adams and Co.

Davies, W. T. and Shepherd, T. B. (1949) *Teaching: begin here*. London: Epworth Press.

De Bruyckere, P. (2018) *The Ingredients for great teaching*. London: Sage Publications Ltd.

De Bruyckere, P., Kirschner, P. and Hulshof, C. (2015). *Urban myths about learning and education*. San Diego, CA: Academic Press.

Didau, D. and Rose, N, (2016) *What Every Teacher Needs to Know About Psychology*. Woodbridge: John Catt Educational Ltd.

Dinham, S. (2016) *Leading teaching and learning*. Victoria, Australia: ACER Press.

Dixon, P. (2019) *Rhetoric*. Abingdon, Routledge.

Donnelly, K. (2009) *Australia's education revolution*. Brisbane, Australia: Connor Court Publishing.

Egan, K. (2004) *Getting it wrong from the beginning: Our progressivist inheritance from Herbert Spencer, John Dewey and Jean Piaget*. New Haven, Conn: Yale University Press.

Elliott, J., Hufton, N.R., Willis, W. and Illushin, L. (2005) *Motivation, engagement and educational performance: International perspectives on the contexts for learning*. DOI: 10.1057/9780230509795.

Fleming, T. (2016). *Ben Franklin: Inventing America*. Minneapolis, MN: Voyageur Press.

Garelick, B. (2016) *Maths Education in the US: still crazy after all these years*. CreateSpace Independent Publishing Platform.

Gill, A. A. (2018) *The Best of A. A. Gill*. London: W&N.

Goddard, V. (2014) *The best job in the world*. Carmarthen: Independent Thinking Press.

Halpern, D. (2015) *Inside the nudge unit: how small changes can make a big difference*. London: WH Allen.

Hattie, J. (2012) *Visible learning for teachers*. Abingdon: Routledge.

Hawkes, H. (2009) *Autism: a parent's guide*. Peterborough: Need2Know.

Haydn, T. (2007) *Managing pupil behaviour: improving the classroom atmosphere*. Abindgon, Routledge.

Hendrick, C. and Macpherson, R. (2017) *What does this look like in the classroom? Bridging the gap between research and practice*. Woodbridge: John Catt Educational Ltd.

Hess, F. M. (2013) *Cage-busting leadership*. Cambridge, Mass: Harvard Education Press.

Hirsch, E. D. Jr. (2006) *The Knowledge deficit: closing the shocking education gap for American children*. Boston, Mass: Houghton Mifflin. Company.

Hirsch, E. D., Kett, J. F. and Trefil, J. (1988). *Cultural literacy: What every American needs to know*. New York: Vintage Books.

Howard, K. (2020) *Stop talking about wellbeing: a pragmatic approach to teacher workload*. Woodbridge: John Catt Educational Ltd.

Hughes, T. (1993) *Tom Brown's schooldays*. London: Wordsworth Editions.

Jones, K. (2003) *Education in Britain: 1944 to the present*. Cambridge: Polity Press.

Kalenze, E. (2019) *What the Academy taught us*. Woodbridge: John Catt Educational Ltd.

Kirschner, P. A. and Hendrick, C. (2020) *How Learning Happens*. Abingdon: Routledge,

Lemov, D. (2010) *Teach Like a Champion: 49 techniques that put students on the path to college*. San Francisco, CA: Jossey-Bass Inc.

Lemov, D., Woolway, E. and Yezzi, K. (2012) *Practice Perfect: 42 rules for getting better at getting better*. San Francisco: Jossey-Bass Inc.

Leslie, I. (2014) *Curious: the desire to know why and why your future depends on it*. New York, NY: Basic Books.

Marland, M. (1993) *The craft of the classroom*. Portsmouth, NH: Heinemann Educational Publishers.

Martin, P. R. and Bateson, P. P. G, (2007) *Measuring Behaviour: An Introductory Guide.* Cambridge: Cambridge University Press.

Marzano, R. J., Marzano, J. S. and Pickering, D. (2003) *Classroom management that works: research-based strategies for every teacher.* Alexandria, VA: Association for Supervision and Curriculum Development.

Maslow, A. (1943) 'A theory of human motivation', *Psychological Review, 50,* pp.370-396. DOI: 10.1037/h0054346.

McCourt, M. (2019) *Teaching for mastery.* Woodbridge: John Catt Educational Ltd.

McCrea, P. (2019) *Memorable teaching: Leveraging memory to build deep and durable learning in the classroom.* Woodbridge: John Catt Educational Ltd.

McGuinness, D. (1997) *Why our children can't read and what we can do about it: A scientific revolution in reading.* New York, NY: Touchstone.

Meyer, E. (2014) *The Culture Map.* New York, NY: Public Affairs.

Miller, A. (1996). *Pupil Behaviour and Teacher Culture.* London: Cassell.

Moore, A. (1987) *Watchmen.* London: Titan Books.

Morris, D. (1969) *The Naked Ape.* London: Corgi Books.

Murphy, J. (Ed) (2019) *The researchED guide to literacy.* Woodbridge: John Catt Educational Ltd.

Nutt, J, (2020) *Teaching English for the real world.* Woodbridge: John Catt Educational Ltd.

Paul, A. M. (2004) *The cult of personality: How personality tests are leading us to miseducate our children, mismanage our companies, and misunderstand ourselves.* New York: Free Press.

Peal, R. (2014) *Progressively worse: The burden of bad ideas in British schools.* London: Civitas.

Peterson, K. D. and Deal, T. E. (2009) *The shaping school culture fieldbook.* San Francisco, CA: Jossey-Bass Inc.

Pink, D. H. (2009) *Drive: The surprising truth about what motivates us.* New York, NY: Riverhead Books.

Pondiscio, R. (2019) *How the other half learns.* New York, NY: Avery.

Postman, N. (1987) *Amusing ourselves to death.* London: Metheun.

Ravitch, D. (2000) *Left back: a century of battles over school reform.* New York, NY: Touchstone.

Rees, T. (2018) *Wholesome Leadership.* Woodbridge: John Catt Educational Ltd.

Ritchie, S. (2016) *Intelligence: All that matters.* London: Hodder and Stoughton.

Robinson, M. (2013) *Trivium 21c: Preparing young people for the future with lessons from the past.* Carmarthen: Crown House Publishing.

Rogers, B. (2011) *Classroom behaviour: A practical guide to effective teaching, behaviour management and colleague support.* London: Sage Publications Ltd.

Rousseau, J. (1988) *The social contract and discourses.* London: J. M. Dent & Co.

Sapolsky, R. M. (2018) *Behave: The biology of humans at our best and worst.* London: The Bodley Head.

Scruton, R. (2016) *Confessions of a heretic*. London: Notting Hill Editions.

Seidenberg, M. (2017) *Language at the speed of sight: how we read, why so many can't, and what can be done about it*. New York, NY: Basic Books.

Shaw, J. (2019) *Making evil: the science behind humanity's dark side*. Edinburgh: Canongate.

Sherrington, T. and Caviglioli, O. (2020) *Teaching WalkThrus*. Woodbridge: John Catt Educational Ltd.

Simler, K. & Hanson, R. (2018) *The elephant in the brain: Hidden motives in everyday life*. New York, NY: Oxford University Press.

Skinner, B. F. (1976) *About behaviorism*. New York, NY: Vintage Books.

Sunstein, C. R (2019) *Conformity: the power of social influences*. New York, NY: New York University Press.

Tallis, R. (2011) *Aping mankind: Neuromania, Darwinitis and the misrepresentation of humanity*. Abingdon: Routledge.

Taylor, C. (2010) *Divas and door slammers: the secrets to having a better behaved teenager*. London: Vermilion.

Thaler, R. H. (2015) *Misbehaving: The making of behavioural economics*. London: Allen Lane.

Thaler, R. H. and Sunstein, C. R (2008) *Nudge: Improving decisions about health, wealth, and happiness*. New Haven: Yale University Press.

Trivers, R. (2011) *Deceit and self-deception: fooling yourself the better to fool others*. London: Allen Lane.

Watson, P. (1978) *War on the mind: The military uses and abuses of psychology*. London: Pelican Books.

Whiting, R. (1987) *Crime and punishment: a study across time*. Kingston upon Thames: Stanley Thornes.

Wiliam, D. (2016) *Leadership for teacher learning: Creating a culture where all teachers improve so that all students succeed*. West Palm Beach, FL: Learning Sciences International.

Wiliam, D. (2018) *Creating the schools our children need*. West Palm Beach, FL: Learning Sciences International.

Willingham, D. T. (2012) *When can you trust the experts? How to tell good science from bad in education*. San Francisco, CA: Jossey-Bass Inc.

Willingham, D. T. (2010) *Why don't students like school? A cognitive scientist answers questions about how the mind works and what it means for your classroom*. San Francisco, CA: Jossey-Bass Inc.